The Fall of Moorish Seville 1023-1091

The Creation and Destruction of a Hispanic-Muslim Kingdom in the 11th Century

Eduardo Manuel Gil Martínez

Helion & Company Limited
Unit 8 Amherst Business Centre
Budbrooke Road
Warwick
CV34 5WE
England
Tel. 01926 499 619
Email: info@helion.co.uk
Website: www.helion.co.uk
X, formerly Twitter: @helionbooks
Facebook: @HelionBooks
Visit our blog https://helionbooks.wordpress.com/

Published by Helion & Company 2026
Designed and typeset by Mary Woolley, Battlefield Design (www.battlefield-design.co.uk)
Cover designed by Paul Hewitt, Battlefield Design (www.battlefield-design.co.uk)

Text © Eduardo Manuel Gil Martínez 2025
Illustrations © as individually credited
Maps by Mark Thompson © Helion & Company 2025
Colour artwork by Giorgio Albertini © Helion & Company 2025

Every reasonable effort has been made to trace copyright holders and to obtain their permission for the use of copyright material. The author and publisher apologise for any errors or omissions in this work and would be grateful if notified of any corrections that should be incorporated in future reprints or editions of this book.

ISBN 978-1-804518-30-4

British Library Cataloguing-in-Publication Data.
A catalogue record for this book is available from the British Library.

All rights reserved. No part of this publication may be reproduced, stored in a retrieval system, or transmitted, in any form, or by any means, electronic, mechanical, photocopying, recording or otherwise, without the express written consent of Helion & Company Limited.

For details of other military history titles published by Helion & Company Limited contact the above address or visit our website: http://www.helion.co.uk.

We always welcome receiving book proposals from prospective authors.

'Better one defeat with honour than a hundred victories without honour'.

In Memoriam: Eduardo Gil

      To Solete, my life.
      To my parents, Salud and Eduardo.
      To Caco, Iñigo, Ibón and June.
      To Merce.
      To my grandparents Mercedes, Salud, Mami, Manuel and Juan.

Thanks to: Marisol García Gómez, Ricardo Ramallo Gil, Cristina Vargas, María Salud Elvás, Hermandad de la Hiniesta and all my dear cousins.

Contents

Preface		vii
1	A Brief Sketch of the Eleventh Century	11
2	Precedent of an Independent State in Muslim Seville	13
3	The City of Seville in the Eleventh Century	17
4	The Fragmentation of Al-Andalus	27
5	Birth of the Taifa of Seville: First Stage, 1023–1042	39
6	Settlement of the Kingdom of Seville: 1042–1069	52
7	The Rise and Fall of the Kingdom: 1069–1091	79
8	Exile	167
Appendices:		
I	Chronology	181
II	Glossary	187
Bibliography		190

Preface

In the year 2023, 1,000 years had passed since the founding of a small Spanish Muslim kingdom with its capital in the city of Isbiliya, now known as Seville. Despite the many difficulties that country would suffer, Seville and the kingdom that grew up around it in the eleventh century came to control vast swathes of the southern half of the Iberian Peninsula. With such a large kingdom, it would be reasonable to think that its history would be sufficiently well known, but it is not. Traditionally, Muslim Hispania has not been treated in the same way as Christian Hispania, and we must not forget that, after the Muslim invasion that began in 711, the population of the territories under Muslim rule were still largely the same as those under Visigothic or previously Roman domination: Hispanics, after all, who were assimilating to a greater or lesser extent the religion and customs of the conquerors. Moreover, the kingdom of Seville only lasted from the end of 1023 to 1091, totalling some 67 years. In this text, we would like to recall the brief but intense history of this kingdom as a representative of the various Muslim kingdoms of the Iberian Peninsula during the eleventh century that, as we have mentioned, in many cases have been overshadowed by the history of the Christian kingdoms of the north of our 'bull skin'. Fortunately, every day, there are more and more works that rescue the 'Muslim part' of our medieval period and specifically of the Sevillian kingdom from its unjust oblivion. Our intention is to compile in a didactic and informative way, without any academic intention, the most outstanding information that has reached us from different sources in order to highlight the history of the Taifa Kingdom of Seville during the eleventh century, which in 2023 celebrated the one-thousandth anniversary of its creation.

After the splendour that Al-Andalus experienced during the period of the Caliphate of Córdoba, a period of chaos and continuous fighting followed, which led to the emergence of the taifa kingdoms. Of all the kingdoms that were 'born', the kingdom of Seville stood out above all others, managing to maintain its military and cultural hegemony over most of its neighbouring taifa kingdoms. During the short period of existence of the Taifa of Seville or Isbiliya or Ishbiliya (in Arabic), the capital of the kingdom became the cultural, scientific and economic reference point for the whole of Al-Andalus and Christian Spain, comparable only to the Caliphate of Córdoba.

THE FALL OF MOORISH SEVILLE 1023–1091

The general oblivion about the Taifa Kingdom of Seville is evident, since important kings of the same are completely unknown by the majority of Seville's own people, a fact that is even more evident on a national level, while the Christian kings of the eleventh century, contemporaries of the Taifa Kingdom of Seville such as Fernando I, Sancho II or Alfonso VI, are well known. Similarly, few know how a small kingdom such as the one that formed around its capital, Seville, after the disintegration of the Cordoban Caliphate managed, with much political and military work, to increase its territorial possessions until its dominions extended from the current coast of the Algarve and the Portuguese Alentejo to the Mediterranean coast of Murcia and from Algeciras to Cuenca during the period of maximum extension of the kingdom.

The wealth accumulated by the Taifa of Seville and the great power that its kings accumulated among the taifas became a double-edged sword, as it became a preferential target for the more socio-culturally backward but militarily superior kingdom of Castile and León at first and later for the Almoravid empire. These riches were conveniently plundered by the king of Castile and León by means of parias.

In this text, we will recall the brief but intense relationship of El Cid Campeador with the kingdom of Seville where, by order of his lord, he not only took part in the sacking of the kingdom of Seville but also risked his life and honour when he fought at the head of the Sevillian troops to defend the territorial interests of the kingdom of the capital of the Guadalquivir against the troops of the Taifa of Granada allied to the Castilian-Leonese troops.

During the present text, we will highlight the continuous military activity of the kingdom of Seville, since, practically throughout its existence, it was involved in confrontation and political–military tensions with neighbouring kingdoms or even without a border between the two. We will also describe the cultural boom that took place in Seville and its dominions during the existence of the kingdom. In both aspects, one of the main protagonists of the text, King Al Mutamid, who led his country to the greatest military and cultural splendour that would not be seen again until the sixteenth century, stands out.

One last point before moving on to the text concerns the names of persons, localities or geographical features that, being originally written in Arabic, raise the question of how to express them in our pages. We have decided not to be so 'purist' and to write them in a more 'normalised' way, as is done in several of the studies consulted. Thus, although the correct way of writing, for example, is al-Andalus or al-Mu´tadid rather than Al-Andalus or Al Mutadid, we have arbitrarily preferred the latter, as it is more appropriate to avoid confusion when reading them. In spite of this, whenever it is considered appropriate, we will use the Arabic name of persons or localities, although always in the background after the Spanish version. Also in our text, faced with the different possibilities of naming the 'son of' as Ibn, Ben or Banu, we have generally opted for the form Ben or ben, although in the case of one of the prominent characters in the text, Ibn Ammar, we have arbitrarily opted for Ibn.

Another aspect to remember is the naming of the years in the calendar used by the Muslims and the one used by us today (Gregorian). The Muslim calendar begins in the year 622 of our calendar when Muhammad fled from Mecca to Medina (the so-called Hegira). Moreover, the years of our calendar do not agree with the Muslim calendar, since 33 Muslim years are equivalent to 32 Gregorian years, which means that, in many cases, the dates used in this text following the Gregorian calendar are not completely defined, although we do not consider this to be a significant problem when counting the course of events. For example, the year in which the kingdom of Seville is 'officially' considered to have begun its existence was 414 in the Muslim calendar, which would correspond to 1023–1024 in the Gregorian calendar.

It is also important to emphasise that, as this is a study that aims to compile, in a didactic and informative way and without academic intentions, the existing information on the subject that concerns us, we have relied on a series of leading works as our main sources, although we have also used numerous minor sources that are no less valuable for this reason in order to draw the most accurate possible portrait of the history of the most politically and militarily dynamic taifa kingdom that the eleventh century saw on the Iberian Peninsula.

Some years ago, I wrote a precedent to the present work entitled *Sevilla, Reina y Mora*, which allowed me to learn more about this small piece of the history of Seville and Spain. On this occasion, I wanted to correct inaccuracies and add to the information that is fortunately emerging about the history of the independent kingdom of Seville that arose after the fall of the Caliphate of Córdoba. I hope that this book will serve the reader as an interesting read that will 'transport' them to the bloody Iberian eleventh century and that it will help them to get to know a rather forgotten part of the history of the kingdom of Seville, as Hispanic as any other Christian or Muslim kingdom that we will talk about during the text.

THE FALL OF MOORISH SEVILLE 1023-1091

Image of the Beatus of Las Huelgas (1220) representing the capture of Jerusalem by King Nebuchadnezzar. Although later than the period dealt with in this book, we can appreciate the growing use of chainmail, numerous rounded shields (called adargas) with hanging tassels, of Andalusian influence, as well as compound arches, of similar origin. (Open source)

1

A Brief Sketch of the Eleventh Century

Before beginning with the history of the Taifa of Seville, we believe it is worthwhile to give a brief outline of the period corresponding to the eleventh century in other geographical areas in order to put our history into context. The eleventh century saw the birth and death of the kingdom of Seville, as well as most of the different taifas that emerged after the fall of the Caliphate of Córdoba. We will recount some of the most important events that took place in Europe, the Holy Land and North Africa.

In Europe, this century is regarded as the beginning of the High Middle Ages, as well as the century in which Christianity witnessed a schism within itself. The split between Roman Catholicism and Greek Orthodoxy occurred in 1054. The heads of both religious movements, Pope Leo IX for Catholicism and Patriarch Michael Cerularius for the Orthodox, excommunicated each other.

The year 1013 saw the total conquest of England by the Danes. Canute the Great was elected ruler of a kingdom encompassing Denmark and England, a kingdom that soon had Christianity as its official religion. The rule of the Danes and their descendants continued in England until 1066, when Duke William of Normandy (a Norman, thus of Scandinavian origin) landed in Britain at the head of an army and confronted Haroldo II (who had defeated an invading Norwegian army at the Battle of Stanforbridge earlier) at Hastings. The result was a victory for William, henceforth known as 'the Conqueror'.

In central Europe, the Germanic Empire held sway, extending from the North Sea to the Mediterranean (occupying the whole of northern Italy as far south as Rome). From 1033, the kingdom of Burgundy was incorporated

The royal standard of 'Abd al-Rahman III, used as a banner for his armies. 'Abd al-Rahman III was the great beneficiary of the disputes between the two main Sevillian families when he became emir in 912, since, in little more than a year, the first attempt at the independence of an independent Muslim state in Seville was finally completed. (Open source by Jin waifu)

into the Germanic Empire. This growing power of the empire gave rise to friction and disputes between the papal and imperial powers.

In the south of the Italian peninsula, from 1057, the Normans under Roger I took political and military control by expelling the Byzantines and Saracens, creating a Norman kingdom.

In eastern Europe, the most important state was the principality of Kiev, which experienced a period of prosperity under Yaroslav 'the Wise', who came to power in 1019. His death in 1054 led to the dismemberment of the principality and a period of decline that continued into the next century.

During this century, the Byzantine Empire began a decline that would culminate in its demise four centuries later. Even so, in 1045, Byzantium's last conquest in the East took place: the conquest of Armenia. In 1071, at the Battle of Manzikert, the Byzantines, led by Roman Emperor Romanos IV Diogenes, were defeated by their emerging neighbours with Sultan Alp Arslan at the head of their troops; as a result of the battle, the Seljuk Turks occupied Anatolia, Bithynia and Isauria. From 1055, the latter took over the political leadership of the Islamic world in the eastern region, taking advantage of the decline of the Abbasid Caliphate, and began a continuous harassment of the Byzantine Empire, which they systematically stripped of its provinces.

Trade in eastern Europe was dominated by the Venetians from 1082, who began to become a European power.

In North Africa, the Fatimids (who claimed sovereignty as direct descendants of Fatima, the Prophet's daughter) were the dominant dynasty. In Tunisia, however, the Zirids ruled, albeit as subordinates of the Fatimids, although they began to act independently in 1041. From 1061 onwards, the Almoravids were the most important state, thanks to their many conquests in the Maghreb area and later in Al-Andalus. But their hegemony soon disappeared at the hands of a movement, also North African, known as the Almohads during the twelfth century.

In the Iberian Peninsula, the disintegration of the Caliphate of Córdoba led to the emergence of the taifa kingdoms, which culminated at the end of the century with the Almoravid invasion of Al-Andalus. This empire from northwest Africa managed to reconquer from the Christians important towns such as Cuenca, Santarem, Oporto, Zaragoza and Mallorca, re-establishing religious unity in Muslim Iberia. Due to its importance and transcendence in the history that concerns us, we will go into more detail on this subject later on.

A final event in the last years of the eleventh century that changed the relationship between Christian and Muslim countries was the birth of the First Crusade. Between 1096 and 1099, a Crusader army composed mainly of French, Lorraine, Flemish and Normans managed to take Nicaea and then Antioch after a seven-month siege. The Crusade culminated with the capture of Jerusalem in July 1099 after five weeks of siege.

As we can see, the eleventh century witnessed many important changes in our Mediterranean geographical environment, with an increase in the clashes between Islam and Christianity that were 'chiselling' the pillars on which Europe, North Africa and, of course, Spain currently stand.

2

Precedent of an Independent State in Muslim Seville

Although the city of Seville in the different historical periods from its foundation until the eleventh century (whether it was the initial Ispal, the Roman Hispalis or the Visigothic Spali before becoming the Muslim Isbiliya) enjoyed great importance, it did not have the opportunity to be the head of a state as it did in the eleventh century.

For this reason, before moving on to the central theme of our text, it is necessary to mention that even more unknown than the history of the Taifa Kingdom of Seville is the adventure of independence that the Sevillian city experienced from 899 to 913, when it still belonged to the Emirate of Córdoba.

The hegemony of Córdoba, which became the most important capital in Western Europe, was evidently based on the multiple riches it obtained from its extensive peninsular possessions. One of the cities that suffered most from the plundering of the caliphate capital was Seville. From 890 onwards, Emir Abdullah of Córdoba had to face multiple internal revolts that limited his real control of the emirate over the city of Córdoba and its surroundings. In the area of Elvira (near Granada), the Muladíes fought against the Qaysid Arabs, and Toledo became independent under the control of the Berbers, the Upper Mark under the Banu Tuyib and the Banu Qasi, and the Lower Mark under Ibn Marwan.

Faced with this situation of generalised revolt throughout the emirate, it did not take long for an atmosphere of hostility to develop in Seville towards the centralist power of Córdoba. Two important Sevillian families of Yemeni origin (the Beni-Khaldun or Banu Khaldun and the

Caliphal style plate con vidriado en verde y negro. X century. Exhibited in the Antiquarium of Seville. (Author's collection)

Beni-Hachach or Banu Hayyay) began to channel this discontent towards the creation of an independent state, despite appearing to maintain cordial relations with the Cordoban government.

It was Kurayb Banu Khaldun, an important landowner from Seville's Aljarafe (the region just west of the city of Seville) who led the revolt of the Yemeni Arabs, managing to defeat the troops of the governor of the emir of Córdoba, supported by the city's Muladíes, in alliance with troops from Mérida, Sidonia and Niebla. These battles took place around 889 in the fields of Tejada, Aznalcollar and Gerena.

As we have already mentioned, revolts against the power of Córdoba were spread throughout Al-Andalus, so it was not until 895 that the emir was able to gather an army to be sent to the Sevillian capital with the intention of bringing it back under the rule of Córdoba. Unexpectedly, this emir's army failed in its endeavour due to the power of both Sevillian families.

Both the Banu Khaldun and the Banu Hayyay behaved in practice as kings independent of Córdoba's power, although they tried to keep up appearances of obedience to Córdoba. The fact was that the city of Seville acted as a free state independent of Córdoba and its ruler as a king would. Not surprisingly, all Sevillian life was now controlled from Seville itself; taxes were collected, officials were appointed, and a small army of its own was maintained, numbering no less than 500 horsemen. In view of the new political situation, a kind of court was created where, in the manner of Córdoba, many scholars and poets attended under the patronage of Ibrahim Banu Hayyay, who eventually became the lord of Seville.

But the de facto independent state of Seville had a more powerful enemy than Córdoba, and it was within its own walls, for between the supporters of the two powerful families there was growing strife and rivalry that led in a practical way to a small-scale civil war. In 899, Ibrahim had succeeded in eliminating his most ready rival, Kurayb Banu Khaldun, and his brother Khalid by assassinating them. As a result, he was joined by the rebels of the new Sevillian lordship in Sidonia, Niebla and Carmona. As a result of these political–military movements, Ibrahim took control of the lands of Seville and Carmona. From his new position, Ibrahim put pressure on the emir to recognise his rights over the possessions of which he was lord.

To make his possessions more secure, he improved the defences of the city of Seville and fortified the city of Carmona, making it a stronghold very difficult to take by force.

Little handle jars with painted decoration used for water. Umayyad Caliphate. X century. Exhibited in the Antiquarium of Seville. (Author's collection)

PRECEDENT OF AN INDEPENDENT STATE IN MUSLIM SEVILLE

Although the Banu Hayyay had seized power, the Banu Khaldun persisted in their clashes against them. As a result, the only beneficiary of this situation was 'Abd al-Rahman III, now in control of the reins of the Cordoban state, who, taking advantage of the weakness of the Sevillian state, did not hesitate to try to put an end to the Sevillian adventure of independence. 'Abd al-Rahman III began his rule in 912, two years after Ibrahim died at the age of 63, leaving his dominions divided between two of his sons; Mohammed was given Carmona, and 'Abd al-Rahman the city of Seville. The Cordoban emir took advantage of the disintegration of Sevillian power, and, soon after, the tribute payments from Seville and Carmona to the Cordoban government were resumed. The growing dominance of Córdoba in the Seville area was compounded by the fratricidal quarrel between the two brothers to the point that, in July or August 913 or 914, 'Abd al-Rahman died, most probably murdered by his brother.

Despite Seville's growing weakness, it still remained a small de facto state, but the Cordoban emir was waiting for the perfect moment to take back the reins of rebellious Seville. Taking advantage of the help requested by Mohammed (whom the Sevillian people blamed for the death of his brother and rejected his intentions to rule them) to confront a cousin of his named Ahmad ben Maslama, who succeeded his late elder brother in the government of Seville, Cordoban troops were sent to the city of Carmona. Finally, the troops from Carmona and Córdoba made their way towards the city of Seville after leaving the city of Carmona through the Tocina Gate to the cheers of the people. These troops approached Seville after covering the approximately 30 kilometres that separated the two cities, first occupying the Aljarafe area and, after receiving the support of those loyal to the Cordoban central power, proceeding to besiege the city of Seville. The outcome of this confrontation was finally settled in the fields of Triana, with the result of a severe defeat for the Sevillian troops, which meant the immediate return of Seville to the Cordoban yoke.

The Cordoban troops under the command of Hashib Badr entered Seville victoriously between 7 and 20 December 913 through the Iron Gate or Córdoba Gate after obtaining the surrender of Ahmad ben Maslama, who was confined to his residence in the alcázar.

Badr's orders from Córdoba were clear and categorical, 'no new discord could be created from Seville towards Córdoba', and so the city was allowed to return to normal life without any reprisals against the population or any bloodshed. Despite this, and with some mistrust, the Cordoban emir, 'Abd al-Rahman III, ordered the destruction of the walls of Seville, foreseeing possible future revolts and insurrections. And he was not mistaken, for between February and April 914 a revolt led by Mohammed banu Ibrahim banu Hayyay, lord of Carmona, took place and tried to bring the Banu Hayyay family back to power in Seville. Unfortunately for the Sevillian rebels, this attempt was easily defeated by troops loyal to Córdoba after some fighting in the very outskirts of the city. Mohammed died shortly afterwards, in July 914, possibly on the orders of the Cordoban monarch with the aim of eliminating possible causes of new revolts. After this, Carmona would fall completely under the control of the Cordoban monarch around November or December 914.

The first dream of an independent Sevillian state had vanished. From 913 onwards, the new governor of Seville would be no more than an envoy of the emir, and Seville would be just another city in the Cordoban emirate.

Little more than 100 years would have to pass before the circumstances of the decaying Caliphate of Córdoba would allow for a new, victorious and long-lasting period of independence in the lands of Seville, which will be described in the following chapters.

Image of the Cántigas de Santa María (second half of the thirteenth century) of a combat between Christian and Muslim troops. Although two centuries after the time dealt with in our book, we can appreciate the similarity between the clothes and weapons of the two sides, except for the North African troops who wore turbans. (Open source)

3

The City of Seville in the Eleventh Century

Before beginning to narrate the history of the Taifa of Seville, it is interesting to know a little about the peculiarities of the city. This sketch of eleventh-century Isbiliya is based on various accounts of the period and existing scientific studies of the city. Although we must not forget that the Muslim remains from the eleventh century in Seville are proportionally smaller than those from other periods of history, thanks to recent work carried out in the vicinity of the Patio de Banderas in the Royal Alcázar of Seville, this lack of remains from the taifa period is going to change substantially.

The city of Seville under the name of Spalis had already had its moment of splendour during the Visigothic period, but it would be in the Muslim period when this city, now under the name of Isbiliya, would be the capital of the arts and knowledge of the whole of Al-Andalus and therefore of the whole of Western Europe.

The foundation inscription of the Great Mosque of Seville, also known as the Great Mosque of Ibn Adabbas, which appears on a column and reads in Arabic, 'God have mercy on 'Abd al-Rahman ben al-Hakam, the just Amir, the well guided by God, who ordered the construction of this mosque, under the direction of 'Umar ben Adabbas, Qadi of Seville, in the year 214 of the Hegira [830 in our calendar]. And he wrote this 'Abd al-Barr ben Harun'. (Author's collection)

THE FALL OF MOORISH SEVILLE 1023-1091

It is difficult to know exactly what the city would have looked like during the period of the Taifa Kingdom of Seville, but there is enough information to at least give us an idea of it.

Seville as a city had been gaining in importance since the period of the Emir 'Abd al-Rahman II, a fact that can be seen by the increase in population that took place. So much so that, in 829, the emir ordered the construction of a mosque of a size in keeping with this demographic increase. This was the Mosque of Ibn Adabbas, which was located in what is today the Parroquia Iglesia del Divino Salvador (parish Church of the Divine Saviour), about which we will comment later.

Thus, when the caliphate fell in the eleventh century, the city of Seville, which had been in the shadow of Córdoba, experienced a period of splendour under the rule of the Abbadids that made it the city of reference in Al-Andalus when we speak of this historical period. In fact, the city began to grow towards the south and northeast due to the growing importance of the capital of the Sevillian kingdom.

Geographically, the city is located in a strategic position thanks to the existence of a navigable river such as the Guadalquivir. The distances by land between Seville and other important cities such as Córdoba, Algeciras, Málaga and Badajoz were three, five, five and six days, respectively. Although these figures may seem exaggerated today, for the traveller of the time, they were not excessively long.

The general appearance of any Andalusian city was similar to that of the Arab cities of North Africa and the Middle East, where the houses were structured around an inner courtyard sheltered from view from the outside. Its basic elements were the defensive wall, the alcázar or government residence, the Great Mosque, the baths and the souk (market). There were also different quarters with main mosques throughout the city.

The first thing you would see on approaching Seville would be its recently built city walls, as these had been demolished earlier in 913 by order of 'Abd al-Rahman III, due to dissent between the Sevillian city and the Cordoban capital. The walls protected the entire urban perimeter, with the exception of the suburb of Triana (Triyana) or the Hawmat Bir Al Wada

Image of the column with the foundation inscription of the Great Mosque of Seville or Ibn Adabbas, now in the Archaeological Museum of Seville. Although it was built before the birth of the Sevillian kingdom, it was its main mosque during its existence. (Author's collection)

THE CITY OF SEVILLE IN THE ELEVENTH CENTURY

Remains of arches, columns and capitals from the courtyard of the Great Mosque of Ibn Adabbas (now the courtyard of the Church of the Divine Saviour). (Author's collection)

('neighbourhood of the well of farewell') outside the Carmona Gate, and had several entrance gates. Inside the city walls, there were large areas dedicated to agriculture, and there were many almunias or farmhouses (in this book, we show some photographs of the remains of a pool belonging to an almunia found in the Casa Hermandad de la Hiniesta). In the outskirts of the city, there were almuzaras (mainly used for equestrian exercises, military training or simply for walking), almusallas (esplanade used for religious celebrations) and some nearby cemeteries such as the maqbarat al sulaha outside the bab Maqarana, or that of the Puerta Osario, which were used to accommodate many people with a bad life, so in general they became real brothels as well as places for quarrelling, gambling and drinking. They had to be closely guarded by the almotacenes. The cemeteries were usually located near the access roads to the city and without any fencing or separation.

Well knob with Arabic inscription on display in the Archaeological Museum of Seville, dated to between the tenth and eleventh centuries. (Author's collection)

Also on the outskirts of the city, next to the river, was the so-called Silver Meadow (Marif al fidda), which was a meadow with a multitude of elm trees that served as a meeting place but, in this case, unlike the staff in the cemeteries, for the elegant and cultured fraction of the city. Its most illustrious visitor was King Al Mutamid, and it was here that he met his wife Itimad, as we will mention in the history of the reign of Al Mutamid.

To the south of Seville, in the area where the present-day Cristina Gardens are located, there were other gardens called Yannat al-musalla, meaning 'Gardens of the Oratory', which were planted with sugar cane.

Returning to the wall, we know that throughout the history of Seville, the number and even the names of the gates have undergone some modifications, but the traveller in the eleventh century could enter the city through at least the following:

> Barqueta Gate, Macarena Gate (Bab Maqarana), Córdoba Gate (Bab al-Hadid or later Bab Qurtuba), Carmona Gate (Bab Qarmuna), Flesh Gate (Bab Chahwar), Jerez Gate (Bab Sharish or Bab al-Farach or al-Furay), Triana Gate (Bab Taryana) and Royal Gate.

The walls had to be improved and renovated during the period of Al Mutamid's rule due to threats from both Christians and Almoravids. This renovation was carried out with rammed earth, and, although it did not cover all the houses in the city (the suburbs were left outside the fence), it has been known in bibliographical sources as the 'Seville Wall' or 'Ben Abbad's Wall'. Another noteworthy feature of the wall is its battlements, at least on the southwest side facing the Guadalquivir riverbed, according to sources handled by A. Tahiri, a true specialist in Abbadid Seville.

The main streets of the city (or medina) started at the gates of the walls and were usually wider than the rest of the streets in the interior.

Bell tower of the Church of the Divine Saviour in Seville. The lower part of the tower corresponds to the original minaret tower of the Mosque of Ibn Adabbas. (Author's collection)

On arriving at one of these gates, specifically the gate of Córdoba (the one through which El Cid Campeador entered after defeating the troops of the king of Granada), patrols of soldiers were stationed to watch over the entry and exit of people and products from the city, where taxes were charged for the entry of products and in many cases for their exit.

Inside the city, there was a labyrinth of narrow, winding alleys whose width and direction were constantly changing, as well as many dead ends. These narrow alleys were paved with the 'pavement' of the time, which was nothing more than layers of sand mixed with gravel. These streets remained narrow until they opened onto small squares or to one of the city's official buildings such as mosques or palaces.

The Great Mosque was built by Ibn Adabbas, from whom it took its name, between 829 and 830. Its founding inscription reads, *'God have mercy on 'Abd al-Rahman ben al-Hakam, the just Amir, the well guided*

THE CITY OF SEVILLE IN THE ELEVENTH CENTURY

by God, who ordered the construction of this mosque, under the direction of 'Umar ben Adabbas, Qadi of Seville, in the year 214 of the Hegira [830 in our calendar]. And he wrote this 'Abd al-Barr ben Harun'. It remained the city's Great Mosque until the Almohads in 1184 transferred the status of Great Mosque to the new mosque that was created on the site of the present-day Santa Iglesia Catedral, whose minaret is the Giralda.

Very few remains of the Ibn Adabbas Mosque remain today; the only ones that have survived after the construction of the Church of the Divine Saviour on its remains are two knockers kept in the rooms of the Sacramental Brotherhood, the base of the minaret and part of the ablutions courtyard (where various shafts and their capitals can be seen), although the authentic primitive floor is about two metres below the present one. In the latter two cases, they have undergone many transformations over the centuries.

Capitals on display in the Archaeological Museum of Seville dating from the tenth and eleventh centuries. Examples of the architecture of post-caliphate and Abbadid Seville. (Author's collection)

Of the square minaret, some 13 metres high, the original construction remains, with a spiral staircase inside around a central buttress. The tower is built of brown ochre-coloured sandstone ashlars.

Although the mosque was obviously not built during the taifa period, there is information in the form of a tombstone stating that Al Mutamid rebuilt part of the minaret of the mosque and that it took about a month to do so.

This tombstone, which is preserved today next to the left side door of the temple, reads as follows:

> ... Baslama, tasliyya. He has ordered al-Mutamid 'ala Allah, al-Muayyad bi-nasri Allah, Abu-l-Qasim Muhammad, son of Abbad - may Allah render continuous help to his Empire and contribute to its strong victory! - the construction of the highest part of this minaret - may the Islamic invocation never be interrupted therein! - when it had just been brought down by a great number of seismic tremors that took place on Sunday eve, at the beginning of Rabi I of the year 472 [1 September 1079]. And this was completed, by the might and assistance of Allah, at the end of the same month. May Allah design to accept for this work his generous occupations of the king and shower him with His favours by building him, for every

stone he has employed, a palace, in His paradise, by His grace and His goodness!

In addition to the repair of the minaret, it seems that the Sevillian king also donated new doors for the mosque, including magnificent door knockers with a hexagonal plan and feline heads.

According to the accounts of the time, the city of Seville did not have a single palace or alcázar but several that were built over the course of many years. The exact size and original layout of these during the taifa period is currently unknown, although recent studies by Miguel Ángel Tabalez Rodríguez and Cristina Vargas Lorenzo have enabled us to locate at least one of them.

The origin of the original Muslim alcázar, known as Dar al-Imara (Governor's House), is to be found in a primitive Roman settlement, on which the Visigoths also left their mark (there is a theory that places the basilica of San Vicente Mártir here, where Saint Isidore was buried). One hypothesis, which is considered to be true, would place its enclosure between the Patio de Banderas, the Palacio del Yeso and the Palacio del Caracol. It was possibly during the reign of 'Abd al-Rahman III when it was built on the remains mentioned above, in the year 913. The layout of this enclosure was irregular rectangular with dimensions of about 120 by 180 metres, of which some remains are still preserved today (some sections of the wall are preserved in the Plaza del Triunfo square, Calle Joaquín Romero Murube and the eastern wing up to the Torre del Agua, as well as its possible entrance gate in the aforementioned street). Its location was determined by its strategic function at one end of the medina. It had its own wall with different entrances to the outside, giving it a certain degree of independence from the rest of the medina.

This enclosure, rather than a palace per se, was the residence of the governor of the city, as well as the residence of the city's main political and administrative offices. For its own defence, the Dar al-Imara also housed a garrison that acted as a praetorian guard for the Cordoban representative (they had not forgotten the previous attempt at independence by the Sevillians in the caliphate capital). Thus, the main political, military and administrative functions of the city of Seville were unified and centralised, under the direct control of the governor. In the eleventh century, the palace was possibly extended in a westerly direction, modifying the Umayyad structure of the palace, just as the rammed-earth wall that today borders the Plaza de la Alianza was built. The Dar al-Imara may have been the palace that, in the Abbadid period, took the grandiloquent name of al-Mukarram (the revered) and was used for governmental tasks.

The work of the aforementioned Miguel Ángel Tabalez Rodríguez and Cristina Vargas Lorenzo has enabled a stratigraphic study to be carried out in several houses next to the Patio de Banderas that outlines the traces of a palatial building dated between the mid-eleventh century and the first decades of the twelfth century and therefore corresponding to at least three of the protagonists of our text: Al Mutadid, his son Al Mutamid and the Almoravid Yusuf.

It is very important to bear in mind that the space of the primitive Abbadid alcázar has undergone enormous transformations in later years that do not allow us to have a full knowledge of its layout at the present time. The alcázar (al-qasr) served as the residence of the representative of the Cordoban Caliphate in Seville until its disintegration. From then on, it became the residence of the new ruler of Seville, Abul Qasim, who did not make many modifications to the original enclosure. It was under the governments of Al Mutadid and his son Al Mutamid that the palace enclosure was extended westwards in Dar al-Imara with the construction of a new palace called al-Mubarak (the Blessing or the Blessed), the entrance to which was located where the arquillo de la Plata is today. Little remains of the latter palace today, except for what was written about it during its existence. It is known that there was a large hall called the qubba of the Turayya or al-Thurayya (Zoraya, the Constellation of the Pleiades), possibly located where the Ambassadors' Hall of the Mudejar Palace of the Christian King Peter I is today. It was in this beautiful dome-shaped hall and its five smaller halls around it (simulating a large star surrounded by five smaller ones) that the king received his most important visitors, and it is also here where some of the verses sung by Al Mutamid took place. Another palace located in this palatial environment was known as al-Zahi, which translates as 'the prosperous' (at least from the time of Al Mutadid), possibly located in what is now the area of the Casa de la Contratación. Al-Zahi came to be compared to the citadel of Aleppo (Syria) and was very much to the king's liking because it overlooked the river. There was a hall called Sa'd al su'ud (the happiness of happinesses) in which the Sevillian king and people very close to him held parties. Other palaces of which only their names remain today are those of al-Wahid (the one and only) with its qubba, gardens and ponds; al-Tay (the crown); Dar al-Sina'a; al-Zahir (the shining one), located in front of the alcázar guarding the river route to Jerez (Sharish), which is thought to have been located in what is now San Juan de Aznalfarache from where the river and the citadel of the city could be seen, also known as Hisn al-Faray (although according to Tahiri, its correct name is 'Hisn al-Furay', which means 'castle of the meadows', and would be near the gate known as Bab al-Furay in the city of Seville); and the one called al-Mukarram (the venerated) in the area of San Martín. Of the latter palace, perhaps the latest to be built, the poet Ibn Ahmad of Denia leaves us this impression:

> … a hall that has two pools, both of great beauty and with limpid gardens where the branches embrace like lovers, recalling the carvings of girls and the necks of inebriated youths. A languid breeze passes through the branches, like the faint flickering of the sun through them, and it is enveloped in extensive shade, among thornless acacias and wet fruits about to fall, while the myrtle exhales its scent. They resemble the molten glow of the stars' hair, the scattered fires, the coloured flowers among which are glowing white and intense yellow,

unmixed red and lustfully green. There are daisies like the teeth of beauties, poppies like wounds or shells of carnelians …

The al-Mubarak palace imitated the West with a military enclosure that served as a parade ground in the area of the Jerez Gate and that linked up with another alcázar that was located in the vicinity of the port (in the area where the Casa de la Moneda (Mint) is located today). From the reign of Al Mutadid onwards, al-Mubarak became the new official residence of the king of Seville (Abul Qasim had resided and ruled in the Dar al-Imara), as well as the temporary residence of ambassadors and personalities from other kingdoms. The lush gardens of this palace were also described by Ibn Ahmad of Denia:

… towering palms, flowers that reach their fullness and multiply in the twinkling of an eye; the rose is like the blush of cheeks; the narcissus like the pupils of beautiful women; the lily is like a hand bending its fingers over gold filings; the anemones are like golden knobs on branches of topaz; the wallflower has borrowed its shape from the eyes and has dressed the garb of the sad; the violet reflects the blue of the hyacinths and the fire of the tips of the teas; the jasmine recalls the white cheeks and has stolen the musk and softness from all the roses …

Or, as Ibn Ammar spoke of them when he compared them to a beautiful Andalusian woman:

The garden is like a beautiful
and its flowers have clothed her
with a striped fabric,
and the dew has made her
a necklace of pearls.

The Andalusian gardens had ornamental plants and aromatic plants (basil, laurel and flowers that gave an intense scent of perfume during the day and night (wallflowers, jasmine, roses and violets)). In addition, fruit trees (quince and bitter orange trees) were often found in these gardens, which perfumed the atmosphere during their flowering. The gardens of Qalat Jabir and Muntazah al-'Arís (Park of the Bride) may have been located in the present-day Maria Luisa Park. The sources consulted also cite Dar al-Muzayna, which must have been an almunia within the palace gardens, the gardens where Al Mutadid and his predecessors are believed to have been buried.

It is now beginning to be considered more feasible that all these palaces could in some cases be the same, but with different names, and that they would therefore be located in the current area of the Royal Alcázar in the form of a real palace complex. Despite this, we end with a couple of palaces whose existence in the Abbadid period is not known for certain but that are mentioned in some documentary sources.

The first of these two palaces, of which little is known about its existence, was located in the area of La Barqueta and the present-day convent of San Clemente, where Al Mutamid had another royal residence.

The second palace that we are discussing and about which there are also many unknowns about its existence is that of the Buhayra (from the Arabic 'Bahr', meaning 'lagoon'), which Al Mutamid ordered to be built using two marshy areas, drained for the occasion, in the meadow of the Masalama (Santa Justa today) and another in front of the Puerta de la Carne (Meat Gate). It seems that this palace also had a large swimming pool and that it served as a recreation area for the royal family.

The growth of the palace buildings was continuous and uninterrupted during the reign of the last two Abbadids, and, by the end of the eleventh century, the palace buildings, and therefore the Abbadid kingdom, extended as far as the area where the Tagarete meets the Guadalquivir. In general, they were characterised by the proximity of some buildings to others, with the practical absence of open spaces in many cases.

Other important buildings of which there are no remains from the period were the shipyards and the naval dockyards (located opposite the Triana suburb). Once on the riverbank, the traveller could take a look at the houses on both sides of the river, which were whitewashed, their white colour shining in contrast to the golden wooden windows. This was due to Al Mutamid's regulation that all the facades of houses facing the river should have a homogenous appearance, both on the facades and on the windows. On a curious note, it should be mentioned that the Rio Grande (Guadalquivir) during the taifa period was still drinkable and that the disposal of detritus into the river was regulated in order to avoid its contamination. Similarly, the two banks of the river were illuminated with oil torches following the course of the river as far as the Santiponce farmstead (Santabus) some five kilometres to the northwest of the city, from the area corresponding to the Torre del Oro (although its construction is attributed to the Almohad period, there are certain sources that place its construction or perhaps its first construction to an earlier period that would include the taifa period).

The Triana suburb was like a small city with its own shops, baths, mosque and so on, which meant that, in some cases, they could be used as defensive redoubts or, on the contrary, as happened on several occasions, they were the target of the attacking troops instead of facing the attack on the infinitely better defended Sevillian medina.

Like Triana, other Sevillian suburbs were those of La Macarena (located in the area where San Lázaro is today), that of al-Mubarak around the Abbadid palace and that of Benaliofar, possibly corresponding to the present-day district of San Bernardo. All of them grew with the passing of time, with the current Triana quarter standing out for its special idiosyncrasy. A little farther down from the Triana suburb was the Tablada farmstead, next to the riverbank, which had another port of arrival in the city.

THE FALL OF MOORISH SEVILLE 1023-1091

The Aljarafe is a fertile area situated in an elevated position with respect to Seville, stretching from the capital to Niebla. There were a multitude of plantations with olive groves and vineyards that covered immense areas. The Aljarafe was dotted with a multitude of farmhouses, which fulfilled a mission similar to that of today's cortijos, numbering close to 200. Many of the rich men of the city lived in their own fortified farmhouses at the foot of their lands. Both in the Aljarafe and in the mountains, there were various fortifications and castles that protected the boundaries of the fertile Guadalquivir valley. One of these fortifications, of which remains are still standing, is the castle of San Juan de Aznalfarache (Hisn al-Faray, meaning 'the castle of Good Sighting', which seems to correspond to the Qasr al-Zahir, which was built in the period of Al Mutadid and was his favourite palace), in the vicinity of the capital, whose southern and fluvial accesses it protected.

Seville in the mid-eleventh century, at the height of the Abbadid state, was the largest urban agglomeration in the whole of the Islamic West, as befitted the capital of a kingdom that aspired to annex a large part of the territory of the ancient and longed-for Caliphate of Córdoba.

Image of the Liber ad honorem where we see a typical medieval (Christian) knight wearing a helmet with a nose, chainmail and armed with a lance with a pennant. (Open source)

4

The Fragmentation of Al-Andalus

The eleventh century was a century of great importance for Al-Andalus due to the political, social, military, demographic and other changes that were to take place on the Iberian Peninsula. The Caliphate of Córdoba reached its maximum splendour during the period of Almanzor, with the puppet regency of Hixam II, in which the Andalusian state dominated a large part of the Iberian Peninsula and had the Christian part, settled in the north of it, on the ropes. The vassalage of Christian lords and lands to the Cordoban state was repeated on many occasions thanks to the powerful army that Almanzor managed to forge in just a few years. Almanzor had managed through political intrigues to become the real ruler of the caliphate, nullifying the political and personal development of the young monarch Hixam II, surrounding him with all kinds of luxuries and without any concern for the government of his state.

After the death of Almanzor in August 1002 in the town of Medinaceli as a result of a raid or aceifa carried out by his troops in the area of the monastery of San Millán de la Cogolla, he was succeeded by his son Saif al-Daula Abu Meruán Abd al-Malik al-Muzaffar (Abd al-Malik) in his military posts and in his high influence over Caliph Hixam II.

Almanzor's son, although he continued to achieve important military victories, had to face certain movements instigated by important Cordoban figures who tried to prevent the position held by his father from becoming hereditary. In the end, these dissident groups were silenced, and their leaders banished to Ceuta on the African coast. It is possible that, had Abd al-Malik remained in office as long as his father, the political and military structure of the caliphate, as well as its powerful influences in Christian territory, would have persisted for a few more decades. But his early death in 1008 led to a series of events that acted like a gale on a caliphate 'governed' by a puppet named Hixam II, who evidently could do no more than comply with the events that fate had in store for him.

Abd al-Malik was succeeded by his brother, Abderramán Sanchuelo, who managed to be appointed successor by Caliph Hixam II due to his inability to have children. But Sanchuelo, despite being of the same blood as his brother and his father, did not live up to it. His life was more akin to the debauchery and luxury of Hixam II than to that of his relatives, with the government of the Andalusian state taking second place. This neglect of political affairs gave rise to many complaints from the citizens, as well as from the leading members of the Umayyad family, who did not recognise Sanchuelo's position as the second man in the state.

The events unfolded at great speed, and soon the various Umayyad pretenders to the throne began to create movements of discontent against Sanchuelo that finally led to an uprising led by Mohammed Al-Mahdi, a grandson of Abderramán III. Al-Mahdi, taking advantage of Sanchuelo's absence in Córdoba because he was on a military campaign against the Christians (with a view to reinforcing his image among the population), organised a rebel army that fell on Córdoba, overthrowing the caliph and taking the city. Sanchuelo, on learning of the revolt, returned to the capital to assert his rights but was killed by his opponents on arrival. That same afternoon in January 1009, his head nailed to a pike was carried through the streets of Córdoba, and Hixam II was forced to abdicate to Mohammed Al-Mahdi (with the title of Mohammed II). The fitna, a term that in Arabic means 'civil war' or 'discord', ended up igniting a fire in the capital of the caliphate that would soon spread throughout its territory and, after several years of disputes, would leave a desolate panorama of what was once the Caliphate of Córdoba.

Mohammed Al-Mahdi's coup d'état, with his ascension to the post of caliph, did not leave other pretenders to the caliphate in any way happy, and they openly confronted him, to the extent that he had to expel many of them from the Cordoban capital. His bad relations with the Berber population groups only increased the discontent of the majority of the population, which finally resulted in an uprising led by Hixam, another grandson of Abderraman III and therefore in the line of succession of the Umayyads, whose father, the Berber Suleiman Al-Mustain, had been imprisoned by Mohammed Al-Mahdi.

Evidently, either side was prepared to go to any lengths to achieve their aims, so they sought allies for their respective causes. They found them in the subjugated lands in the north of the peninsula, which had been ruled by Christian rulers until a few years before. This reversed the trend that had traditionally existed, whereby it was the Christians who needed the caliph's troops to solve their political problems.

Sancho García of Castile sided with the Berbers and managed to defeat the troops of Mohammed Al-Mahdi in the vicinity of Alcolea, in coalition with the counts of Barcelona (Ramón Borrell) and Urgell (Armengol I). The latter had to flee with the survivors of his troops, abandoning the idea of returning to Córdoba and heading towards the northern border areas, specifically towards Toledo (Tulaytula), where he had the support of the governor of the lower border, the Slav Wâdih.

Barely a week after the Battle of Alcoléa in November 1009, Suleiman was proclaimed caliph in the Great Mosque of Córdoba. Only the lands to the south of the Cordoban state would follow the new caliph, while the rest of Al-Andalus would remain under the control of Mohammed II.

THE FRAGMENTATION OF AL-ANDALUS

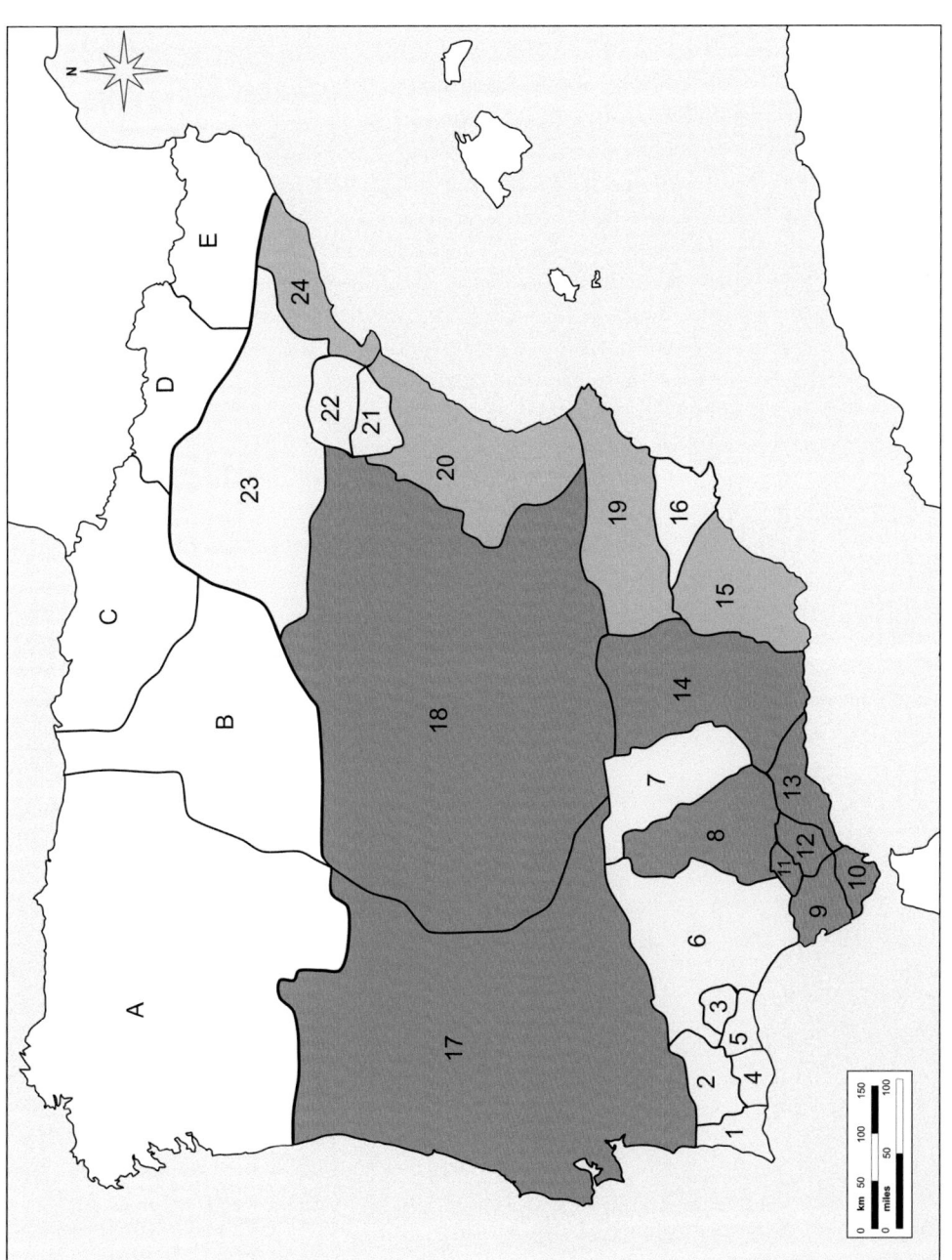

Taifa kingdoms that emerged after the disintegration of the Caliphate of Córdoba. (Created by the author)
a) ANDALUSIAN: 1. SILVES; 2. MÉRTOLA; 3. NIEBLA; 4. ALGARVE; 5. HUELVA; 6. SEVILLE; 7. CÓRDOBA; 16. MURCIA; 21. ALPUENTE; 22. ALBARRACÍN; 23. ZARAGOZA
b) BERBER: 8. CARMONA; 9. ARCOS; 10. ALGECIRAS; 11. MORÓN; 12. RONDA; 13. MÁLAGA, 14. GRANADA; 17. BADAJOZ; 18. TOLEDO
c) SLAVIC: 15. ALMERÍA; 19. DENIA; 20. VALENCIA; 24. TORTOSA
d) CHRISTIAN KINGDOMS: A. LEÓN; B. CASTILE; C. NAVARRA; D. ARAGON; E. CATALAN COUNTIES

THE FALL OF MOORISH SEVILLE 1023-1091

In 1010, after the Battle of Acabalbacar near Córdoba, Mohammed II regained control of the caliphate, thanks to the collaboration of the counts of Barcelona and Urgell, although only for the three months it took for the faction controlled by the Slavs to overthrow him and put the deposed Hixam II back in power. After that, and in less than three years, Suleiman's Berbers returned to power. Suleiman's entry into Córdoba on 19 April 1013 was in blood and fire, allowing his troops to sack and destroy houses and palaces, which were razed to the ground within days (as was the case with the royal residence at Medina Azahara, which has survived to the present day with many signs of such destruction). The indiscriminate slaughter of the population was another of the guidelines followed by the Berbers, 'thirsty' for revenge against their enemies. It is said that it was probably during these massacres after Suleiman's return to Córdoba that Hixam II was strangled to death on the orders of Mohammed, Suleiman's son. However, his corpse was not exposed to the population, which would give rise to the tricks and myths that were created, which, due to their transcendence, will be discussed later on.

Suleiman's return was decisive for the subsequent fragmentation of Al-Andalus, as, during his second rule (between 1013 and 1016), he granted the status of lordships to the Berber-ruled regions, thus allowing the seeds of the political fragmentation of the Andalusian territory to growarmy.

The division created by Suleiman to please his Berber 'countrymen' quickly backfired, as it predictably caused his power to diminish. This situation of political weakness was conveniently exploited in the form of a new coup d'état, in this case by Ali ben Hammud (belonging to the Hammudid family of Málaga, descendants of the Idrisids of Fez, considered to be direct descendants of Muhammad), who proclaimed himself caliph of Al-Andalus in 1016. Subsequent plots against the new caliph were crushed before they came to fruition, but one of them led by Slavs succeeded in assassinating the caliph, who was succeeded by his brother Al-Qasim ben Hammud (who ruled from 1018 to 1021), He was succeeded by his nephew Yahya after dethroning him and imprisoning him in Jerez (ruling from 1021 to 1023), who sent a Berber general to take charge of the government of Córdoba, which greatly outraged the population of the ancient capital of the West. Once again, events were moving at breakneck speed, and the ongoing changes led to a spiral of violence in the lands of Al-Andalus that would destroy them over the next few years. The compact and powerful state that 'Abd al-Rahman III had succeeded in

Arquillo de la Plata. During the taifa period, it was one of the access gates to the Royal Alcázar. The layout and extent of the Seville royal palace(s) during the eleventh-century taifa period is still unknown today. (Author's collection)

THE FRAGMENTATION OF AL-ANDALUS

Walls separating the gardens from the Royal Alcázar. These gardens already existed in the eleventh century, although with a different layout to the present one. (Author's collection)

establishing had vanished, and in its place appeared various factions that always violently tried to take control of the country, and the proof of such instability is again demonstrated by the fact that, in the period 1021–1033, three new caliphs assumed power. This power was increasingly limited to a smaller area of territory, as the turmoil of the caliph's throne was followed by the gain of small chiefs and governors in the regions more distant from the Cordoban capital, who were in practice independent of the Cordoban government. This ambition, maintained by so many who coveted power on a greater or lesser scale without any concern for the interests of the common people, was to the detriment of the central state as well as Muslim religious and ethnic unity, which gradually drifted apart. The lack of this sense of Muslim unity among the new chiefs and rulers was the final straw that put an end to the Cordoban Caliphate in the first instance and to the presence of Muslim states on the peninsula in general as time went on. Despite the demise of the caliphate, the Umayyad tradition survived in the form of court and governmental rules to be followed by the taifa monarchs that emerged from the civil war.

With the fall of the Cordoban Caliphate, the axis of power shifted from the Arabs to the Berbers and thus to the confrontation between them. The Christian states did not miss the opportunity and took advantage of the general weakening of the once powerful and flourishing Andalusian state to become the arbiters of the many disputes that arose, always making a handsome profit from them.

The last caliph of Córdoba, Hixam III, elected in 1027, was deposed after the uprising in Córdoba by Banu Yahwar in November 1031. After this overthrow, the figure of the caliphate was abolished, freely allowing a fact that had already been in place for many years in different Andalusian regions, the formation of independent states or taifas of greater or lesser territorial extension with a certain tendency on the part of some of them to take control of their neighbours. These states, although mainly populated by Hispanics descended from the Hispano-Visigoths or Hispano-Romans, were mainly marked by the ruling ethnic group of each of them, allowing us to divide them into three groups of taifas: Arabs, Berbers and Slavs.

This period of revolts and clashes between one and the other ravaged the land of Al-Andalus from 1009 to 1031, which led to the disintegration of the state of Al-Andalus. It was the beginning of the brief but intense history of the Taifa Kingdom of Seville, a Hispano-Muslim kingdom where a family of Arab origin had managed to maintain power but that found itself surrounded by different states where kings of Berber origin ruled for the most part, events that would mark the existence of the Sevillian taifa.

The final consequence of this division was the loss of power and disunity among the Muslim states in the face of the growing power of the Christian states that would literally overwhelm the taifa kingdoms bordering their lands. It also led to the reappearance of parias or payments from one state to another basically so as not to be attacked by the state to which they would have to pay it, but the flow of these tributes changed drastically. These tributes that used to be paid by the Christians to the Muslims (the times of Almanzor barely 35 years earlier were not so distant) reversed their direction, and now it would be the Muslim states that would have to pay them to the Christians. These tributes would mean a progressive impoverishment of the Muslim kingdoms with a crushing fiscal pressure on their populations, while at the same time allowing slow but steady progress for the Christian states of the north, which came to control the military actions during the following years until the arrival of the Almoravids.

The Taifa Division

At this point, it is important to remember what the population of Al-Andalus was like and its peculiarities, which marked to a large extent the course of events during its existence. Andalusian society in the eleventh century was a melting pot, made up of different groups with marked differences between them. Thus, we find the large Muladí group, made up of the former inhabitants of the peninsula before the arrival of the Muslim troops who had converted from Christianity to Islam and who were generally characterised by their limited access to power. Two other groups are made up of both the descendants of Arab families and those of Berber families who had settled in the peninsula since the Muslim invasion. A fourth ethnic group is the Slavs, who, from the high command positions they held in the army from the time of 'Abd al-Rahman III, were able to exert a great deal of influence over palace decisions. Other ethnic groups, although not Islamic, were the Christians and Jews who lived in Andalusian territory.

What is certain is that this ethnic division, so marked among the Muslim inhabitants of Al-Andalus, was what determined a new political map of the Iberian Peninsula in which the former territory of Córdoba was divided

THE FRAGMENTATION OF AL-ANDALUS

Marble inscription in Arabic on display in the Archaeological Museum of Seville, dated 1022. It commemorates the death of an officer of the Sevillian army in 'the battle of Triana [in what seems to be the first written mention of the Triana quarter] at the edge of the river and near the aforementioned quarter, in the obedience of Amir al-Muminin al-Mamun al-Qasim, on Friday the twelfth night of 24 February 1022'. (Author's collection)

into multiple taifas. The last to proclaim its independence was, of course, the seat of the 'phantom' Caliphate of Córdoba, which was now limited to just a few kilometres around the city. As the years went by, most of the taifas developed a policy of continuous confrontation with the neighbouring taifas that definitively weakened Muslim power on the peninsula, which ended up decisively benefiting the Christian kingdoms of the north.

The main taifas that were generated over the years after the disintegration of the Caliphate of Córdoba were:

a) Taifas of Arab and Hispanic Muladí origin: Murcia, Córdoba, Seville, Niebla, Huelva, Santa María del Algarve, Mértola, Silves, Alpuente, Albarracín and Zaragoza
b) Taifas of Berber origin: Granada, Badajoz, Toledo, Ronda, Morón, Arcos, Málaga, Algeciras and Carmona
c) Taifas of Slavic origin: Valencia, Denia, Almería and Tortosa.

Andalusian Society

It is important to give a brief outline of the demographic component that existed in Al-Andalus during the eleventh century, as it was a determining factor in the events that took place on the Iberian Peninsula. The society that we find in the kingdom of Seville, as in the rest of Al-Andalus during the eleventh century, is a mixture of different types of population groups. Religiously speaking, we can divide this population into Muslims, Christians and Jews.

Muslims

These are all those who professed Islam, although within this group we can distinguish between Arab Muslims and non-Arab Muslims (Berbers, Slavs and Muladíes):

Arab Muslims

This group corresponds to the Arabs of Qaysi and Yemeni origin who arrived in the Iberian Peninsula during the years of conquest, as well as their descendants. When they arrived in the Iberian Peninsula, they behaved like the new aristocracy that replaced (in most cases) or coexisted (in fewer cases) with the Visigothic aristocracy.

They monopolised the best farmland while controlling all military and judicial functions, making them de facto the new rulers of the Iberian Peninsula. As mentioned above, the lineage of the Abbadids settled in the area of Tocina (Tossana), that of al-Ilhaniyun in the farmstead of La Macarena (Maqrana) and the Banu Yumhur in the Aljarafe area.

It is a proven fact that the different Arab lineages had their ups and downs on many occasions, but, despite the differences between them (Syrians, Yemenis and so on), above all they considered themselves Arabs and fought as a single people against their main Muslim enemies: the Berbers.

The progressive Hispanisation of the Arabs and the Islamisation of the Hispano-Visigoths led to the breaking down of the barriers between the two population groups that existed in the early years after the arrival of the Arabs in Al-Andalus. This rapprochement led the Muladíes (Hispano-Visigoths who converted to Islam) to identify themselves closely with the Arab aristocracy, and, in many cases, they acted in unity against those who could be a dangerous element to their hegemony, such as the Berbers or the Slavs.

The Hispano-Arabs would form the basis of the population of the Taifa Kingdom of Seville, as well as of some other taifa kingdoms, many of which would be absorbed with little difficulty by the Sevillian warlords.

Non-Arab Muslims

Berber Ethnicity

This population group accompanied the Arabs in their domination of Al-Andalus, albeit as mere auxiliaries. This meant that, once they had settled on the peninsula, they were relegated to the poorest, most undeveloped, mountainous and generally sparsely populated lands.

They were a people who, after their Islamisation, continued with a similar way of life to the one they had before their conversion. They remained far removed from the way of life of the Arabs, which soon led to clashes between them. From the ninth century onwards, they took part in many revolts against the dominant Hispano-Arab rulers, being reinforced on many occasions by the numerous contingents of troops of their own ethnicity who were recruited as mercenaries by the various caliphs, especially during the most successful period of the caliphate with Almanzor at the head of his armies.

After the division of the taifas, many of them came under the control of this ethnic group.

Slavs or Slaves

Slavery was an accepted fact of life in the Islamic world, and slaves became very important in Andalusian society.

At first, they were needed for agricultural and industrial tasks, although, as time went on, they also supplied the harems (concubines and eunuchs), palace posts and the armies of the Andalusian rulers. In the latter case, due to their extreme loyalty to their master, many slaves reached high positions in the various Andalusian armies. Eventually, they became so necessary in the positions they held that they gradually displaced their masters from their posts and were replaced by them.

In general, this social class did not initially mix with the other Andalusian social strata; it was from the eleventh century onwards that they became more closely linked with the Muladí population.

Some of the taifas that were created after the Caliphate of Córdoba were governed by Slavs, who had gained great power from their high military posts; these taifas were concentrated in the eastern part of the peninsula.

Another group of male slaves (although some ceased to be so over time) were black men from sub-Saharan Africa. Some of them became part of the Sevillian troops, who were in constant need of men due to their expansionist policy.

Muladíes

This social group is made up of the Hispano-Visigoths and their descendants who converted to Islam. They were the most numerous demographic elements in all of Al-Andalus. This group can also be divided into two clearly differentiated factions:

- The descendants of the Visigoth nobility with large estates that they partially kept when they converted to Islam.
- The small landowners and serfs with few possessions joined Islam as a way of improving their social status. In many cases, they had a very weak Christianisation, so it did not cost them much to change their religion. The conversion process required the completion of various notarial forms, also known as conversion contracts.

THE FALL OF MOORISH SEVILLE 1023-1091

As we can see in both cases, Islam represented a way to maintain or improve the social status of individuals. The new religion brought economic and social advantages that were undoubtedly accepted by many Hispanics.

As the Arab and Berber population mixed with the Hispanic population, another type of Muladí appeared, that of the children of a Hispanic mother with an Arab or Berber father. In general, we also consider them to be Muladíes, although we point out their special characteristics with respect to converts of pure Hispanic origin.

The end result of the mixing of Muladíes with Arabs and Berbers would be a social integration so high that it was not possible to distinguish them from the other social groups.

Christians

Despite the Muslim control of a large part of the peninsula, many people living in Islamic areas remained faithful to the Christian religion. This was made possible by the Muslim political and religious authorities' compromise in this regard. The influences of both Christians and Jews that Muhammad had on him were the mainstay of Islam's acceptance of the latter within its own society. However, another factor also had a decisive influence, since, in exchange for maintaining the Christian religion and its customs, these people had to pay a special territorial tax (jaray) and a personal tax (yizyah), which was imposed according to the profession and social status of each individual. Exempted from this tax were those under 20 and over 50 years of age, monks, invalids, the sick and beggars. In addition, they would also have to pay the same extraordinary taxes as the Muslims. Thanks to this 'freedom', the Christian community was able to remain structured despite Muslim territorial control, even having judges who legislated internally according to the old Visigothic law; a clear example of this is the persistence of the metropolitan seats of Toledo, Merida and Seville despite the interference of the high Andalusian rulers. The church of uliya on the outskirts of the Abbadid city of Seville, near the present-day Montequinto (formerly the farmhouse of Kuntis ma 'afir), was well known. In

Tower of the Church of Santa Catalina, which, although dating from the Christian period, shows us what the minarets of the mosques in Seville's 'neighbourhood' may have looked like. (Author's collection)

THE FRAGMENTATION OF AL-ANDALUS

the same way as the Jews, both communities were authorised to practise their own religions (although without publicly proclaiming them), as well as having the legal capacity to officiate marriages, divorces or any other civil matters within each of their communities. In contrast, with respect to the Jews, the Christians did not settle in their own neighbourhoods but were fully integrated with the rest of the Sevillian population.

During the taifa period, there were still many Christians in Al-Andalus, although the passing of the years under Muslim control had to some extent orientalised them. This led to some movements to halt this orientalisation in the Andalusian Christian community in the Islamic style.

Jews

The Jewish community suffered a situation very similar to that of the Christians who decided to continue with their religion. Perhaps the Jews were more favoured by the new masters, due to their help to them from the first days they arrived on the peninsula as a result of the harsh restrictions they suffered from the Visigoth monarchs. So important was their help to the Muslims that they left the administration of many newly conquered cities, such as Seville, Granada, Córdoba and Toledo, in charge of the Jews. The Jews were deeply integrated into Muslim culture, allowing them to have numerous scholars in the different fields of knowledge of the time, such as medicine, philosophy, geometry and music.

Similar to the Christians, most of them dedicated themselves to professions such as craftsmen, merchants and doctors, although some of them came to have an important political role and therefore great power despite not sharing a religion with the Muslims. Abbadid Seville was no

A basin of ablutions on display in the Archaeological Museum of Seville dating from the tenth century during the caliphate period. The city of Seville went from being a city of some importance within the Caliphate of Córdoba to possibly becoming the most important capital of the entire Iberian Peninsula during the eleventh-century taifa period thanks to the expansive policy pursued by the three kings of the Abbadid family. (Author's collection)

THE FALL OF MOORISH SEVILLE 1023-1091

exception, with important figures in the political life of the capital of Jewish origin and religion.

As mentioned when writing about the Christians, the Jews, unlike the Christians, tended to group together in close proximity, avoiding dispersion throughout the city. In Seville, from the emirate period onwards, the Jews settled mainly in the area within the walls of the Carmona Gate.

Another image of the Beatus of Urgell depicting on this occasion a castle with a besieged Muslim appearance. The defenders are armed with spears and rounded shields, swords and stones. (Open source)

5

Birth of the Taifa of Seville: First Stage, 1023–1042

Abul Qasim

During the fitna, Seville was ruled by Al-Qasim ben Hammud, brother of Ali, a Cordoban caliph (a Hammudid) who was assassinated in 1018. Like the other members of this Berber dynasty, Al-Qasim ben Hammud left the city with the intention of succeeding Ali on the caliphate's throne.

In the climate of decay in which the once powerful Caliphate of Córdoba was immersed, it did not take long for the Sevillian capital to show its rebellious side in the face of central power. Thus, in 1022, a revolt took place in Seville by the cadi against the Cordoban government represented by the Hammudid Berbers. After the Battle of Triana (in 1022), in a short space

Current walls of the Royal Alcázar. Although almost all the walls are of Christian origin, they give an idea of what they might have been like during the taifa period. (Author's collection)

of time, Seville proclaimed itself independent of Córdoba, giving birth to the taifa state of Seville, which in a few years would reach its maximum splendour only to be almost immediately destroyed and subsequently largely forgotten.

The cadi who stood up to the caliphate troops belonged to one of the most influential Arab families in the area and was named Abul Qasim Muhammad ben Ismail ben Abbad. The Abbad family, to which he belonged, was one of the first to arrive on the peninsula at the time of the Muslim invasion, from their native lands in the district of Hims (in present-day Syria) to settle in the area of present-day Tocina (at least one man from this family took part in the invasion, after which he settled in the farmhouse of Yumin in the district of Tocina, some 30 kilometres from the capital). From there, some of the members of the family moved to Seville and Córdoba, where, thanks to their efforts and hard work, they prospered to the point of directly serving the Umayyad family in which the power resided. The Abbadids claimed to belong to a high-status family of the Yemeni Lajm tribe (and thus of pure Arab origin), which was at the time one of the most important families in early Islam.

Although the family was not considered a noble family, thanks to their work and constancy, the different generations of the family gradually raised their 'status' in Spanish-Muslim society in Seville. This happened to such an extent that Abul Qasim's father, Ismail ben Abbad, was already an influential man who became imam of the mosque of Córdoba in the time of Almanzor, as well as cadi of Seville. In fact, Ismail ruled the city and its Cora together with Allah al-Zubaydi and Allah Ben Maryan. After he was disabled by sight problems, it was his son Abul Qasim (his full name was Abul Qasim Muhammad ben Ismail ben Ismail ben Muhammad ben Ismail ben Qurays ben Abbad ben Amr ben Aslam ben Amr ben Itaf ben Naim al-Lajmi) who was given the post of corregidor (magistrate who exercised royal jurisdiction in his territory) and cadi (actually he acted as double vizier like his father) by decision of the Cordoban caliph himself (contravening the last decision of his father who had granted the post to another high-ranking citizen in Seville), a post that he carried out with efficiency and admiration of his fellow citizens. To such an extent was he respected by the people of Seville that, when the uprising against the Berber oppression from Córdoba took

Detail of the inside of the gateway along the walls of the Royal Alcázar showing the two holes used to pour boiling liquid in case the gate had to be defended. (Author's collection)

BIRTH OF THE TAIFA OF SEVILLE: FIRST STAGE, 1023–1042

Remains of the arches of the Islamic courtyard of the taifa palace in Seville. (Photograph used with the permission of Cristina Vargas Lorenzo from her article 'La recuperación del palacio primitivo del Alcázar de Sevilla')

place, he was chosen to lead the destiny of the newly created independent state of Seville. Abul Qasim had been the highest authority in the city and its lands since he became cadi of Seville, but the fragility of the Caliphate of Córdoba meant that he acted as the leader of an independent state from 1022, although the official date currently considered to be the beginning of the independent kingdom of Seville is the beginning of November 1023. It was in this month that the gates of the city were closed to Al-Qasim ben Hammud (leader of one of the factions that, after the civil war of the Caliphate of Córdoba, had risen as the 'legitimate' caliph of Córdoba since 1018 and controlled the territory of Seville) and a rebellion took place against the representative of Al-Qasim ben Hammud, who was none other than his son Muhammad. Thus, the city of Seville, after breaking the ties of submission with Al-Qasim and expelling his two sons from Seville (the aforementioned Muhammad and Hasan), began its journey as a completely independent state.

The population of the city consisted mainly of Hispano-Muslims (descendants of the Roman-Visigothic population who had converted to Islam), Sevillians, an Arab minority (who held high political and economic positions), Mozarabs and Jews. In general, all groups were happy to separate from Córdoba, as they considered that they would benefit from it. The reason for the start of the Seville revolt seems to have been the order

Entrance gate to the Dar al-Imara. This is one of the few remains still standing of the citadel from the caliphate period. This palace continued to be used during the taifa period, despite the construction of several new ones. (Author's collection)

given by Al-Qasim ben Hammud to evacuate 1,000–1,500 houses from Seville to give them to Berbers loyal to him.

Abul Qasim, whom Jacinto Bosch in his history of Seville called selfish and ambitious as well as shrewd and intelligent, accepted the appointment by his countrymen willingly, but he made it conditional on surrounding himself with a group of men that he himself would choose to carry out his function. Evidently, the personalities who were chosen to govern the city were part of the nobility, thus ensuring that they did not pose problems by not being in power. Thanks to this astute way of acting, Abul Qasim together with Allah al-Zubaydi and Allah Ben Maryan formed a triumvirate that continued to govern (as in his father's time) the city and the territory belonging to his Cora (the administrative circumscription in the time of the Emirate and Caliphate of Córdoba and that corresponded to the territory belonging to the city of Seville). In any case, Abul Qasim was still the most important figure, and, though surprising considering his balanced character, he gradually dispensed with them, until the government of the city was run by him alone.

Independence had not been easy to achieve, but it would be even easier to maintain it. To avoid falling under the sway of Córdoba again, Abul Qasim wisely decided that it was a priority to form an army that would be powerful enough to maintain independence and, at a later stage, to be able to take possession of other territories annexed to the Sevillian taifa.

The situation in Al-Andalus was very complex, and every decision would have its consequences. At the end of 1023, both the Cordobans and the Sevillians clashed with Al-Qasim ben Hammud (from the Hammudid and therefore Berber side), who had become the 'governor' of this territory during the fitna.

Model at the Fundación Biodiversidad of the Patio de Banderas showing what the area of the entrance gate to the Dar al-Imara would have originally looked like during the taifa period. (Author's collection)

BIRTH OF THE TAIFA OF SEVILLE: FIRST STAGE, 1023–1042

The Sevillian army was organised not only with the remnants of the caliphate army that had helped Abul Qasim in his revolt but also with mercenary troops. These troops, made up indistinctly of Arabs, Hispano-Muslims, Berbers or Slavs, came to the call for a good purse of money for themselves and with promises of more benefits for the future. The success of this appeal to the army was only partial, as at first they obtained little more than half a thousand knights, as well as levy troops as infantry, which was considered a very small number of men to defend a territory such as Seville. As would happen later with Al Mutadid and Al Mutamid, the command of the Sevillian army fell to the heir, in this case, Ismail ben Abbad.

It is curious to know how Abul Qasim obtained more than half of these 500 knights, who were also Christians. It was because he was in need of new troops in 1025 and decided to make an expedition northwards to look for more men, so, when he arrived north of the town of Viseo or Viseu in Portuguese (in the northern region of what is now Portugal), he attacked two fortresses that were separated by a ravine. These were controlled by Christian troops of supposed Gassanid Arab origin, who had maintained their fortresses of Al Akowén (translated as 'the two brothers' and today located in Alafoens) by pacts made with caliphate troops many years before and who did not owe obedience to any Christian or Muslim kingdom. Thus, after conquering both fortresses, the 300 remaining defenders were 'convinced' to act as mercenaries in the service of Seville. More than half of Abul Qasim's army was Christian during this time, and this did not pose a problem for them to fight for their new lord in the years to come. As was usual during the Caliphate of Córdoba and in the newborn kingdom of Seville, there were people who, because of their worth, managed to rise in the structure of the country's government regardless of their origin. This was the case of Sisnando Davidiz, one of the men captured in Viseo, who

One of the access gates to the city of Toledo. The kingdom of Toledo became the greatest rival to the kingdom of Seville for power in the city of Córdoba. (Open source by Daderot)

became vizier to King Al Mutadid of Seville and later went on to serve the Castilian Kings Ferdinand I and Alfonso VI. He would even act as governor of the city of Toledo after its conquest by Alfonso VI.

In 1027, the Sevillians realised how difficult it was to maintain their independence. Yahya ben Ali's moves to seize power from the dying Caliphate of Córdoba in conjunction with the caliph of Málaga and the chief of Carmona (of Berber ethnicity) decided to set their sights on weak Seville in order to establish the capital of the Cordoban Caliphate there under the figure of Yahya ben Ali. Evidently, the situation became a matter of life and death for the small Seville state, as its meagre army could hardly defend itself for a few days against the superior attacking army. Abul Qasim acted in the wisest possible way, which was to recognise Yahya as caliph, avoiding the sack and destruction of Seville and its region, but this was no easy task, as Yahya, following an old custom, demanded the delivery of hostages from important families to answer with their lives if they did not comply with what had been agreed in the city of Seville. These conditions were another cold-water pitcher for the main Sevillian families, who refused to offer their relatives in such a dangerous barter. It was again Abul Qasim who managed to straighten out the situation and, in a brave gesture, offered his own son Abbad as a hostage, which Yahya accepted in view of Abul Qasim's great influence; he then refused to enter the city of Seville in blood and fire. Seville had been saved in extremis possibly from destruction, and the people had witnessed Abul Qasim's gesture, which definitively made his figure stand out above that of any other renowned personage in Seville. Thanks to this popular support, Abul Qasim definitively took the decision to dispense with all those who craved power in Seville, remaining the sole ruler of Seville, or, in other words, from cadi he became a king in a practical capacity (in fact, he adopted the title of malik or king).

Although opinions are divided on this matter, we must consider that Abul Qasim from 1027 became the first taifa king of Seville; as such, he would rule without any external influence, and finally his position would become hereditary in the purest monarchical style, ceding the position to one of his sons (according to other studies, the most probable date for the beginning of his reign is 2 November 1023 as a de facto prolongation of the rule of the city as he had done up to that time).

The pact between Abul Qasim and Yahya of submission of the former to the latter did not really have much more scope. As stated above, the comings and goings in the power of the caliphate (especially in the later years) did not allow either side to be powerful enough to maintain its theoretical rights for long over its rivals. Thus, Abul Qasim reigned over his territories, although, for Yahya, he was only a cadi who owed him obedience.

On 30 November 1031, the now fictitious Caliphate of Córdoba was officially abolished, a fact that gave even more support to the reality of the fragmentation of Al-Andalus into independent taifa kingdoms. For Abul Qasim, despite being theoretically subject to Yahya's control, it served to set his sights with determination on a completely independent Sevillian kingdom, both practically and theoretically.

BIRTH OF THE TAIFA OF SEVILLE: FIRST STAGE, 1023–1042

With this aim of further establishing his territories, Abul Qasim recognised the need to extend the territorial margins of Seville with the dual purpose of allowing for a better defence of his kingdom as well as to obtain more land, wealth and population. But the other independent kingdoms that had been forged after the collapse of the Caliphate of Córdoba had similar intentions, and, in some cases, they were very powerful new kingdoms, such as the Zirid kingdom of Granada or the Hammudid kingdoms of Málaga and Algeciras (all of which were ethnic Berbers and as such were naturally at odds with the Arabs). Moreover, these new states of Berber control had the moral support of a large part of the common people, as they were subject to a leader with a caliphate title, who represented not only political power but also religious power. Faced with this situation, Abul Qasim initially had a difficult solution, as he did not even come from a noble family, let alone a caliphate family. But once again, the Sevillian monarch's ingenuity was fundamental, as he recovered the deposed Caliph Hixam II or someone who pretended to be him for 'active service'. Some (as seems to have been the case) thought him dead in the second Suleiman Caliphate, others believed he had fled to the East, where he would have spent the last years of his life, while others believed he was still alive and in full possession of his rights to religious power.

Hixam II was still reminiscent of the golden days of the caliphate for part of the population, so it is not surprising that he continued to have supporters. Moreover, the intense rumours about him (sometimes politically motivated, sometimes spontaneous) did not agree with his status. Abul Qasim had only to take advantage of these legends circulating in his

Painting made in 1885 by Dionisio Baixeras Verdaguer and exhibited in the Auditorium of the University of Barcelona that shows us the opulence and splendour of the throne room of Abd al-Rahman III that in a few years would disappear giving rise to the appearance of multiple kingdoms of taifas in the Iberian Peninsula. (Open source)

THE FALL OF MOORISH SEVILLE 1023-1091

favour and unleash his ruse in a public act during which he made it known that Hixam II was with him and that Abul Qasim himself recognised him as caliph. In order to make the plot more truthful, they gathered some well-paid people who declared under oath that the man was the real Hixam II, among them some women belonging to the old seraglio maintained by the caliph. Of course, after creating the 'false' Hixam II, Abul Qasim 'ascended' to a higher rank such as that of hayib or prime minister of the said caliph.

Despite the untruthfulness of the Sevillian leader's ruse, the common people felt that they could continue with their old Umayyad caliph leading their prayers. The mosques once again held prayers for the caliph, coins were minted in his name, and even Abul Qasim 'renounced' his rule of the city and placed himself at the disposal of Hixam II as hayib or chancellor of the caliph. In order for the whole scheme to work, they had to be very careful not to show it in public and to spread the good news of the caliph's 'return' to the other territories of Al-Andalus with the intention that the other Muslim kingdoms would also recognise him as caliph and thus strengthen Abul Qasim's political position. But, mysteriously, the ruse worked, or at least the rulers of taifas such as Carmona, Denia and Tortosa, the Balearic Islands and Valencia allowed it to work. Even Abul Qasim tried to take up residence in the palace of the Umayyads in Córdoba, but the regent of Córdoba prevented him from doing so, demonstrating the fraud to his citizens, and, from that day on, a deep enmity between Córdoba

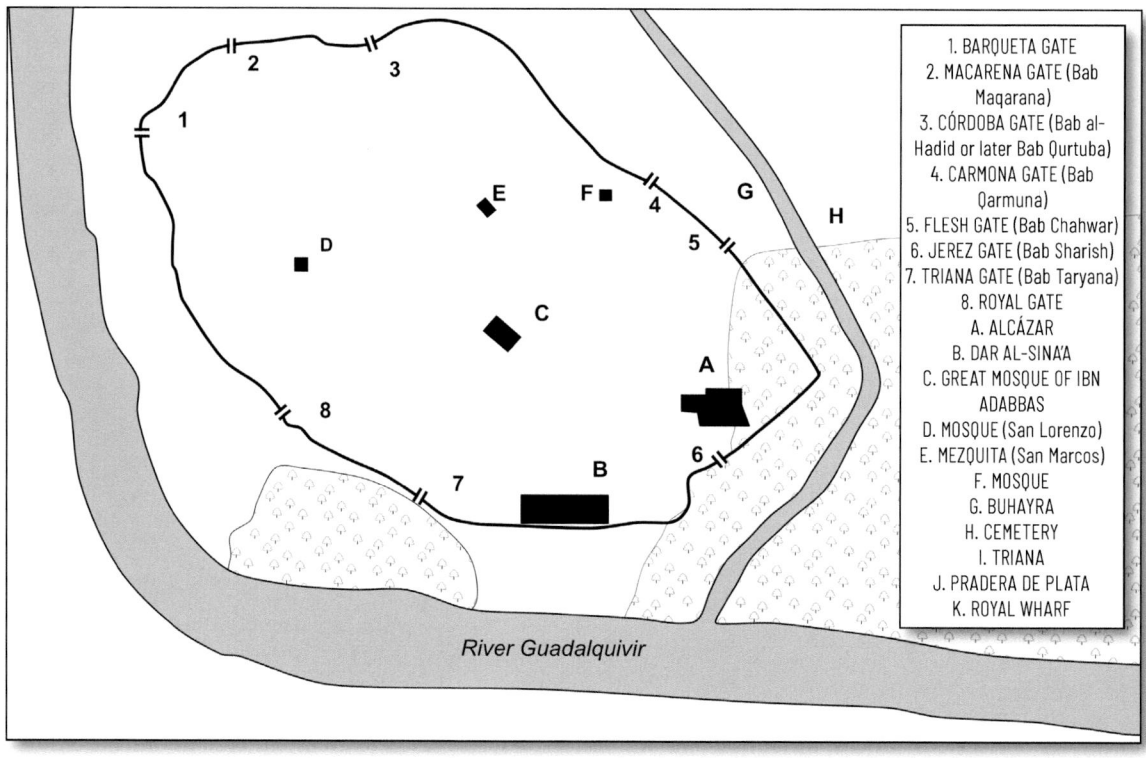

Hypothetical drawing of the extent of Abbot Seville in the eleventh century based on Levi Pr. (Drawn by the author)
SCHEMATIC PLAN OF THE CITY OF SEVILLE IN THE ELEVENTH CENTURY (BASED ON LEVI PR.)

and Seville began. Ibn Yahwar, the Cordoban regent, did indeed accept the 'return' of Hixam II at first, but, shortly afterwards, he renounced it. The reason for this renunciation is that both Ibn Yahwar and some of the Cordoban nobles went to visit Hixam II in a Sevillian palace as a 'courtesy' of the regent of Seville, who showed the caliph to the Cordobans. But the Sevillian, citing problems with the caliph's eyesight, caused the whole room to be kept in darkness, which was the trigger for the Cordobans to further increase their doubts about the caliph's authenticity, a fact that was confirmed shortly afterwards by their refusal to believe in him. As was to be expected, something similar happened in other taifas, and the whole plot collapsed. This attempt to unite the efforts of the different kingdoms for a common purpose, after its failure, only led to a greater desire to annex one taifa to another and to achieve union by force and not by the unity of faith and goodwill.

Abul Qasim, angry with Zohair of Almería, the only Slavic prince who did not obey Hixam II, decided to give him a lesson with attacks on his lands, but the Almerian allied himself with the Granada troops of Habbus, and they met him, forcing him to retreat back to his lands.

The Calatrava Esterero

We briefly relate what the chronicles tell us about the great farce that was created about Caliph Hixam II, a political ruse that Abul Qasim was able to use to his advantage. But this was only possible thanks to the existence of a man who bore a strong physical resemblance to the missing caliph, and his name was Khalaf.

Khalaf, or Khlaf, was a sterling born in the city of Calatrava who, knowing his extraordinary resemblance to Hixam II, decided to take advantage of it. His ambition led him to convince his neighbours that he was the caliph dethroned by Soleiman. The inhabitants of Calatrava were so convinced by the insistence of the esterero (a person who works esparto grass, reeds, palm and so on, which are then used to cover the floor of rooms, among other uses) that they recognised him as their legitimate sovereign, disassociating themselves from their current lord, Ismail, the king of the Taifa of Toledo. Ismail ben Dhi nun sent his troops against the population of Calatrava to put an end to the revolt.

It was at this point that the paths of Abul Qasim and Khalaf met, as the Sevillian king took advantage of this farce for his own political purposes, as mentioned above. Khalaf thus came under the protection of the Sevillian king, and a story began to be created to justify the presence of Hixam II in Calatrava as a simple esterero; it was October–November 1035 when these events took place.

Word spread that Hixam II, after the disturbances in the caliphate capital, had decided to secretly leave for Asia. From there, he made his way to Mecca, where he fulfilled the precept of pilgrimage. There, he had an unfortunate encounter with the emir's black warriors who stripped him of everything he possessed, which was nothing more than a bag of money and some jewellery. After being left in such a pitiful situation, he heard about a caravan that was soon to leave for Palestine, which he joined. He arrived in Jerusalem, where he took up residence. There, after wandering through the city's markets, he met a silversmith with whom he struck up a friendship and from whom he learned the trade. He stayed there for a few years working as an assistant to the matador until 1033, when he decided to return to the Iberian Peninsula under a false name: Khalaf. After arriving in Al-Andalus, he settled in the town of Calatrava, where, as we have already mentioned, he convinced his neighbours that he was the real Hixam II.

When he was transferred to the city of Seville, he entered secretly so that the people could not see him, as there was a danger that someone might recognise the farce.

Subsequently, Abul Qasim completed the ruse by attempting to impose the replacement caliph on the various taifas with the results already discussed in the sections on Abul Qasim and Al Mutadid.

Expansionist Policy

The geopolitical situation of Abul Qasim and the Arab-Andalusian Taifa of Seville was as follows. To the north, it had the powerful Taifa of Badajoz (Berber) and that of Córdoba (Arab-Andalusian); to the southwest, the small Taifas of Mértola, the Algarve, Huelva and Niebla (all Arab-Andalusian); to the south and southeast, the Taifas of Carmona, Arcos and Morón (Berber). In addition, there were some territories in the west that had remained outside the influence of other kingdoms, such as the city of Beja (Madinat Baya), which had been ravaged by the Berbers in the many disputes that became so frequent in Al-Andalus in those years. This 'solitude' of the city of Beja put it in the sights of the Sevillian taifa, which considered that the best defence was a good attack and that the more distant its borders were from the capital, the greater the security would be (similar to the concept of 'Lebensraum' followed by National Socialist Germany in the twentieth century). But this thought was also held by the king of the Berber Taifa of Badajoz (Batalyaws), Abdalá ben Aftas, especially after being informed by his spies of Abul Qasim's ideas, which was why he sent troops under the command of his son Muhammad (the future King Al Muzaffar) to take Beja ahead of the Sevillians. The clash between the two kingdoms was imminent, and its continuity over time would continue throughout the life of the Sevillian taifa, as we shall see below.

Returning to the race that had begun for the siege and subsequent capture of the city of Beja, we know that once again a son of Abul Qasim, Ismail, together with the cadi of Carmona, Abdalá al-Birzali, were chosen to command the allied troops from Seville and Carmona. The confrontation with the troops from Badajoz, assisted by troops from the lord of Mértola, Abén Taifur, did not take long, ending with the Sevillian victory over them, the capture of Muhammad and the capture of Beja and bordering areas between Évora and the sea, as far as Lisbon itself. Muhammad was taken to Carmona, where he remained a prisoner, until it was possible to take advantage of the advantage of having him captured against his father, the king of Badajoz. After the triumph, the Sevillian army launched itself against the area north of Évora and other areas of the Algarve, weakening the Aftasid presence in the area.

This victory only inflamed the spirits of the Sevillian monarch, who became emboldened and began to carry out raids in the lands south of Badajoz and Córdoba, seeking above all to 'mark' his territory and his power against possible rivals. In the case of the king of Badajoz, Abdalá ben Aftas, he agreed to sign a peace with the Sevillian king in which, in exchange for his son's freedom, he would respect the lands conquered by the Sevillians while allowing his troops the right of passage through the lands of Badajoz if requested to do so. Between March and April 1030, Muhammad ben Aftas was taken to the lands of Badajoz with the honours of a prince.

But Abdalá ben Aftas did not forget the affront of the defeat of Beja, the capture of his son and the conditions of peace with which he had to come to terms, and, as soon as the opportunity arose, he prepared to strike back at Abul Qasim. In 1034, in order to enforce the right of passage of Sevillian troops under the command of the Sevillian heir, Ismail, through the lands of the kingdom of Badajoz to carry out attacks on the Christian kingdom of León, Abul Qasim's troops headed north. Despite Ismail's misgivings about the hospitality and good treatment of the troops from Badajoz compared to those from Seville, they continued to advance towards the interior of the lands of Badajoz, where, cowardly passing through a gorge in the Sierra de la Estrella, close to the lands of León, they were attacked and massacred jointly by the troops from Badajoz and the warned troops from León. Ismail and a few of his men were lucky to escape on horseback in the direction of the nearest city under Abbadid control. The fate of future relations between Seville and Badajoz was sealed, and the bloodletting of men on the borders between the two kingdoms would last to a greater or lesser degree throughout the existence of the Sevillian kingdom.

After the 'return' of Hixam II, and despite the fact that the kingdom of Seville enjoyed de facto independence, the situation of the Caliph Yahya's theoretical dependence was maintained in the capital of Seville in a more or less stable manner, until, with the caliphate having disappeared (in 1035), Yahya was recognised as the imam or leader of the Berber Andalusian party. This new situation brought him into direct confrontation with his main rival faction, that of the Arab party, which by then was headed by Abul Qasim.

Yahya established himself in the Berber town of Carmona, a few kilometres from the Sevillian capital, forcing the troops he encountered into his service. Once his army was reinforced, he set out on the road to Seville, ravaging everything in his path.

Although over time the Sevillian kingdom had improved in terms of its army (both in number and quality), Abul Qasim knew that any conflict within his territories would always lead to destruction and starvation for the

Sevillian people, whoever won. So, knowing from confidants from Carmona of Yahya's weakness for wine (various sources refer to him as a man who was almost always drunk), he ordered his son Ismail and Muhammad al-Birzali (former cadi of Carmona, expelled by Yahya himself) together with a detachment of cavalry to set up a nightfall raid on Yahya's troops. With a small detachment of cavalry, they provoked Yahya's troops who were in Carmona to go out after them, with such good fortune that soon a force of some 300 men led by Yahya himself went after the Seville column. The latter faced the onslaught of the enemy force until they agreed to retreat in the direction of where Ismail was ambushed. Taking advantage of the help provided by the darkness to the outnumbered troops and the hasty decisions taken by a drunken Yahya, the Sevillian army, which included Christian mercenaries (the aforementioned Christians of Al Akowén), won the battle. They managed to kill Yahya, and, taking advantage of the lack of control of the Berber armies, they took the city of Carmona, of which Muhammad al-Birzali was to become its first independent king.

But the Andalusian lands were too small a 'corral' for so many 'roosters', and, if any one raised its head more than usual, it was quickly hounded by the others. Such was the case in August 1036, when Seville was beginning to look like a taifa with greater power with each passing day and had turned its gaze westwards. But how long would it take to look eastwards? The taifa leaders of Carmona, Granada and Almería wondered. They thus agreed to ally themselves in order to make a show of power to the Sevillian king and to remove from him any idea of expansionism towards their respective territories. It is striking that the al-Birzali, who was often allied with the king, found himself in this alliance, although he was under pressure from the kingdom of Seville as well as from its eastern flank, which is why he was involved in the alliance. The coalition troops assembled in Carmona, from where they advanced towards the Abbad lands, first taking the village of Tocina (of such historical importance for the Abbad family) and other small fortresses such as Al-Qala (no exact location) until they reached the vicinity of the capital, where they attacked with blood and fire localities such as Aznalcázar. Finally, they made their way to the suburb of Triana, ravaging it.

In the same way, and to further affront Abul Qasim and discredit him even more in the eyes of his people, the three kings, the Berber al-Birzali, the Zirid from Granada Habus and the Slav from Almería Zuhayr, in the town of Aznalcázar proclaimed Idris ben Alí ben Hammud as caliph. After the demonstration of power against the Sevillian kingdom, they finally decided to return to their lands without even being harassed by the Sevillian troops, who had been surprised and were outnumbered.

In 1039, there were again disputes between the kingdoms of Seville and Carmona, but the latter took the Taifa of Málaga and Granada as allies. All of them had outstanding accounts with Abul Qasim, so such a coalition was not difficult. Carmona, due to its proximity to the Sevillian taifa, was a priority target, and Granada and Málaga sought to punish Seville for having taken in Aben Abbas, former vizier of the kingdom of Almería and

BIRTH OF THE TAIFA OF SEVILLE: FIRST STAGE, 1023–1042

at odds with both the Granadans and the Malagan taifa, as a 'political exile'. Everything was resolved with a confrontation between the two sides with the final defeat of Ismail ben Abbad's army, again motivated in part by the numerical inferiority of his host and the treachery of some of his men. Ismail ben Abbad, who was the heir to the crown, died in this battle, which took place between 1039 and 1040 (possibly between September and October 1039) in the vicinity of Ecija, after a small siege of the city of Córdoba had already taken place. This combat is described in Maillo Salgado's translation of the Bayan, as quoted in the work entitled *Los reinos de taifas* (*The Taifa Kingdoms*) by Guichard and Soravia, as follows:

Another image taken from the Cantigas where we see a group of Christian horsemen chasing a group of Muslim horsemen. The use of the turban on the Muslim side is noteworthy. (Open source)

> There was in the company of Ibn Abbad a troop of Berbers who deserted him and betrayed him, then defeat seized him because of them; for they were not faithful to him in fighting the Berbers his fellows, and there remained with him only a small group of his officers and slaves. His endurance was worthy of honour, while the attacks came upon him and the swords took the same trajectories. He charged at them left and right until his wounds covered him and the swords ate up his entire army, except for the Berbers who fled before that.

In this account, we can see that it was a betrayal by his Berber troops that led to Ismail's defeat and death; in the same way, we can get an idea of the composition of a Sevillian army contingent at that time, where the strong elements were mainly composed of slaves and Berbers. According to some sources, the head of the Sevillian prince was sent to the king of Málaga.

Three years of relative tranquillity passed in the Sevillian kingdom, with minor border frictions of no further significance, until Abul Qasim died on 24 January 1042. The first Abbadid monarch had done no more than plough the furrows in a land that would flourish under the reign of his son Al Mutadid and later his grandson Al Mutamid, who would bring the small kingdom of Seville to its apogee and to its sad end. He left his heir and an Andalusian Arab kingdom at odds with many of its neighbouring kingdoms of Berber origin.

6

Settlement of the Kingdom of Seville: 1042–1069

View of one of the primitive towers of the Royal Alcázar of Seville, where the representative of the emir-caliph of Córdoba and later the Sevillian kings resided. (Author's collection)

Al Mutadid

Great changes were to take place in the kingdom of Seville when, after the death of Abul Qasim, his son and successor, Abu Amr Abbad ben Muhammad ben Ismail ben Abbad, known by the nickname or honorific title of Al Mutadid (after the caliph of Baghdad of the same name, who was very possibly his role model), took control of the destiny of the kingdom of Seville. Al Mutadid, born on 31 July 1016 in Seville, may well have come to power only two days after his father's death, on 26 January 1042, at the age of 25, and took the title of háchib (prime minister or chancellor) from Caliph Hixam II, maintaining the fiction that his father had begun years before. Thus, Seville, with Al Mutadid at its head, would continue to be the banner of the Arab-Andalusian party in Al-Andalus, in opposition to the Berber party.

Although the name by which he is remembered in history is Al Mutadid, this is no more than a nickname (Al Mutadid bi-Llah or the one who seeks God's support), although prior to this he had other titles such as Fajr al-Dawla (the pride of the state) or al-Mansur bi-Fadl Allah (the victor by the grace of God), du l-wizaratayn (the one of the two vizierates, used at the beginning

SETTLEMENT OF THE KINGDOM OF SEVILLE: 1042–1069

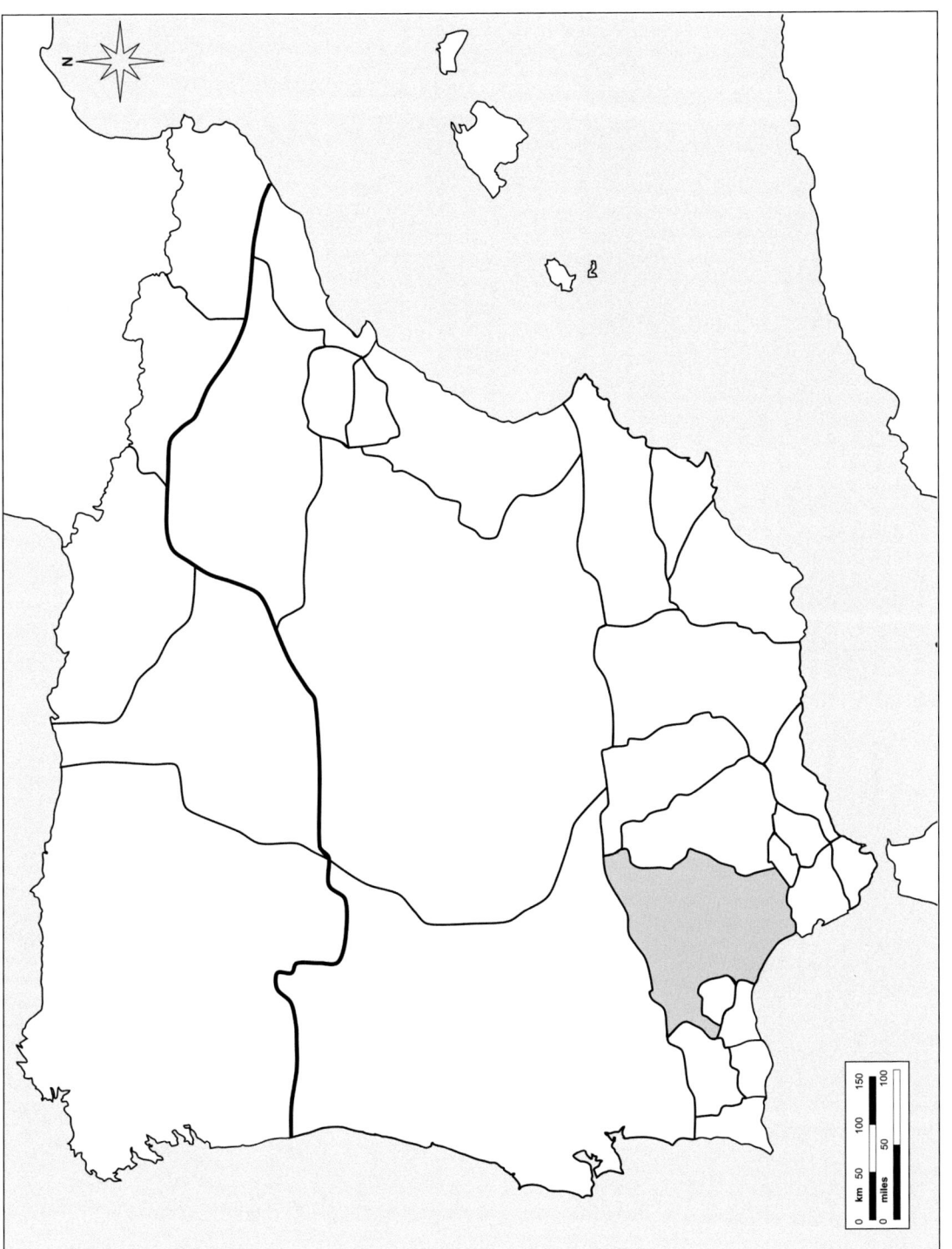

Extension of the kingdom of Seville in 1041. (Map drawn by the author)

THE FALL OF MOORISH SEVILLE 1023-1091

View of the two towers that guard and protect the now closed Dar al-Imara gate. They are located in Calle Joaquín Romero Murube. (Author's collection)

of his rule) or asad al-muluk (the lion of kings). These honorific titles were merely the imitation by the taifa kings of many of the aspects linked to the tradition of the first kingdoms of Islam in the East, the Abbasid caliphs and later the Caliphate of Córdoba. After all, they invested the rulers of the small taifas of the Iberian Peninsula with ancestry and greatness, putting them on a par in practice with the powerful caliphs of the past.

Al Mutadid had a personality very much in keeping with his historical context in which everyone was against everyone else: he boasted of his extreme cruelty, he was vengeful, intriguing, perfidious and ambitious, but, at the same time, he had the gift of audacity, his refined education, his capacity for reflection and his intelligence. The possibly egocentric, violent, sadistic and paranoid character of the new Sevillian monarch was to have a great influence on the history of the Sevillian kingdom, both outwardly (with numerous conquests) and inwardly (by executing his first-born son). Also, despite his religious precepts, he was fond of drinking, and, according to some revised texts, he kept a harem through which no less than 800 women passed during the years of his reign. The texts that have come down to us tell us that Al Mutadid was a man of formidable appearance and with a great fondness for women and the pleasures of the flesh. He had many women throughout his life and from different origins (as was generally the case in any taifa court), although his favourite was the daughter of the lord of Denia and the Balearic Islands, Mujahid al-'Amiri. The celebration of the wedding feast with the princess of Denia is said to have lasted a week. When he died, he left no less than 70 of them and some 20 sons and 20 daughters, for whom, despite his reputation for cruelty, he showed a deep love, considering them an extension of what he was in life. Although the kingdom of Seville did not take any warlike action against the kingdom of Denia due to the friendship and kinship between their kings (Mujahid of Denia was the father-in-law of the king of Seville), Al Mutadid did intrigue some time later, without success, to make a brother of his wife (Hassan) accede to the throne as opposed to the true heir to the throne.

On the other hand, he was enlightened, composed poems and loved the arts and letters like his father. As fond as he was of carnal pleasures, he also devoted himself to the affairs of government, which he always handled personally. His love of culture and his patronage of artists has sometimes

Obverse and reverse of a divided dirhem of the Taifa of Seville in the name of Al Mutadid in AH 456 (AD 1062). (Author's collection)

led him to be likened to the Italian Renaissance princes, of course, with a cultural and spatial–temporal distance.

Due to his developed ability to analyse geopolitical situations, Al Mutadid from the beginning of his reign determined that the best defence was always a good attack, both inside and outside his small kingdom. His years of rule were marked by his heavy-handedness, inflexibility and ruthlessness both in the control of his own kingdom and in the harassment he subjected his neighbouring taifas.

The kingdom that he had inherited from his father was internally stable, although it had to be continuously monitored to avoid any kind of revolt, so present in Al-Andalus in those years. In this sense, according to Bosch, Al Mutadid expressed himself in such a way: 'the enemy must be eliminated before he tries to do away with you'. During his years of rule, and thanks to his expansionist policy (which was largely due to the abundance of raw materials and wealth in the kingdom), he managed to bring Seville to a period of significant economic and social development, which led to the prosperity of the kingdom's population and therefore to a stability that the subjects of his kingdom had not enjoyed for many years. However, it is true that his people also suffered some periods of hardship, such as the famine of 1056–1057. Economic prosperity was naturally accompanied by intellectual prosperity. As was the case during the period of the Umayyad Caliphate, the arts and cultural activities reached very high levels in Seville, which would be but a prelude to what happened during the reign of his son Al Mutamid. Poets, musicians, dancers, scholars and so on all had their place in this cultural capital of Al-Andalus, with a certain similarity to the Spanish Golden Age in Seville a few centuries later.

The influx of goods from conquered territories and trade with other kingdoms increased the population and consequently the city itself. The inhabited areas were extended, and, above all, important buildings were built for the royal family, worthy of the importance acquired by the people who lived there. Unfortunately, little or nothing of those days has survived to the present day, and we can only recreate these buildings in our imagination.

Returning again to Al Mutadid, a fact that shows us his 'double' personality was the panorama offered by a garden on the façade of his palace, where he had several pikes placed in well visible places, where the heads of his most visceral enemies were exhibited for years, to which he dedicated verses of great poetic level. His rancour had no end, and he not only sought revenge against his enemies in life but also extended it far beyond their deaths. Among the heads that were 'planted' in his garden were those of al-Birzali (the former lord of Carmona) and of Yahya ben Ali (the Hammudite caliph who was defeated in battle outside Carmona by Ismail and al-Birzali himself).

Gold dinar issued by Al Mutadid, taifa king of Seville, between 1045 and 1046. Sevillian coins enjoyed a good reputation for their manufacture, although Castilian pressure forced a change in the percentages of the alloys in the Sevillian coins. (Open source by Numismatica Pliego)

To prevent the early putrefaction of these heads, he saw to it that they were cleaned and perfumed with ointments to keep them 'mummified'. Moreover, to make his action more dastardly, he ordered flowers to be planted on the heads of those of lesser importance or rank, while those of the most important rivals were highlighted in a more conspicuous position, and he placed a piece of paper tied to the ear of each one with his name on it.

Although this cruel and aberrant behaviour seems despicable to us, Al Mutadid intended to undermine the morale of possible people who might want to take up arms against him, as well as to frighten his opponents from other taifas, since anyone could end up 'grafted' in his garden. It was therefore a warning to sailors that, in good faith, fulfilled its purpose, as Al Mutadid was truly feared by locals and foreigners alike.

Campaigns to Expand the Kingdom

Al Mutadid's military campaigns began at the same time as his reign, especially marked throughout his reign by his special hatred of the Berbers.

SETTLEMENT OF THE KINGDOM OF SEVILLE: 1042–1069

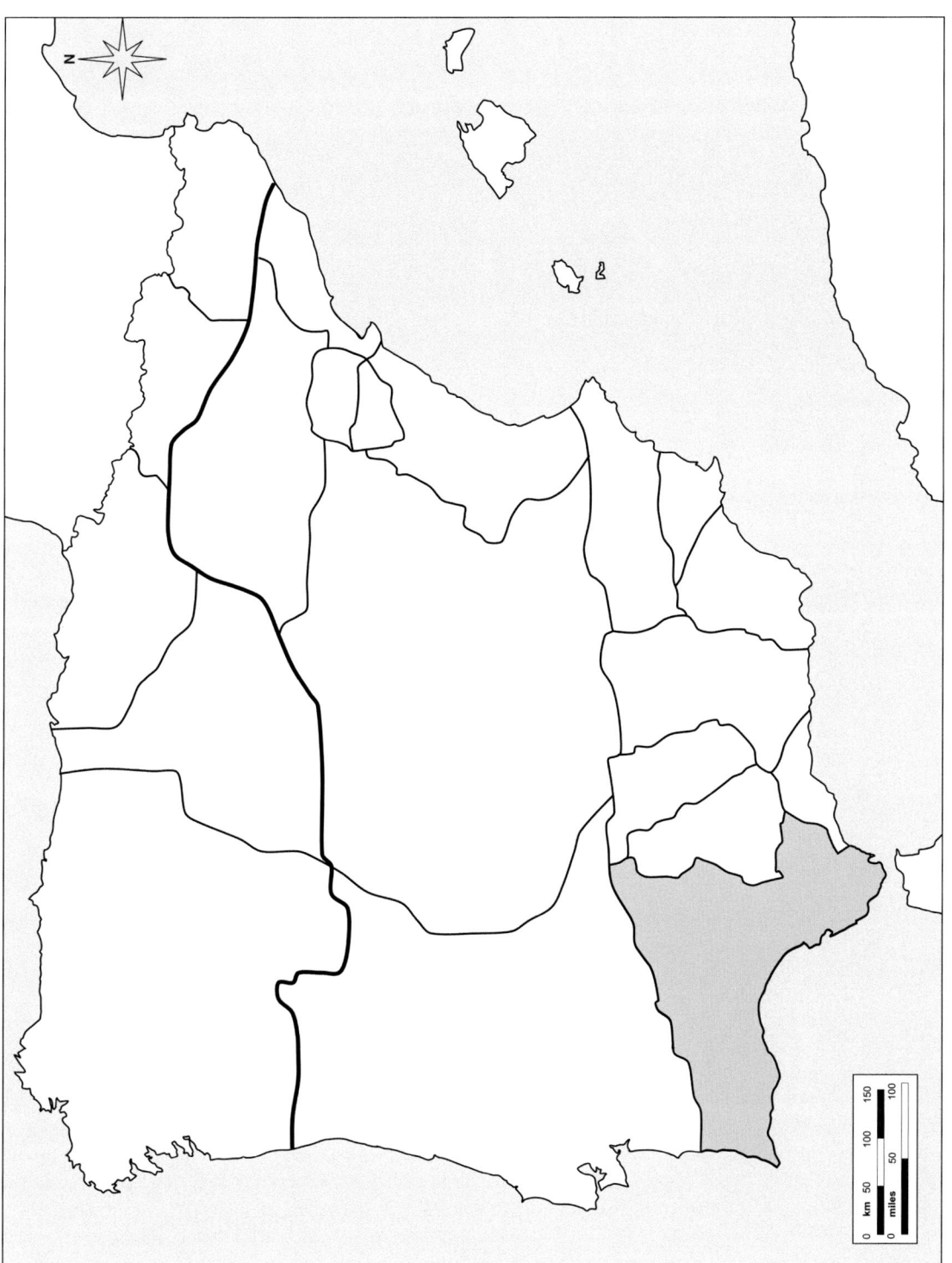

Extension of the kingdom of Seville in 1068. (Map drawn by the author)

THE FALL OF MOORISH SEVILLE 1023-1091

Image of the Alcazaba of Málaga from the port. In front of it, Al Mutamid, as heir to the Sevillian throne, suffered a major defeat against the Berber troops of Málaga and Granada between 1065 and 1066. (Open source by José Luis Parra Olmo)

The latter may have been motivated by an astrological prediction that he or his dynasty would be overthrown by men born outside the peninsula (such was Al Mutadid's Andalusian sentiment that he considered himself Sevillian, unlike the Berbers who had been settling in the Muslim part of the Iberian Peninsula since the time of the Caliphate of Córdoba).

In 1042, he began his offensive against the nearby enemy Taifa of Carmona, continuing the dispute that his father had already maintained. Although he still did not manage to take Carmona, Al Mutadid did manage to kill al-Birzali in an ambush in 1043, which, as we have already mentioned, would be an important 'potsherd' in his macabre garden. The battle did not end because of this, as al-Birzali's son Isaac defended himself very well against the Sevillian king, mainly thanks to the support received from the kingdom of Badajoz, in the form of Muhammad Al Muzaffar, the son of King Abdalá of Badajoz, and his army.

Around 1044, he attacked the Arab Taifa of Mértola with its capital Mértola (in the present-day district of Beja), located in present-day Alentejo, which, after its corresponding siege, fell to him within a few days. Ibn Tayfur, its king, would be the first of the many Andalusian kings forcibly displaced from their respective thrones by the action of the Sevillian taifa. Unfortunately for Ibn Tayfur, there would be no mercy whatsoever, ending his days crucified on the banks of the River Guadalquivir in the Sevillian capital.

After this brief and relatively comfortable campaign, Al Mutadid turned his sights on the Arab Taifa of Niebla (Lebla), also located to the west of the Sevillian capital. Niebla was ruled by Mohammed of the Ben Yahya al Yahsubi family, who, faced with the danger that lay ahead, managed to form an alliance with the Taifas of Silves, Granada, Málaga, Algeciras and Badajoz, as well as some troops from the recently conquered kingdom of Mértola. The fate of the Algarve (al-garb) was at stake, many interests were on the table, and no one wanted a powerful kingdom of Seville that would swallow up the various kingdoms of the southwest of the peninsula one by one.

SETTLEMENT OF THE KINGDOM OF SEVILLE: 1042–1069

Walls of Niebla. Between 1051 and 1053, fighting intensified over the territory of this taifa, culminating in its annexation by the kingdom of Seville. (Open source)

The Berber kingdoms of Al Muzaffar of Badajoz and Badis of Granada, the Hammudites of Mohammed of Málaga, Mohammed of Algeciras and the Arab kingdoms of Silves and Niebla against all odds joined forces for a common goal: Seville and its kingdom were to be defeated, and its lands divided among the other kingdoms. The war would be long, and the outcome, a priori, not very favourable for the kingdom of Seville.

The head of this alliance was taken by the king of Badajoz, a kingdom that had been at odds with the Sevillians for years and was anxious to prevent their expansion. After sending an army to support Niebla, he managed to break the siege it was suffering from the Sevillians. Al Mutadid resigned himself to withdrawing his troops, as the circumstances were not appropriate, but he was not prepared to give in so easily and prepared his next move. This consisted of ravaging the southernmost lands of the kingdom of Badajoz, causing chaos, death and the destruction of everything in their path. This led to open warfare between the two taifas, which, due to the hatred that both monarchs had for each other, sought the destruction of each other.

Although the coalition troops had made small incursions into Seville, it was the kingdom of Badajoz that bore the brunt of the conflict against Al Mutadid. Finally, a deeper campaign against Seville was prepared, and the troops of Granada, led by Badis, joined with their allies on the eastern bank of the Guadalquivir to threaten the city of Seville. They ravaged the lands of Seville seeking the destruction of any villages or lands they found in their path, in a similar way to what Al Mutadid had done in the lands of Badajoz.

But the situation for Al Muzaffar had deteriorated so much that he could no longer withstand the Sevillian onslaught. Many of his fortresses (mainly those located farther south) had been occupied by the Sevillian troops, and he began to fear for the capital. Taking advantage of the good situation on the northern front, Al Mutadid decided to divide his troops into two army corps, the first would continue his task of conquering and destroying the kingdom of Badajoz while the second, under his own command, would attempt to deliver the final coup de grâce to the city of Niebla. After attacking his enemies in a gorge where he inflicted multiple casualties, he ended up cornering them against the River Tinto, where more of his enemies perished. The conquest of the city of Niebla seemed to be in sight, but, at the last moment, an army corps from the kingdom of Badajoz once again forced the Sevillian troops to retreat and even ravaged some of the territories of the Abbadid kingdom.

But Al Mutadid was not going to give up his efforts and used diplomacy to achieve what arms had denied him. After intense diplomatic pressure on Niebla, he succeeded in 1051 in getting it to break away from the alliance to which it belonged (with the Berber taifas) and to ally itself with him. This is another great example of the great negotiating skills of Al Mutadid, who, like his father, achieved with cunning what arms denied him.

When Al Muzaffar learned of Niebla's treachery, he appropriated the money it had entrusted to him and began to ravage its lands. Evidently, the Sevillian's new ally had to ask him for help against those of Badajoz. Al Mutadid sent an army to defend Niebla, but it came up against the army of Badajoz, which he ambushed and managed to practically annihilate.

In 1050, at the same time, the son of Al Mutadid named Ismail (who like his father also had several titles such as al-Mansur or the victorious, al-Muayyad or the supported and al-Zafir or the triumphant) marched on the region of Évora (belonging to the kingdom of Badajoz) so that the king of Badajoz could not use his troops to attack Sevillian territories and use them to defend his own, Ismail's troops then being repelled by troops from Badajoz. The first-born son of the Sevillian kingdom, following family tradition, took over the position of commander of the Abbadid army. The king of Badajoz asked for help from the Berber Isaac of Carmona, who sent an army under the command of his own son. The Carmonans, aware of Ismail's powerful army, tried to convince Al Muzaffar (who reigned over Badajoz from 1045 to 1068) how unproductive a direct encounter between the two formations would be. Al Muzaffar, with the hatred he felt towards the Sevillians, was unable to accept the advice of Isaac of Carmona and sought a head-on clash with Ismail. The result was a crushing Sevillian victory, leaving more than 3,000 dead on the allied side (remember that the figures according to the chroniclers of the time can never be considered very reliable, although they give us an idea of the extent of the defeat), in which even the son of Isaac of Carmona perished, whose head went on to join that of his grandfather in Al Mutadid's garden of skulls. The Badajoz troops were forced to retreat after their defeat, so their Carmona allies marched back to their territories, and the Sevillian troops continued to harass the lands of their enemies.

The situation in the kingdom of Badajoz had worsened drastically, the capital showed its shops closed, and the markets lifeless; the situation had become untenable. Finally, in August 1051, Al Muzaffar asked for peace through the mediation of Abucheuar of Córdoba, which was signed with important territorial and economic benefits for Al Mutadid. This was a small triumph for the Sevillian kingdom, as it weakened the kingdom of Badajoz and, at the same, time managed to keep the incursions of Granada at bay, normalising the situation on these borders, which remained more stable. After seven years of continuous fighting, perseverance and confidence, as well as the aggressive nature of his tactics against his rivals (and mainly against the troops of Badajoz) and his diplomatic skills, allowed Al Mutadid to triumph in a situation so critical that it could have completely destroyed the still small kingdom of Seville.

Once the situation on the northern front of the kingdom had stabilised, Al Mutadid turned his attention to the small Arab taifas in the southwest of the peninsula. These small kingdoms no longer had the support of the large Taifas of Málaga, Granada, Badajoz or the smaller and less powerful Carmona, and, at this point, they must have found themselves 'alone' against the powerful and reinforced, after recent victories, Sevillian army.

But, before embarking on the conquest of the small taifas of the southwest, let us return again to Niebla. The situation in the small state was becoming more tense by the day, for King Nasir ad Dawla, after making peace with Al Mutadid, realised how futile it was. Al Mutadid, after accepting an annual sum of money from Niebla to alleviate the costs of the wars with it, preferred to return to fighting and the widespread devastation of its lands. The continuous raids against Niebla were answered to a lesser extent by similar raids against the Aljarafe in Seville by the Niebla people. But the situation was suffocating for Nasir ad Dawla, who opted to surrender himself (possibly between 1053 and 1054) and therefore his kingdom to Al Mutadid, ending his life in Córdoba, exiled and taken in by Ibn Yahwar.

The victories of the Sevillian armies and the fall of the kingdom of Niebla were the first dominoes to fall, followed by the next, which would be the Taifa of Huelva and the island of Saltés (located in the low maritime-river area formed by the mouths of the Rivers Tinto and Odiel, the latter separating it from Huelva to the east, and the estuary of Punta Umbría to the west, and open to the south by the Atlantic Ocean). Their king, Abdelaziz al-Bakri, was convinced that his time was running out and, after congratulating Al Mutadid on his recent conquests, reminded him of the old friendship between their respective families and of the non-aggression pacts they had had between them since the time of Ismail ben Abbad. In any case, al-Bakri, knowing his position of inferiority in this 'relationship' between kingdoms, made a pact with Al Mutamid, which consisted of handing over the kingdom of Huelva, leaving him on the island of Saltés as his vassal (we must clarify that the kingdom of Saltés and Huelva had almost no army, its armed troops being reduced to the king's personal guard). Al Mutamid pretended to accept the deal, and, when he took possession of Huelva (between 1050 and 1051), he simply limited himself to not letting al-Bakri leave Saltés. Despite this, there is evidence of the 'collaboration' of Sevillian troops and al-Bakri in operations aimed at capturing an important rebel highwayman in the Mértola area who was sowing terror in the region (successfully, as the rebel was captured and subsequently crucified in Seville). Despite his continued collaboration, al-Bakri knew that the attitude of the Sevillian king was aimed at bringing about the complete isolation of the small territory of Saltés in order to end the complete 'strangulation' of his dwindling kingdom and that no deal was possible under such circumstances. So he took the decision that would bring the least misfortune to his kingdom and his people: in 1052, he accepted Al Mutadid's offer of 10,000 gold dinars (in exchange for his ships, weapons of war and his last lands) and permission to go into exile to the city of Córdoba, where he would coincide with the also exiled Yahya of Niebla, also after having been dispossessed of his lands. But, despite accepting the deal with the monarch of Saltés and Huelva, Al Mutadid did not want to leave any loose ends and did not make it easy for him. So the journey was not an easy one, as Al Mutadid tried to capture him on his way to Córdoba (during his passage through Tejada, known at that time as Talyata), which did not happen, as al-Bakri asked for help in the form of an escort from the troops of the king of Carmona (always ready to participate in any action against the Sevillian kingdom), which allowed him to arrive safely in the old caliphate capital. In this way, al-Bakri's head possibly did not end up in the macabre garden of the Seville regicide, and he was taken in by Ibn Yahwar of Córdoba, who was quite rightly described as 'The plugger of the gaps and the asylum of the exiled'.

The Patio de Banderas of the present-day Royal Alcázar of Seville, which seems to have served as a parade ground for the Dar al-Imara and therefore during the taifa period. (Author's collection)

Following the plan that Al Mutadid had drawn up, he indicated his new objective, which was the kingdom of Silves, which, under the rule of Abulasbag Iza, offered strong resistance until the last moment. But the circumstances were not at all favourable for the small kingdom, since, after multiple raids by the Seville cavalry on the lands of Silves, they finally had to face a large army under the command of Muhammad Al Mutamid, the second son of Al Mutadid, who at that time was 13 years old and fulfilled the functions of governor of the recently conquered kingdom of Huelva. Between 1052 and 1053 (1063 according to Tahiri, although this is unlikely), the kingdom of the southwest of the peninsula fell definitively after taking the city by force by means of almajeneques, which demolished part of its walls, and by digging through other parts of the city (the city had previously been isolated, cutting off any means of supplying it with coal, firewood and foodstuffs). The capture of Silves required the construction of two towers from which to direct the siege by the Sevillians, which lasted about eight months. After the conquest in which King Al Muzaffar of Silves was captured in his fortress (known as Qasr Al Sarayib), he was immediately taken to Seville, where, after suffering multiple tortures, he was executed. After the victory over Silves, Al Mutamid was left as governor of the once independent kingdom, a fact that we will see how important it would be in the history of the Sevillian kingdom. Iza had no choice, after surviving the siege and battles in his capital, but to go into exile in the city of Seville, where he would die (according to other versions, he did go to Seville, specifically to the Royal Alcázar, where Al Mutadid, after subjecting him to various humiliations, finally slit his throat). Another domino had fallen.

It was inevitable that the next target would be the last remaining independent Arab-Andalusian kingdom. We are referring to the kingdom of the Algarve (Santa María del Algarve or Santamariyyat al-Garb), with its capital at Faro or Santa María de Faro and governed by Said ben Harun, who is not recorded as being either Arab or Berber according to the chronicles of the time. After a brief period of resistance in which many battles and massacres took place, the Sevillian troops placed their banners on the city walls. This kingdom was united with that of Huelva and Silves and thus also came under the rule of Al Mutamid (possibly between 1053 and 1054). Ben Harun was finally forced to abdicate in favour of the Sevillian and return with him to Seville, where he lived for 10 more years until his death.

All the new lands that had been annexed more or less violently in recent years had made the Sevillian kingdom one of the richest in the peninsula. The only kingdom that remained to the west of Seville, that of Badajoz, was never to be annexed by the Sevillians, largely because it was too large and still powerful enough to avoid conquest.

It was therefore time to look eastwards, and the first taifas to set their sights on were those belonging to the so-called Berber 'half moon' made up of the Berber Taifas of Morón, Ronda, Arcos, Jeréz, Algeciras and Carmona. Farther east, the powerful kingdom of Granada was becoming the pillar of support for many of these small Berber kingdoms and was beginning to show worrying signs of expansion; in particular, King Badis succeeded in annexing the Hammudid Taifa of Málaga to the kingdom of Granada in 1057 while maintaining border clashes with the kingdom of Almería.

Al Mutadid, being on good terms with the previous taifas, except for that of Carmona, devised a new ruse to obtain them in the least bloody and costly way possible. After his return from the conquest of Silves, he decided to make an 'unexpected survey' in person of the real situation in the Taifas of Morón and Ronda, as he knew that many of the population of these taifas were of Arab origin and were equally afraid of the Berbers and hated them, so they could be a strong point of support when it came time to strike a blow against them. Given the ancestral hatred that the Berbers and the Arab-Andalusians had for each other, it was a dangerous visit indeed. Al Mutadid stepped boldly into the lion's den, accompanied by only a few hundred of his men, who could have been easy prey for the Berbers. He first set out for Morón, where he met its lord, Ben Nuh, who received and entertained him as he deserved and assured him that he would always be a loyal vassal. A few days after this fruitful visit of Al Mutadid in Morón, he set off for Ronda with the same purpose. His reception and welcome were equal if not better than the ones he received in Morón, and the words that Ben Abí Corra, as lord of Ronda, had with the Sevillian king were certainly reassuring for the Sevillian. As the days passed in Ronda, the men of Al Mutadid were in contact with important people of Arab origin in Ronda, who told them how oppressed they were under the hard hand of Ben Abí Corra. It happened that, one day, after a great feast with plenty of wine, Al Mutadid felt sleepy and excused himself to the diners to retire. He retired to a sofa where he would rest, while the rest of the diners, all Berbers, took off their hypocritical masks and began to say what they really thought of the presence of the Sevillian in their lands, where he entered as their master and strutted before them. Taking advantage of Al Mutadid's sleep, they took the courage they lacked when he was awake and conspired to take advantage of the opportunity of having him defenceless and on their lands to assassinate him. The occasion could not have been more propitious and required a quick response, so much so that they decided to end the life of their most recalcitrant enemy. It was already decided when one of the diners, a relative of the lord of Ronda, named Moadh Ben Abi Corra, 'flared up' against the others, expressing the dishonesty of the words he had heard. He would on no account allow a guest who had placed his trust in the hospitality of the lord of Ronda to be killed so viciously. For him, that was to lose the honour of the family, and he made this clear in his exposition by trying to convince the others with the phrase 'God damn him who dares to commit such a crime'. Finally, between Moadh Ben Abi Corra's exposition and the fear imposed on them by the figure of Al Mutadid (even in his sleep), they decided to let this unique opportunity pass and forget the conversation. But, to their dismay, Al Mutadid, once he was lying on the sofa, had not been asleep and had listened perfectly well to the conspiracy plot against him. He also kept in his memory the name of the one who had interceded for his life, Moadh Ben Abi Corra; perhaps one day, Al Mutadid would do something for him by returning the favour. The next day, Al Mutadid left for Seville, satisfied to have observed the 'reality' of his relations with the Berbers, with the false satisfaction, in their eyes, of maintaining good relations between Sevillians and Berbers.

SETTLEMENT OF THE KINGDOM OF SEVILLE: 1042–1069

For Al Mutadid, who hated the Berbers, the talk he had the good fortune to hear at that feast had made clear to him what he should do with the Berbers: wipe them out. With this obscure aim in mind, very possibly around 1057–1058 (according to the various sources that speak of the event, it may also have taken place in 1052, 1053, 1055, 1056, 1057, 1065 or 1066), he called a meeting in Seville with the lords of Arcos, Morón and Ronda, with the excuse of repaying the favours received during the visits as well as to endorse the 'harmonious' relations between all of them. What really happened next is a matter of controversy, depending on the source consulted, but we will comment on the most widespread 'version', which in the end tells us in broad outline what happened. The royal guests were received in the palace as befitting their rank, and, as was customary, they were invited to the hammam (known as ar-Raqqaqin or bath of the pergaminers) along with the principal men of their entourages. Taking advantage of the fact that he had them all assembled, he had the doors to the baths and the vents bricked up, killing them by suffocation. Shortly before going to the baths, however, Al Mutadid requested the presence of one of the young men accompanying the lord of Ronda to discuss certain unimportant matters; this young man's name was Moadh Ben Abi Corra. He was the only one of the more than 60 men who made up the Berber embassy in Seville who managed to keep his life. The perfidious and Machiavellian Al Mutadid had eliminated at a stroke the three main families and corresponding entourages of three of the kingdoms he claimed and had returned the favour Moadh Ben Abí Corra had unwittingly done him shortly before in Ronda. For the Sevillian monarch, justice had been done. After the slaughter of the hammam, Al Mutadid sent two army corps to each of the three capitals of the murdered kings to take possession of them, after overcoming some resistance from the Berbers aided by King Badis of Granada. The new king of Morón, Imad ad-Dawla (son of the murdered Izz ad-Dawla), put up fierce resistance against the Sevillian troops despite the continuous incursions of the enemies who ravaged his lands and burnt his villages. This situation prompted Imad ad-Dawla to send a letter to the king of Seville requesting peace on condition that his family and his possessions were respected. Al Mutamid accepted willingly, allowing him to live in the Sevillian capital in a magnificent house, where he maintained great luxuries in his living (these events took place around November 1066, leading to the annexation of the taifa between 1065 and 1066).

Undoubtedly, the most difficult city to take was Ronda, perhaps because it was the most difficult to reach, as it was situated on an elevation surrounded by cliffs. But, thanks to the Sevillian army, the Arab population of Ronda who rebelled against the Berber 'oppressor' and the many traitors that arose in the villages when 'the wind changes direction' who went over to the Abbadid side, Ronda was taken for the king of Seville (the capture would take place in an absolute manner between December 1064 and December 1065). So great was the impact on Al Mutadid of the capture of the once very hostile Ronda that he composed one of his verses in honour of such a shocking event that he so strongly longed for. The verse is as follows:

THE FALL OF MOORISH SEVILLE 1023-1091

> Better fortified than ever, thou art now the best jewel in my crown, O Ronda! The spears and cutting swords of my valiant warriors, have procured me the advantage of possessing you; your inhabitants now call me their lord and will be the firmest support for me. Ah, let my life endure, and I will know how to shorten that of my enemies! As long as I have breath left I will never cease to fight them. I have put battalions and battalions to the sword, and the heads of my enemies, strung like pearls, form a necklace on the door of my palace.

Despite the formal conquest of these territories, there would still be periodic uprisings against the Sevillian 'yoke' until 1068–1069. In any case, the move had worked out perfectly. On the one hand, Al Mutadid had got rid of three Berber kingdoms close to his eastern border, and he had done so at no human or material cost. In addition, his kingdom had gained new lands and therefore new wealth and population, which would allow him to maintain the expansionist policy that had been so successful for himself.

Moadh (Muadh) Ben Abi Corra, grateful to the Sevillian king, remained forever in his service. He became a man of trust for the Sevillian monarch, who even lodged him in one of his palaces, later placing him at the head of a corps of his armies with an annual salary of some 12,000 ducats. The good service he had done for Al Mutadid required a good payment like this. A few years later, we will see him commanding an expeditionary force from Seville to take part in the battles for Barbastro.

After the Sevillian onslaught on the kingdoms of Morón, Ronda and Arcos, the southern Berber Taifa of Algeciras had come within a stone's throw of the Sevillian kingdom, and it was not long before the latter was attracted to it. In 1054–1055 (1058 according to other sources, although less credible), the Hammudid Al Qasim, after a brief resistance, surrendered his kingdom to Al Mutadid and went into exile in the city of Córdoba (other sources suggest that he set off for Ceuta, although he ended his journey in Almería, as he was not well received by the people of Ceuta and came under the tutelage of the Almerian sovereign, Almutasim). The defence of the kingdom could not have been more effective due to the small number of cavalry troops at his disposal at the time, which amounted to only 200 horsemen. When the Sevillian king heard of this, he sent his troops under the command of the vizier Abdalá ben Sallam, who besieged Algeciras both by land and by sea, thanks to ships from the Sevillian fleet that completed the siege.

During these years of Al Mutadid's rule, the Sevillian army's main enemies in the east were the small Berber taifas and, above all, the more powerful kingdom of Granada, where its monarch, Badis, acted on several occasions to help the Berber taifas closest to Seville. As was the custom of the time, Berber cavalcades entered Seville's territory causing disorder and destruction in their wake. The Sevillian army also suffered a defeat in 1054–1055 against the troops of Arcos and neighbouring Sidonia, ruled by the Banu Irniyan, in one of the frequent clashes that took place during this period. However, chroniclers also record (although this cannot be

SETTLEMENT OF THE KINGDOM OF SEVILLE: 1042–1069

confirmed with certainty) that, around 1054, Almería lost the area of Los Vélez to the king of Seville.

In January or February 1060, the 'theatre' of the existence of Caliph Hixam II came to an end. There was no longer any need for a figure to unite the Muslims, because that task was being carried out by Al Mutadid and his troops. The statement could not have been more 'absurd', a fitting climax to the whole story of the false Hixam II, since Al Mutadid declared that the real caliph had died in 1044 and that he had not been made known to the people because he was engaged in continuous wars. Despite this, the name of Caliph Hixam II as Prince of the Believers remained on the coins of the Taifa of Seville until 1068–1069.

However, although everything seemed to be going in Al Mutadid's favour, the kingdom was soon to suffer from the rapid growth it had undergone, and this was largely due to two events that marked the future of the history of the Sevillian kingdom. On the one hand were the disagreements that arose between Al Mutadid and his first-born son (Ismail), and on the other was the interference of the Christian King Don Fernando I in the politics of the Sevillian taifa.

Ismail, despite knowing he was the heir to the kingdom his father was forging, was not in tune with him. The disagreements between the two were becoming more and more important, despite that the unity of the family was maintained. This balance between father and son was broken by the bad influences Ismail received from an intriguer from Málaga, possibly sent to Seville for that purpose, who went by the name of Abú Abdalá al-Bizilyani. He suggested to Ismail that he should rebel against his father and subsequently become independent in some part of the kingdom. This flame of rebellion caught fire in the 'dry leaf' that was Ismail, who took advantage of the fact that his father had entrusted him with a campaign of harassment in the lands of Córdoba to disobey his orders and set off for Seville. There, taking advantage of the fact that his father was residing in the castle-palace Qasr al-Zahir (the shining fortress) on the other side of the river in what is now the Aljarafe, he seized everything he could find in his palace and many of the women in the harem. After the betrayal, Ismail set off for Algeciras, the city he had chosen as the capital of his new kingdom. But Al Mutadid, after recovering from the surprise of the filial betrayal, ordered his men in Algeciras and in all the fortresses on the way to Seville not to allow him access to the city. Seeing himself lost, Ismail could only ask his father for forgiveness. The latter, despite his cruel personality, agreed to pardon him, trying to forget the attempted sedition he had caused. But he was not so generous with al-Bizilyani, who was immediately beheaded along with those who had supported him in his treachery.

But Ismail was no longer the same, he distrusted his father and did not feel safe, so again he tried to betray him. One night in the palace, he gathered several of his men (well paid with the first-born's gold), and, after arming them and drinking with them to encourage them, he resolved to climb up to his father's chambers, where he would kill him. But Al Mutadid surprised them in their preparations, forcing them to flee again. This escape was short-lived, however, as within minutes Ismail and his followers were captured. This new failure in Ismail's revolt was to be the last, as Al Mutadid, in a fit of rage against his son, killed him with his own hands in one of the rooms of the Abbadid palace (the first-born son would have been between 25 and 30 years old or perhaps older, but it is not possible to specify in this case) and, at the same time, ordered the public executions of his supporters and even some of the women in his son's harem. The date given by the philologist Pilar Lirola Delgado in her book *Al-Mu´tamid y los Abadíes* for Ismail's death is 23 September–22 October 1039, although it seems to us to be too early (considering that Al Mutadid is considered to have been born in 1016 and to have begun his rule as monarch in 1042). This event catapulted Al Mutamid to the position of heir to Al Mutadid, changing the destiny of the Sevillian kingdom, although this is a matter of supposition. The Sevillian monarch never recovered from the execution–murder of his first-born son and was plagued by remorse for the rest of his life.

The revolt instigated by his son and his son's tragic end was assumed by Al Mutadid to be necessary, but, on the other hand, he was aware that he had killed his son, the one he had loved and trained to be his replacement when Allah had decided. He had been not only wise and prudent in his actions and advice but also brave and fearless on the battlefields. He could have been a great king, but that possibility had vanished because of his father's intransigence and the terrible distrust and hatred that Ismail had built up over the years, possibly due to the bad influences of certain characters close to him.

Possibly this fact, together with his excessive fondness for wine and the cruel and obsessive behaviour of the Sevillian monarch, which apparently bordered on paranoia, made him a dangerous man to be close to, as is attested in numerous sources.

It did not take Al Mutamid long to try to earn the stripes he had recently acquired as the new heir to the kingdom. For some time, there had been a general malaise in the territory of Málaga due to the subjugation they had been subjected to by the Granadan taifa. Despite their Berber origin, they had contacted the Sevillian taifa on several occasions to try to reach a pact of convenience in which the latter would help the former to expel the Granadans. One day in 1065–1066, there was a simultaneous revolt in several towns and even in the capital of the Malagan taifa (we must not forget that this period in the kingdom of Granada was particularly critical due to the uprising in 1066 of part of the population against the Jews). This was the signal for the Sevillian troops to enter Málaga to support the people. Al Mutamid, as we have already mentioned, saw this as an opportunity to enhance his military stature and launched his army corps towards Málaga, 'liberating' as many towns and villages as he passed through. At least 25 fortresses in Málaga submitted to the Sevillian king in about a week. Alongside Al Mutamid, as second-in-command of the Sevillian troops, marched another son of Al Mutadid, by the name of Yabir. Within a week, Al Mutamid, thanks to his surprise attack, had taken the whole of the Malagan taifa, except for the citadel of the capital, which was

SETTLEMENT OF THE KINGDOM OF SEVILLE: 1042-1069

Image of the Beatus of Osma (completed in 1086), representing the four horsemen of the apocalypse. As it is an image contemporaneous with the time dealt with in this book, and therefore of weapons used by both Christians and Muslims, it is worth highlighting the use of a hand crossbow by one of the horsemen, another carries a sword and a third a long spear. (Open source)

THE FALL OF MOORISH SEVILLE 1023-1091

still holding out, defended mainly by the Sudanese black guard under the command of Majluf ben Mallul. The Sevillian troops camped in the vicinity of the citadel in preparation for the final coup de grâce, while, at sea, Sevillian ships anchored in the port of the city of Málaga to tighten the siege even further. On the one hand, the difficult accessibility of the citadel made it very difficult to capture, especially since there was always the possibility that Badis of Granada, warned of the situation by emissaries from Málaga, would raise an army to help his Málaga 'brothers'. But the ill-intentioned advice of some Berber chiefs in the Sevillian army (who intrigued on the Seville side and wanted an Abbadid defeat) convinced Al Mutamid that the citadel would not hold out for many days. The indolent and trusting Sevillian prince was thus left to wait for the 'apple' to fall of its own weight, while his army spent the time of the siege in continuous feasts where wine was flowing everywhere (despite having been warned by many of the Málaga Arabs who advised a definitive attack on the citadel). It is even known that, while Al Mutamid was in Málaga, the Friday sermon was delivered in his name and was received with great pleasure by a large part of the population, who felt sympathy for the Abbadid. In one part of the sermon, it was said, 'Today is when I have perfected your religion, I have completed my benefits to you and I have been satisfied to see that at last you profess Islam as a religion'.

But Badis of Granada came by surprise with a formidable army to the aid of the besieged after being informed by some men (sent from the citadel of Málaga on a special mission) of the state of relaxation of the Sevillian army. The Granadan army commanded by Al Naya caught the inertia and drunkenness (in many cases) of the Sevillians unawares, although, according to some sources, some of the Berber troops who were part of the Sevillian army changed sides and betrayed Al Mutamid. The fact is that the hitherto triumphant Sevillian army suffered a great defeat that almost ended with the death of most of the troops, although Al Mutamid, possibly with a small part of his troops, had time to react, making a sortie in extremis against the Granadans, although without success. Al Mutamid's overconfidence had led to the failure of the conquest of the Taifa of Málaga, and he was forced to flee with some of his personal guard and his brother Yabir, galloping towards his fortress in Ronda. After this debacle, Málaga would never again become a Sevillian objective, as Badis prevented the circumstances that favoured the Sevillian raids on Málaga with the support, in many cases, of the local population.

Al Mutadid suffered a severe blow, venting all his anger against his son for his ill-advised tactics during the siege of Málaga. And, although for a moment Al Mutamid was able to follow in the footsteps of his brother Ismail, it is true that his well-measured words and poems softened the heart of his father, who finally forgave him and allowed him to return to the capital of the kingdom. Al Mutamid wrote this poem to his father after obtaining his pardon:

SETTLEMENT OF THE KINGDOM OF SEVILLE: 1042–1069

I have sent a gift with joy,
to thank you for your love.
It is a small thing, but with it came your pardon.
If the gift were my own self,
it would be worthless compared to you.

As mentioned above, the second event that changed the destiny of the Taifa of Seville was the intervention of the Christian kingdoms of the north of the peninsula in the politics of the different taifas. The Castilian-Leonese King Ferdinand I had begun a policy of continuous aggression against the various Muslim kingdoms. In 1057, he advanced on the lands of King Almodaffar of Badajoz, taking towns such as Viseo, Geisa, San Martín de Moros, Travanca and Petralba, as well as other castles in the area. The king of Badajoz, faced with increasing Christian pressure from the northeast and pressure from the south from the always warlike Taifa of Seville, agreed to declare himself a tributary of the Christian king. This vassalage involved the surrender of wealth and other products as a 'voluntary payment' from one kingdom so that the other would agree not to attack it (the so-called parias). Although it was the custom of the time (the opposite had already happened in the time of the Caliphate of Córdoba, when it was the Christian kingdoms that paid the Muslims), it was nothing more than vile blackmail, the terms of which could be freely modified by the kingdom that imposed it. But there was no other solution for the dispersed and, in many cases, feuding taifa kingdoms.

Close-up of the front of the alberca belonging to an eleventh-century almunia in Seville. We can appreciate the magnificent conservation of the paintings based on geometric designs. (Photograph by Marisol García Gómez)

After obtaining the vassalage of Badajoz, the Christian armies headed towards the kingdom of Ahmed Almoctadir Ben Hud, located in Zaragoza. After the former seized a multitude of fortresses that the latter had in the south of the Duero, Ahmed Almoctadir Ben Hud also had to become a

THE FALL OF MOORISH SEVILLE 1023-1091

General image of the front of the alberca found in the Casa Hermandad de la Hiniesta. Its construction technique is based on applying a layer of lime and sand on the adobe walls. This mortar was mixed with straw, and, on this white stucco, the black and red paint was applied. (Photograph by Marisol García Gómez)

tributary of the Castilians. After this, the next to enter the game of vassalage was the kingdom of Toledo.

The choice of the three taifa kingdoms mentioned above, which agreed to pay parias, evidently corresponded to the fact that they were the three border kingdoms with Christian lands and therefore the most easily attacked.

But the ambition for riches so easily obtained easily caught on in Ferdinand I, as he passed the parias beyond the limits of the taifa kingdoms bordering the Castilian kingdoms. Thus, in 1063, it was Ferdinand I's turn to confront the demands of Al Mutadid. The Castilian letter of introduction was that of continuous raids on the lands of Seville, burning villages and plundering the population of the kingdom. This was Ferdinand I's way of showing the royal weakness of the Sevillian kingdom against the Christians, even though, among the Muslim taifas, the kingdom of Seville was particularly powerful.

Al Mutadid agreed to an interview with Ferdinand I in which he tried to escape the extortion of the Christian kingdom. This took place in a region in what is now the lands of Badajoz, but Ferdinand had the 'upper hand', and, after accepting countless rich gifts from the Abbadid, he reaffirmed the need to collect tribute from Seville in exchange for 'protection' from Castile and León over his new vassal state. The Sevillian king, quite contrary to what he really wanted to do, had to accept the conditions imposed on him, and, without any struggle, he became a vassal of the king of Castile and León. But Ferdinand I, knowing he was superior to the Sevillian king, set a final condition for considering the first instalment of the annual Sevillian tribute to have been paid, and that was none other than the 'return' to Christian hands of the relics of the Sevillian saints Justa and Rufina. Al Mutadid 'graciously' agreed but reminded Ferdinand I that he was completely unaware of the possible location of these objects. To demonstrate the Sevillian monarch's goodwill in this regard, he allowed Christian scholars and prelates to investigate the possible location of the relics in Seville.

Once the arrival of the Christian experts presided over by Bishop Alvito of León and the counts of Astorga, among others, had been agreed, Fernando I returned to his lands with his objective accomplished.

The Christian expedition led by Alvito was lodged in one of the royal palaces in the capital, and, after assigning a suitable number of masons and other workers, they were guided to the existing plots where Christian churches had previously existed. After many days of excavation, they had found nothing, until they excavated the ground of a mosque located in the present-day Church of San Vicente, where they found a coffin with the incorrupt body of Saint Isidore of Seville (another version of the same story places the events in a hermitage where the monastery of San Isidoro del Campo is located today in Santiponce in the vicinity of Seville).

The entire Christian retinue was seen off from San Vicente to the Macarena Gate by the Sevillian king himself and the main men of his kingdom, heading north.

The system of parias in which both the kingdom of Seville and the other taifas found themselves immersed led to a substantial increase in the currency in circulation in the Christian kingdoms, which was subsequently used to repopulate the occupied territories as well as to defray the costs of new campaigns against the Muslim taifas. The Muslim kingdoms themselves paid the Castilians money that would be used to subjugate them even further.

In 1065, the Sevillian taifa tried to seize the stronghold of Ceuta (ruled by its owner Saquit), already on the African continent. To do so, they made use of the ships they had at their disposal (from the former Taifa of Salta) and a large army. After heavy fighting, the Sevillian troops had to give up and return to mainland Spain. In the same year, 1065, a small Sevillian army of around 500 Berber horsemen commanded by Caid Muadh ben Abi Qurra (who was a member of the family of the Ifran Berber emirs of Ronda, now part of the Sevillian kingdom) was sent north to help the friendly army of Moctadir of Zaragoza to take the city of Barbastro, at that time with a small garrison of Normans belonging to the papal troops who had taken it a short time before. But the great military campaigns that had characterised the years of his reign were over and would not be repeated.

The Final Years of the Reign and the Holy War in Barbastro

Because of their importance in history, we will briefly describe the events that took place in Barbastro in which some Sevillian troops took part. During the eleventh century, Islam in the Iberian Peninsula and southern Italy was in a state of fragmentation in the face of the inexorable push of Christianity. Pope Alexander II was largely to blame for this Christian belligerence,

THE FALL OF MOORISH SEVILLE 1023–1091

Beautiful image of the River Guadalquivir as it passes through Seville, very possibly in the vicinity of the so-called Silver Meadow (Marif al fidda), which had a multitude of elm trees and was a place frequented by the city's population as a meeting place. (Author's collection)

mobilising Christian troops from the Iberian and Italic Peninsulas, as well as from France and other European Christian lands under the banner of a 'holy war' against Islam. This active policy against the European Muslim world took the form of two practical crusades, one against Sicily (which culminated in its conquest in 1061) and the other against the Upper Mark of the Iberian Peninsula with the aim of taking the city of Barbastro.

Barbastro was the main advanced bastion of the Hudi kingdom against the Christian kingdom of Aragon; it was therefore an important axis in the defence of the Andalusian territory in the Upper Mark, which was known for the superiority of its defences in comparison with the rest of the towns in the Upper Mark.

The peninsular Christian troops were aided by troops from beyond the Pyrenees (among whom the Normans were prominent), which culminated in the capture of Barbastro in 1064; the latter were commanded by William of Montreuil, the head of the papal troops at the time. Ben al-Kardabus described the Christian troops that took the city as huge armies that arrived in Al-Andalus from France; he also described the 40-day siege that ended with the capitulation of the Andalusians on the condition that their lives and property be respected. But, although the Christians accepted these conditions for both the garrison and the civilian population, as soon as the unprotected and trusting Andalusian soldiers were outside the city, the Christian troops violated the agreement and killed them. They also broke the pact with the inhabitants of Barbastro, and, when they were leaving the city, some 6,000 people were massacred by the Christians.

Evidently, this blow suffered by the Muslims shook the deepest foundations of the Iberian Muslim world, creating great concern and worry not only in the Taifa of Zaragoza but also in the rest of Al-Andalus, and immediately plans were made to recapture such a significant stronghold. This Christian crusade required a response of at least equal intensity from the Muslims, and, to this end, the king of the Taifa of Zaragoza, Ahmad Al-Muqtadir, called for a holy war or jihad against the invaders, which met with a strong response in the Iberian Muslim world. Al-Muqtadir was a king with good 'press' in Al-Andalus since 1063, when he apparently put a definitive stop to the Aragonese kingdom's attempts to expand into the Andalusian territory of the Taifa of Zaragoza by defeating King Ramiro I of Aragon in the stronghold of Graus.

Thus, the capture of Barbastro by a coalition of Christian troops was immediately responded to by a coalition of Andalusian troops only a year after the fall of the important Hudi town, which not only allowed Barbastro to be retaken but also gave an image of the strength of the Iberian Muslim world, which acted united against a common enemy.

Troops of Al Muzaffar from Lleida, his brother Al-Muqtadir from Zaragoza, Al Mutadid from Seville and other Iberian Muslim territories came to Barbastro in 1065 to reconquer the fortress. Among the Muslim troops, the chronicles highlight the 500 Berber horsemen commanded by Caid Muadh ben Abi Qurra, who came from the Sevillian taifa, and the more than 6,000 archers who were recruited from different places.

According to the accounts that remain of the reconquest of Barbastro – such as that of Ibn Idhari, *Al-Bayán Al-Mugrib* – Al-Muqtadir led the siege operations. Among the tactics employed, it should be noted that tactics of siege of the walls were used, as, when the Christians saw the arrival of the Muslim contingent, they had preferred to flee from combat in the open and take cover behind their walls. As mentioned above, Al-Muqtadir ordered his men to undermine the fortress walls under cover of his well-stocked formation of archers. The defenders could barely get their hands out from the top of their battlements and could do little against the 'sappers'. The Normans tried to open a breach in the walls, through which they could defend themselves, with so little success that part of the wall collapsed against them; this, together with the work of the Muslim archers, who gave no respite, allowed the Muslims to assault the city through this breach.

At that moment, part of the defenders entered the battle, while another contingent went out through one of the city gates with the aim of razing the Muslim camp to the ground, taking advantage of the possible carelessness there, as most of the troops were engaged in the assault. However, they were repelled and subsequently pursued by the Andalusians, who left few survivors.

The reconquest of Barbastro by Al-Muqtadir of Zaragoza took place on 19 April 1065 (only nine months after its fall into Christian hands) and had such repercussions that it led to him taking the honorary title of Al-

THE FALL OF MOORISH SEVILLE 1023-1091

Current walls of the Royal Alcázar of Seville. Behind these walls is the original palace of the Royal Alcázar of Seville, recently recovered from centuries of neglect. (Author's collection)

Muqtadir billah (the mighty by God) to commemorate such an important victory.

After this brief account of the struggle for Barbastro, we return to the history of the kingdom of Seville. In 1067, after intense diplomatic exchanges, the warring Taifa of Carmona was finally incorporated into the Sevillian kingdom. The incorporation of this much desired city was the result of a 'game of several sides' in which it was handed over by the Toledan King Al-Mamun thanks to a pact that would allow Toledo to take Córdoba with the connivance of Seville. Al-Izz, the last ruler of Carmona, handed over his kingdom to Al-Mamun between 1066 and 1067, precisely to prevent it from falling into the hands of Seville, although ironically the exiled Al-Izz died in 1067 in Seville itself. The resistance that this taifa had offered to the kingdom of Seville for many years had finally been eliminated. This would be the last act in the conquests carried out by Al Mutadid to enlarge his kingdom.

In 1068, after the death of Muhammad Almodaffar, king of Badajoz, his successor, Yahya, was to succeed him, but his brother Omar, at that time governor of Évora, did not abide by this decision and proclaimed himself independent ruler of the western part of the kingdom. Evidently, the situation was very favourable for the Sevillian taifa to once again interfere in the politics of Badajoz. Al Mutadid thus supported Omar in his uprising

SETTLEMENT OF THE KINGDOM OF SEVILLE: 1042–1069

against his own brother (the latter supported by the king of Toledo). But the early death of the Sevillian monarch meant that this new attempt to control the Taifa of Badajoz did not prosper.

The last years of Al Mutadid's reign were relatively calm compared to the preceding years. Since the Christians had begun to be paid parias, the kingdom of Seville had been restrained in its desire to conquer. Now humiliated by Ferdinand I, Al Mutadid lived a few years of tranquillity, which ended on 7 February, 20 February or 28 March 1069 (depending on the version) after suffering an acute myocardial infarction or a cerebral haemorrhage (depending on the version), possibly caused by the death of one of his daughters, whom he adored like all his other offspring (other sources point to a possible contagion of the disease from which his daughter died). Although he was not an old man because of his age, as he was approximately 52 years old, he was an old man because of his body, which he had subjected to the most varied excesses since his youth, so now this painful news did nothing more than give the final blow to a tired and ageing body. As the writer Ben Hayyan reflected, the 'lion of kings', the 'fire of fitna', the 'avenger', received the fatal arrow from God's quiver, felling him and bringing down his pride.

After his death, he left his now eldest son, Al Mutamid, an 'immense' kingdom of Seville in territorial and economic terms, feared by the other

View of the current Patio de Banderas (in the present-day Royal Alcázar of Seville), which corresponds in extension to the parade ground of the Caliphate Alcázar and the beginning of the taifa period. (Author's collection)

THE FALL OF MOORISH SEVILLE 1023-1091

taifa kingdoms. But he also left a kingdom of Seville humiliated by the Christians and tributary to the kingdoms of Castile and León. The pressure exerted by the Christian 'noose' on the 'neck' of the Sevillian kingdom was increasing. The Taifa of Seville began its countdown, and it was Al Mutamid who would be in charge of those intense and bittersweet final years.

Image of the Cantigas where a Muslim rider (wearing a turban typical of North African troops) embraces another rider with a helmet and chainmail. This second rider could be an Andalusian Muslim or a Christian, since there could be few differences between the two on many occasions. (Open source)

7

The Rise and Fall of the Kingdom: 1069–1091

Al Mutamid

Abul Qasim Muhammad ben Abbad ben Muhammad ben Ismail ben Muhammad ben Ismail ben Ismail Qurays ben Abbad ben Amr ben Aslam ben Amr ben Itaf ben Naim al-Lajmi, also known by his nickname Al Mutamid ala Allah (the one who relies on the help of God), took the reins of the kingdom the day after his father's death. The life of the people of the Sevillian kingdom continued to be similar to that under the rule of Al Mutadid, the early years of Al Mutamid's rule being a continuation of the later years of his father's rule. The kingdom that Al Mutamid had received was a very powerful state in comparison with its Muslim neighbours but a weak kingdom in comparison with the Christian kingdom of Castile and León.

Al Mutamid was born in Beja in December 1039, in January 1040 or December 1040 (other sources place the date between 20 November and 19 December 1039), possibly because Al Mutadid was governor of that city during that period, and was educated at his father's court, although he was not originally destined to rule over Seville but instead his unfortunate brother Ismail, whose story we have already told. Due to the important cultural imprint that reigned in the palatial environment in which his early years were spent, where pleasures and luxuries were a daily constant, Al Mutamid came to know and learnt to love music, poetry, evenings where wine was never lacking, flowery gardens and therefore a life that did not correspond to the reality behind the walls of the Sevillian palaces.

The new Sevillian monarch saw the need for poetry, with which he could freely and harmoniously express all his feelings; his love of poetry has survived to the present day, and he is remembered today as the 'Poet King'.

But, despite the life of luxury in which he lived like a fish in water, the permanently active military situation of the kingdom of Seville under the command of Al Mutadid meant that, from an early age, he had political and

THE FALL OF MOORISH SEVILLE 1023-1091

Commemorative plaque with an inscription made in 1079 commemorating the repairs carried out by order of King Al Mutamid on the minaret of the Mosque of Ibn Adabbas after several earthquakes. The plaque reads in Arabic:

... Baslama, tasliyya. He has ordered al-Mutamid 'ala Allah, al-Muayyad bi-nasri Allah, Abu-l-Qasim Muhammad, son of Abbad - may Allah render continuous help to his Empire and contribute to its strong victory! - the construction of the highest part of this minaret - may the Islamic invocation never be interrupted therein! - when it had just been brought down by a great number of seismic tremors that took place on Sunday eve, at the beginning of Rabi I of the year 472 [1 September 1079]. And this was completed, by the might and assistance of Allah, at the end of the same month. May Allah deign to accept for this work his generous occupations of the king and shower him with His favours by building him, for every stone he has employed, a palace, in His paradise, by His grace and His goodness!
(Author's collection)

military duties. It should be remembered that he was governor of Huelva at the age of 13 and led the Sevillian troops to take Silves at a similar age and that he was governor of the recently conquered Silves in 1052–1053. Between 1052 and 1058, he was in charge of the conquest of the entire territory of the Algarve. He thus achieved a very important military and political training, only dwarfed by his great skill in poetry.

During his reign, he faced numerous difficulties both at home and abroad. The existence of the tribute to Castile and León meant that the tribute imposed on the population of the Sevillian kingdom was too high, which led to discontent among the population, who saw how the Christian enemy was being paid, giving it even more power. In addition, another important aspect that increased tension within the country was the legitimisation of the Abbadids to hold power. Let us not forget that Al Mutamid's grandfather was elected by the people for his good deeds, but both his father and he had inherited the kingdom. In the face of this, Al Mutamid had to silence some dissenting voices with a few executions. This situation of tension between the people and the ruling hierarchy would have another twist a few years later when many alfaqids, or faqihs, proclaimed slogans against Al Mutamid, delegitimising him as a 'bad Muslim', thus opening the door to the arrival of the Almoravids.

THE RISE AND FALL OF THE KINGDOM: 1069–1091

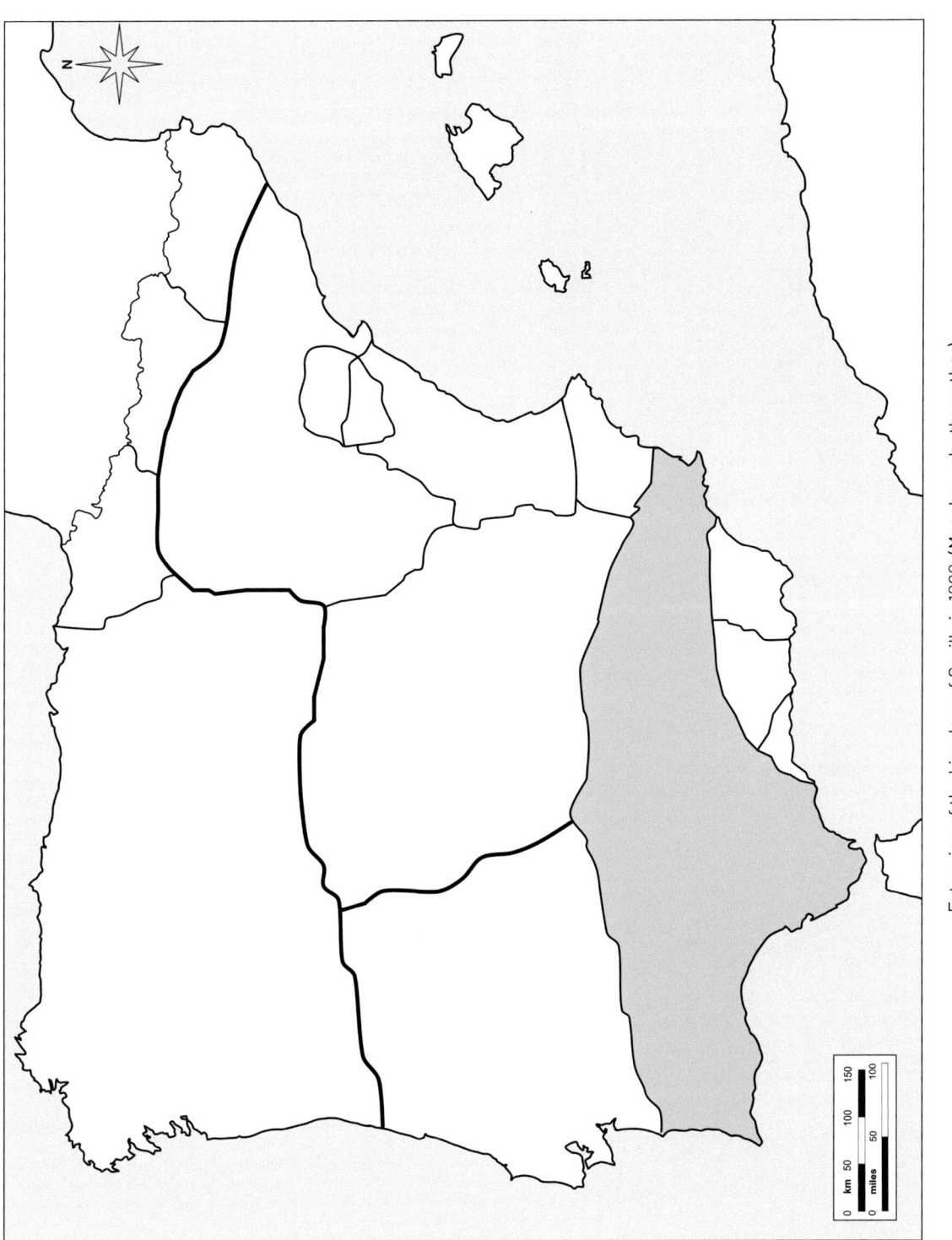

Extension of the kingdom of Seville in 1080. (Map drawn by the author)

THE FALL OF MOORISH SEVILLE 1023-1091

Cordoba Gate, part of the wall of Seville, which has not retained its original layout from the taifa period after successive modifications. It was through this gate that El Cid Campeador entered after his victory over the Granadans under King Abdalá and the Christians under Count García. (Author's collection)

Al Mutamid's personality displayed great virtues such as his broad culture, his bravery and indulgence, but he was also branded as indolent, candid and excessively devoted to the pleasures of wine and meat. There is surely some truth in all this, though all these adjectives were said either to praise or to vilify him, so, as always, they must be considered in their rightful measure. Before he became king, he bore honorific titles such as al-Zafir bi-hawl Allah (the triumphant with the power of God) and al-Muayyad bi-nasr Allah (the supported by the help of God).

His period as governor of Silves was short, for, soon after, he was succeeded by Ben o Ibn Ammar, nine years older than Al Mutamid, with whom he developed a deep friendship, partly helped by the fact that he was also a poet. This gave rise to genuine poetic evenings between the two.

Ibn Ammar was to become one of the most important and powerful figures in the Sevillian kingdom. He was born to humble Arab parents in the vicinity of Silves, where he began to study literature, continuing his studies in Córdoba; he later travelled through many of the lands of Al-Andalus reciting poems. After many wanderings, he was introduced to Al Mutamid, at which point his friendship began. This led him out of his poor life and into a life of fantasy in which all pleasures could be achieved, but he never forgot that fortune could also be adverse, which gave him a character of mistrust and scepticism towards many situations.

When the two friends did not coincide in Silves, they did so in Seville, where they used to enjoy all the pleasures of the capital of the kingdom. There, they used to go, disguised so as not to be recognised, to the so-called 'silver meadow' on the banks of the Guadalquivir, where the whole town used to go to have fun and relax. They had a lively social life and were great fans of banquets. Several of the poems that Al Mutamid composed were dedicated to the 'forbidden' wine, which, as we will see below, was by no means hidden; this is one of them:

> As I passed drunkenly through a vineyard,
> I snagged my clothes.
> <you're going to hurt me> I said to him.
> Why did you pass without greeting
> though your bones
> shed my blood?

Or like this one:

> The reflection of the wine through the light
> Colours the cupbearer's fingers red,
> As juniper leaves the antelope's snout tinged.

Also the figure of the cupbearer who served them the forbidden liquid:

> He appeared, exhaling aromas of sandalwood,
> As he bent his waist about the slender waist,
> How many times he served me, that dark night,
> In crystallised water, liquid roses!

Ibn Ammar's influence over the young Al Mutamid was not at all to his father's liking, so he finally decided to exile Ibn Ammar. The latter did not return to Seville until Al Mutamid succeeded his father, and, in this case, he returned as prime minister of the Sevillian kingdom.

Line of the wall of the Royal Alcázar of Seville, behind which recent studies place the royal palace of Al Mutamid. (Author's collection)

It is said, although more of a legend than a historical fact, that, on one of the many afternoons spent similarly, Al Mutamid and Ibn Ammar, suitably masked so as not to be recognised, were strolling along the banks of the Guadalquivir in the vicinity of the bridge of boats that linked Seville with Triana (possibly located today between the Triana and Cachorro bridges). This riverside area, as mentioned above, was known as the 'silver meadow'. The two friends were walking there, playing a popular pastime in Seville at that time, which was to improvise a poem based on verses improvised by another person. We are well aware of the irremediable fondness that both

THE FALL OF MOORISH SEVILLE 1023–1091

Al Mutamid and Ibn Ammar had for poetic composition, so Al Mutamid improvised some verses praising the splendour of nature that surrounded them, to which Ibn Ammar replied in return. But, after a gust of wind arose, it passed over the water of the river and caused the water to move. Al Mutamid improvising gave the foot of a poem to his friend; it read:

> The wind weaves the waters with lorigas [the lorigas were a type of defensive coat of mail made up of small parts in the form of 'scales'].

Ibn Ammar had not yet replied to his king when they heard a female voice behind them, who completed these phrases recited by the Sevillian king with an inspired verse. It went like this:

> What a breastplate if they were frozen.

The two men turned and began to converse with the beautiful woman. They soon learned that her name was Itimad (which means 'confidence' or 'support') and that she was a slave of Berber origin who worked in the house of a merchant called Romaik, in the suburb of Triana. Al Mutamid was completely smitten by her, not only by her beauty but also by her wit and her natural way of being, her cheerfulness and her prudence (she did not know the real identity of the two men). This moment, although highly poetic and romantic, was yet another pillar on which the future of the kingdom of Seville would be built. As we will discuss later, Itimad would give rise to certain confrontations between Al Mutamid and the religious power, although we will continue with this encounter on the banks of the Guadalquivir.

Itimad said goodbye to the two men, and, from that moment, Al Mutamid instructed Ibn Ammar to go to Itimad's owner to buy her. And so it was that, within a few hours, this Berber slave girl became the favourite of the king of Seville (today it would be considered a fairytale courtship). Just a few days later, he made her his wife, though not as one more in his harem but giving her the title of queen; Itimad, until a few days ago known as Al Romaikiya (which means 'belonging to Romaik'), had become the first lady of the kingdom.

Another, more plausible, version of the first meeting between Itimad and Al Mutamid took place between 1054 and 1055 in Silves,

Sevillian tile narrating the beautiful love story between Itimad and Al Mutamid, whose legend is interwoven with history. What does seem to be true is the immense love they professed for each other until the end of their days in North Africa. (Author's collection)

shortly after he was chosen by his father to rule that territory. Al Mutamid would have been about 15 years old when he met a slave girl known as Al Romaikiya, possibly a little more than a year younger than him. Even during Al Mutamid's time in Silves, they married (not exactly with his father's permission) and at least had the first of their children. Soon after, Al Mutamid was reclaimed to Seville, leaving his family in Silves (between 1057 and 1059). When they later arrived in the capital of the kingdom, Al Mutamid introduced his wife and son to Al Mutadid, who, after meeting them, empathised with Itimad, diametrically changing his opinion of her.

Be that as it may, we can say that the crush that Al Mutamid felt was certain, as Itimad was never replaced by another woman in the heart of the Sevillian king, becoming his favourite and mother of the crown prince. When he found himself in the not too distant future exiled in the lands of North Africa, she would remain by his side, loving him to the end. Al Mutamid had at least nine sons with her, most of whom served as governors of the various cities of the kingdom. He had other children with other women, which according to the sources ranged from 64 to 173, so it is practically impossible to know the real number, although it is assumed that it was a good number.

Returning to the thread of the story, after Itimad and Al Mutamid married, she became very popular among the Sevillian population, perhaps because of her humble origins, perhaps because of her joviality, court antics, humility and natural graces. However, she was also a capricious young woman, and Al Mutamid, her fervent lover, was willing to do anything to make them a reality. Two examples suffice to show how Al Mutamid spared no expense or effort to satisfy his wife. In one case, Itimad, perhaps longing for the 'freedom' she had to move around the streets of Seville during her childhood and youth, told her husband how much she longed to tread mud in a pottery as the other girls did in Triana. Al Mutamid was left with his wife's wish, and, after a week, on some pretext, he made Itimad go down to one of the courtyards of the alcázar. There, the young queen found the whole floor covered with a large layer of mud. On approaching, she realised that this 'mud' was not mud at all, and that it was a paste created with expensive cinnamon mixed with costly perfumes and spices brought from all parts of her kingdom. In the other case, a few months after the first case, Itimad again showed signs of melancholy that did not go unnoticed by her husband. When he asked her what was wrong, Itimad told him how unhappy she felt at times, since, despite being the queen of a powerful state, she would like to have a snowy landscape in winter like other queens in the peninsula. Aware of the difficulty of what she was asking, he told her that the snowy areas belonged either to the Christians in the north or to the lands of her enemy, the Taifa of Granada. Although at first it seemed to be all in that conversation, after a while, Itimad went out onto one of the balconies of her palace in Córdoba and saw the whole landscape on the horizon in white. Itimad ran to her husband to tell him that it had snowed, but, when he heard her, he laughed and took her to where the 'snow' was. As she got closer, Itimad realised that all that was white was nothing more

THE FALL OF MOORISH SEVILLE 1023-1091

Remains of the caliphate walls of Marbella, which belonged during the taifa period to the kingdoms of Málaga and Granada, bitter enemies of the Sevillian kingdom. (Author's collection)

than hundreds of thousands of almond blossoms. In order to satisfy his wife's wishes, Al Mutamid had brought more than a million almond trees from the fertile plains of Málaga and planted them in the Córdoba countryside, so that, when their flowers blossomed, they would give rise to a spectacle very similar to what the countryside would have looked like if it had snowed.

Al Mutamid's love for Itimad is reflected in many of the poems he composed for her, such as the following two, in which he longs for her when he is away from her on a military campaign:

Invisible to my eyes,
You are present in my heart.
May your happiness be as great
As my sorrows, tears and sleeplessness.
Thou art mistress of me, who am hard to reach,
And you find it easy to guide my affection.
My longing at every moment, is to have you by my side,
Would that my wish were fulfilled.
Keep the pact that binds us, and do not change
Despite my long absence.
Your sweet name I have hidden
Inside my poem, where I have written
The letters of Itimad.

I am writing to you and I have only your absence
And my desire is comparable to that of one who has been separated from paradise.
My calamus cannot write without my tears tracing a poem
On the page of the cheeks
And if it were not for the glory that claims me
I would visit you in the folds of the night
Passionately,
As the dew visits the petals of the rose;
And I would kiss beneath the veil your red lips
And I'd snatch your waistline
From waist to neck.

Or as in the following poem, in which he renews his love for her, possibly after some 'conjugal' argument:

Itimad thinks I am bored with her.
How wrong she is!
How could I abandon a gazelle
that lives in my heart,
or the full moon
that dwells in my eyes
or the delightful garden
that I cultivate,
or the unbidden kiss!
If I did, may my hand be cut off,
Splendid in alms, terrible in war.

The passion for Itimad remained throughout their existence. Proof of this are the several children they had together. Names of some of the sons were Abbad (the first-born), Malik, Al Radi and Al Motadd; and daughters such as Fetona (the second), Zaida (the youngest) and Butayna. Al Mutamid had the same great love for all of them as he had for his wife. They were also reflected in some of his poems, and even one of them, Butayna, was particularly successful in her poetic compositions.

Like the rest of the royal family, Itimad also favoured the construction of certain buildings, as well as improvements to existing ones for use by the people. An example of this can be found in one of the inscriptions preserved in the Provincial Archaeological Museum of Seville, which commemorates the construction of a minaret sponsored by Itimad for the mosque possibly located in the church of San Juan de la Palma. As Rodrigo Amador de los Ríos' book indicates, the inscription on this tombstone would read:

One of the entrance gates to the fortified enclosure of the city of Ronda. This was one of the last towns to remain in the hands of Sevillian troops when the Almoravids conquered the country. (Author's collection)

> In the name of Allah, the gracious, the merciful, the blessing of Allah (be upon) Muhammad, the seal of the prophets. The august lady, mother of Ar Raxid Abú-L-Hoseyn, Obaydo-L-L-Láh, son of Al-Motamid-Alay-L-L-Láh Al-Mulled-Bi-Nassri-L-L-Láh, Abú-L-Cásim Mohámmad-Ben-Abbad (may Alláh perpetuate his empire and might and the glory of both of them), commanded to erect this assegah in her mosque (may Alláh preserve it), hoping for abundant rewards. And it (this work) was finished with the help of Allah, under the supervision of the Guacir Al-Katib Al-Amir Abu-L-Casim, Ben-Battáh (may Allah be propitious to him). And this (was) on the moon of Xaaban in the year four hundred and seventy-eight (between November and December 1085 AD).

Despite her 'good deeds', the queen was always in the sights of the ultra-orthodox of the religion, who saw her as a harmful and negative element for the Sevillian monarch. Not surprisingly, one of the excuses that would be used in the future to overthrow Al Mutamid would be the multiple accusations made against his wife.

Old engraving of the castle of Beja, the birthplace of King Al Mutamid in late 1039 or early 1040. The area of today's Portuguese Algarve belonged entirely to the kingdom of Seville in the eleventh century. (Open source)

The Capture of Córdoba

After his accession to the reign of Seville at the end of March 1069, when he was 29 years old, he continued his father's expansionist policy. For this reason, Al Mutamid's military campaigns began to follow one after the other from the beginning of his reign. From Seville, he managed to seal an agreement with the taifa king of Toledo to help the latter take the city (and part of the kingdom) from the Taifa of Córdoba. In exchange for this help, Toledo would cede the small kingdom of Carmona to Al Mutamid, which happened in 1067 (the kingdom of Carmona had belonged to the kingdom of Toledo since 1066–1067 because this kingdom was given to Al-Mamun of Toledo by Al Azziz of Carmona in exchange for the fortress of Almodovar, since the king of Carmona preferred this deal to handing over his lands to the Sevillian monarch, against whom he had been in continuous conflict for years before). In the second half of 1069 (although some sources place the event in the autumn of 1070), backed by Al Mutamid's promise to support him with troops from Seville and due to the existing disputes between Abderramán and Abdelmelik, sons of Abucheuhar, after the latter resigned to continue in command of the Cordoban taifa, King Yahya Ibn Ismail Al-Mamun of Toledo saw the opportune moment to realise his dream of taking

THE RISE AND FALL OF THE KINGDOM: 1069–1091

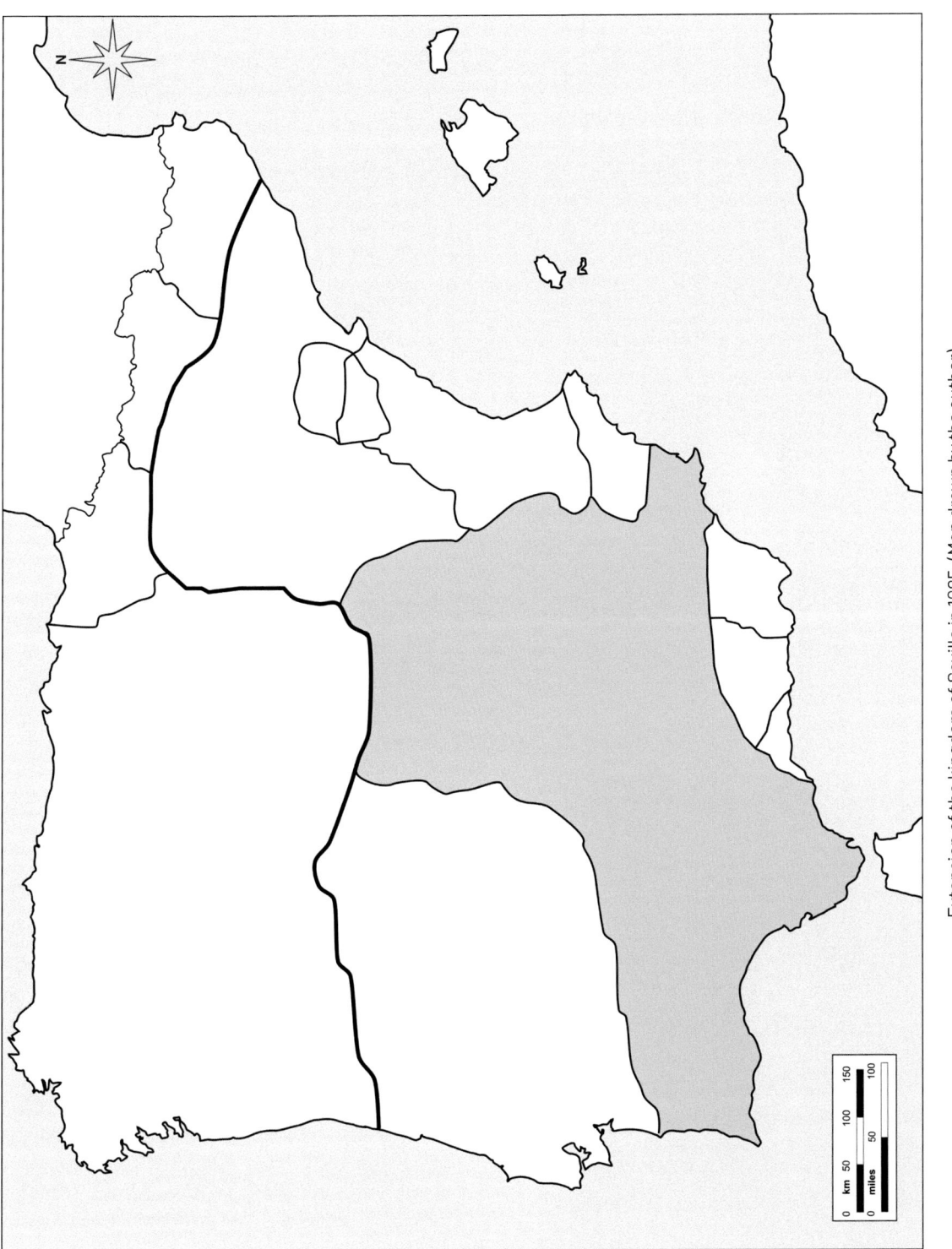

Extension of the kingdom of Seville in 1085. (Map drawn by the author)

possession of the old capital of the Cordoban Caliphate. So, at the head of an army of barely 200 cavalrymen plus foot troops (a small number of troops, as he had not been able to muster more in such a hurry), he set out for Córdoba to take it with the help of the Sevillian troops. Al-Mamun was able to take several minor towns in the kingdom of Córdoba with little difficulty, due to the virtual absence of Cordoban troops who could defend them with minimal chances of success. That autumn, he proceeded to lay siege to the Córdoba square, occupying its outlying districts (such as al-Zahara), which also had an army greatly reduced in number of men and incapable of dealing with the troops from Toledo. The Cordobans, seeing themselves between a rock and a hard place, decided to seek the help of the Sevillian king, who had already shown signs of having backed out of the pact he had made with Al-Mamun just three years earlier to help the Toledan king in the capture of Córdoba. Al Mutamid unhesitatingly came to the aid of the Cordobans, confronting the Toledan troops, whom he managed to get to lift their siege and flee northwards.

The Sevillian troops settled in the suburb of Levante and received strict orders not to plunder or commit excesses, trying to make the Sevillians look like friends and allies of the Cordobans. Since the arrival of the Sevillians in the vicinity of Córdoba, emissaries of King Al Mutamid had been in contact with some Cordoban personalities with the aim of preparing a suitable breeding ground in Córdoba once the Sevillian troops had defeated the troops from Toledo and entered Córdoba in triumph. And so it was, since, after the victory (possibly achieved between June and August 1069), Al Mutamid entered the caliphate city in triumph, reaffirming Abdelmelik as lord of Córdoba. But this was only a stratagem, since, during the seven days that the Sevillians had been in the city since the flight of Al-Mamun, contacts with the seditious Cordobans continued. So, on the same day that the date for the return of the Sevillians to their capital was fixed (which according to Ibn Idari was Sunday), the Sevillian troops, and above all many Cordobans, went to Abdelmelik's house. Abdelmelik with his small army tried to make himself strong, but the mob managed to enter his house from the neighbouring house, and he was finally seized by his own men to finally hand over the throne to Al Mutamid.

Abucheuhar's two sons and his closest relatives were banished to the island of Saltés.

Al Mutamid, for his part, left his first-born son, Abbad, as governor of the former caliphate capital when he was possibly around 15 years old, just as his father had done with him. Abbad arrived with great pomp and circumstance on 27 July 1069 in Córdoba to take up his post along with his entourage, which included important figures trusted by Al Mutamid to advise his son properly.

One of the doors of the Great Mosque of Córdoba, where, during the years of Sevillian domination, Friday prayers were held under the rule of Al Mutamid. (Author's collection)

THE RISE AND FALL OF THE KINGDOM: 1069–1091

Al Mutamid, in keeping with his great love of poetry and emulating his father in the capture of Ronda, also composed a poem to glorify the capture of the ancient caliphate capital. The poem is as follows:

> I have won the hand of beautiful Córdoba, of that brave Amazon who, with sword and spear in hand, refused all who sought her in marriage. Now we both celebrate our marriage in her palace, while the other kings, my rivals, discouraged, weep with rage and tremble with fear. Tremble, and rightly so, vile enemies, for soon the lion will fall upon you.

But Al-Mamun had not said the last word on the matter of the possession of Córdoba, and, while the Sevillian troops were taking over the city of Jaén after its capture in 1074, he allied himself with the Castilian-Leonese King Alfonso VI. Thanks to the help provided by the Christian troops and new dissident movements inside the city of Córdoba, he began to ravage the lands near the capital, then ruled by Abbad al-Zafir (the triumphant), a son of Al Mutamid and Itimad, although, due to his young age and experience, the real power rested with the garrison commander Mohammed Ben Martin (a Christian surname). Al-Mamun had come into contact with a seditious Cordoban, a former raider in the lands of Córdoba, by the name of Ben Ocacha or Ukasa, who was gradually carrying out his intrigues and gaining some followers. It so happened that, although suspicions were raised against Ben Ocacha, they were never brought to an end, possibly due to the laziness of the Sevillians. One night, taking advantage of the darkness and the bad weather, Ben Ocacha and his followers, knowing the customs of the guard to retreat to the inner chambers, managed to sneak into the city. They made their way to Abbad's palace, which was similarly ungarrisoned at its gates. In the vicinity of Abbad's quarters, Abbad and a few soldiers and slaves came upon them, and a fierce battle ensued. The advantage went to the Sevillians, until bad luck caused Abbad to slip, a moment that one of the assailants took advantage of to throw himself upon him and skewer him with his sword. Once Abbad was dead, it was easy to finish off his men, who were demoralised by the lack of a leader. After the assassination, his corpse was left in the street, almost naked (he barely had time to put on clothes as the assault on his quarters was imminent). When the body was abandoned there, an imam happened to pass by and, recognising him as Prince Abbad, despite the blood and mud that covered him, was kind enough to cover his body with his cloak so that he could 'rest in peace'.

Since hardly anyone noticed the surprise attack, they repeated it in the quarters of Mohammed Ben Martin, who at the time was watching some girls dance. When he became aware of the attack, instead of fighting back, he tried to flee, but the result was similar to that of Abbad, as he was also killed. Having finished off the two visible heads of the Sevillian government in Córdoba, they went house to house seeking to convince the Cordoban nobles to join the revolt. Having achieved his objective, Ben Ocacha, his

THE FALL OF MOORISH SEVILLE 1023–1091

View of the exterior of the Great Mosque of Córdoba from its courtyard. One of the high points of the Sevillian kingdom was when Córdoba was annexed and the call to prayer in the name of the Sevillian King Al Mutamid was heard in the great mosque. (Author's collection)

men and the many followers he had recruited began to take to the streets. To put an end to the resistance offered by the Sevillian troops, Ben Ocacha ordered the head of Abbad's corpse (who was about 20 years old at the time) to be cut off and carried around Córdoba on a pike. This led to the battle-hardened Sevillian troops becoming demoralised and fleeing (those who could) or surrendering their weapons to the rebels (the less fortunate). After the capture of the entire city, Ben Ocacha gathered the Cordobans in the mosque to make them swear allegiance to Al-Mamun of Toledo. Although there were quite a few Cordobans who were loyal to Al Mutamid, pressure and fear of revenge forced them to swear allegiance to the Toledan.

A few days later, Al-Mamun entered 'his city', which was now incorporated into the kingdom of Toledo; it was the beginning of the year 1075 (between January and February).

When Al Mutamid was told of the events of that fateful night in the city of Córdoba, his heart was inflamed with rage and anger, for, apart from losing his beloved and longed-for Córdoba, he had been robbed of his beloved and madly loved first-born son. He was also aware of the act of mercy that this unknown imam had performed on the lying body of his son, and he felt a deep gratitude towards this man. Since it was unknown who he was, Al Mutamid made his gratitude public by dedicating a poem to him, which is as follows:

> Alas, I do not know who it is that has covered my son with his cloak,
> but I know that he is a noble and generous man.

These events called for revenge, and Al Mutamid would not rest until he avenged his son's death and recaptured the city of Córdoba.

The Toledan king remained from that moment on to reside in Córdoba, and, in June of that same year of 1075 (about six months had passed since the new capture of Córdoba and Al-Mamun was living in the city), apparently due to intrigues devised by Al Mutamid or perhaps by Ben Ocacha (despised by Al-Mamun after the capture of the city), he was poisoned and died immediately. After the death of Al-Mamun, the inept and corrupt al-Qadir came to power in the Taifa of Toledo and had to resist the ambitions of Al Mutamid to retake the city of Córdoba. Ben Ocacha, despite his disagreements with Al-Mamun, managed to win the favour of the new Toledan monarch, becoming the monarch's delegate in Córdoba.

THE RISE AND FALL OF THE KINGDOM: 1069–1091

Finally, after several attempts to take the caliphate city, in September 1078, Córdoba and its kingdom were once again taken for and by the king of Seville. The triumphal assault took place on 4 September 1078 and allowed Al Mutamid to achieve another objective, which was the capture of Ben Ocacha. When the latter saw the city taken by the Sevillians, he fled, as he knew there would be no mercy for him. And so it was, since Ben Ocacha's escape lasted as long as it took a detachment of Sevillian cavalry to capture him on the outskirts of the city of Córdoba. Once he had been executed, Al Mutamid had one more punishment in store for him, to 'take revenge' for the murder and mockery of his son's corpse in early 1075. He ordered that Ben Ocacha's corpse be crucified and a dog placed next to it, with the negative religious connotations that both events had for Muslim believers.

As happened in the first Sevillian conquest of Córdoba, on this occasion, Al Mutamid gave the post of governor of the caliphate city to his son Fath Al Mamun, who, as we shall see, suffered a similar fate to his brother Abbad while he governed Córdoba.

But this acquisition of new lands by force, on the one hand, made the Sevillian taifa stronger; on the other hand, it made it more coveted by the Castilian-Leonese kingdom. We must not forget that, although strong in Muslim territory, the kingdom of Seville was, after all, a tributary. At first, it belonged to King García of Galicia (in fact, he was exiled in the kingdom of Seville in 1071 when he was dethroned by his brother Sancho of Castile), but, after Alfonso usurped the kingdoms of his brothers, García and Sancho, now under the name of Alfonso VI, he was the recipient of the wealth from Seville.

Let us take a brief look at Alfonso VI to situate him more in this decisive eleventh century in the history of the Iberian Peninsula. He was the son of King Ferdinand I 'the Great' of Castile and Sancha of León, and he became king of León from 1065 to 1109 and of Castile from 1072 to 1109. After the death of Ferdinand I, the kingdom he possessed was divided among his sons, with Alfonso obtaining the kingdom of León and the parias of Toledo, the first-born, Sancho, the kingdom of Castile and the parias of Zaragoza and García the kingdom of Galicia and the parias of Badajoz and Seville. For his daughters, Urraca and Elvira, he created two infantates, that of Covarrubias and that of Campos, respectively.

It did not take long for clashes to occur between Sancho and Alfonso to gain control of the whole of his father's kingdom. On 19 July 1068, in Llantada, they had a first confrontation, in which Sancho was victorious; after this, in 1072, they met again in Golpejera, with victory again falling on the same side. Alfonso had to emigrate after being stripped of his kingdom, choosing the city of Toledo, with whose king, Al-Mamun, he had good relations. In his absence, his sister Urraca worked

Minaret of San Juan, located in the city of Córdoba in the vicinity of the Aljama Mosque. It is a fine example of the type of tower from which the muezzin called to prayer. (Author's collection)

THE FALL OF MOORISH SEVILLE 1023-1091

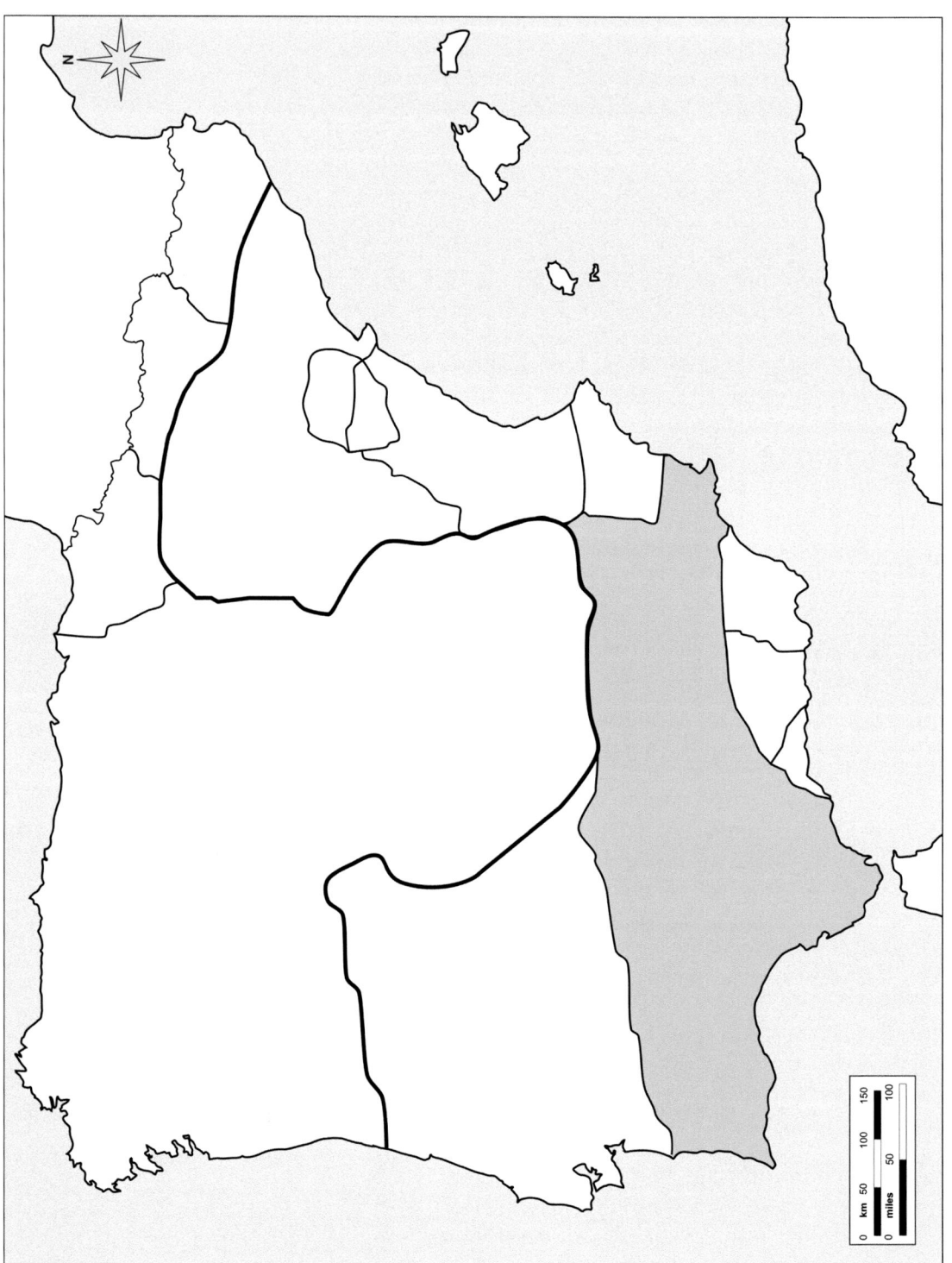

The kingdom of Seville in 1080. (Map drawn by the author)

THE RISE AND FALL OF THE KINGDOM: 1069–1091

in his favour, as, after raising the city of Zamora against Sancho, the king was killed by Vellido Dolfos during the subsequent siege. This led to the return of Alfonso, who took over Sancho's lands and completed them by annexing those of his brother García (who, as we have already mentioned, ended up in exile in the kingdom of Seville, which he held as a vassal).

In 1072, Alfonso VI became the flamboyant king of Castile and León and took over the collection of the parias from the various taifas that were vassals to him, managing to consolidate this trend, which ultimately allowed the already fragile foundations that supported the taifa kingdoms to be shaken.

Alfonso VI was not a comfortable rival, because he was eager to extort more and more money from the Muslim taifas, especially the most powerful of them all, Seville, and, in addition to the annual tribute, he periodically intimidated the Muslims with invasions of their territories. Playing on the weaknesses of the taifas and their many intrigues, he gradually made himself master of the peninsula. In this way, in 1078 (after the capture of Córdoba by Sevillian troops), he acted against the kingdom of Seville, since, despite receiving the tribute in full, he decided to 'squeeze' Al Mutamid a little more by raiding and plundering his lands. The Sevillian army, although powerful among the Muslims, as we have mentioned, was no match for the increasingly powerful armies of King Alfonso VI.

Approaching the vicinity of the city of Seville and seeing how useless it would be to send his troops against the Christian army, Al Mutamid decided to use diplomacy to stop them. For this mission, he sent his right-hand man, Ibn Ammar, with the aim of relieving the Sevillian kingdom of the destruction that the Christians were causing in their lands, whatever the cost. Ibn Ammar was the protagonist of an unusual story that allowed the Christian army to retrace their steps without having to fight them. The Sevillian vizier set off with a colourful retinue laden with gifts to meet the Castilians.

One of the Arab gates of the city of Córdoba (de Almodóvar), which had to resist the Toledans, Sevillians and Almoravids during the reign of Al Mutamid. (Author's collection)

Once he arrived at Alfonso VI's camp, Ibn Ammar pitched his colourful tent, made of rich silk, and invited the Castilian king to join him for a chat. There, Ibn Ammar spent several days trying to elicit his tastes, among which he discovered King Alfonso VI's inordinate fondness for chess. As Ibn Ammar was also a great fan of the game, he agreed to play a game with the Castilian. To this end, the vizier carried among his belongings a chess set made of mother-of-pearl and ebony and the figurines made of ivory, which was a real jewel that amazed Alfonso VI.

They agreed to play for something, so they decided to bet on something, but Ibn Ammar with his loquacious conversation convinced the king that, as a mere servant, he could not have enough money to bet against a whole king. So he proposed a wager, according to him, 'simpler'. He said to Alfonso VI, 'if I win you will give

THE FALL OF MOORISH SEVILLE 1023–1091

Arches of the upper basilica building in the city of Medina Azahara, which was destroyed at the beginning of the fitna. This ancient palace-city was stripped over the years of all its wealth and building material, which would end up in many other cities, such as Seville. (Author's collection)

me two grains of wheat for the first square of the board, four grains for the second, sixteen for the third, and so on, multiplying the number by itself in each of the squares. If I lose I will give you the same, and the chess game will be yours too'.

The king accepted the pact without much interest; after all, he was a powerful king and capable of paying off his debts. During the game, Ibn Ammar's brilliance surpassed that of his rival, finally defeating him.

The Castilian prepared to 'pay' the debt he had contracted and told Ibn Ammar how much wheat he should give him. Ibn Ammar made the account under the pretext that he did not want to receive one grain of wheat more and certainly not one less. As they went through the accounts, Alfonso VI saw that the figures were immense, practically unmanageable. There would not be enough wheat in all Castile to satisfy the gambling debt to the Sevillian vizier.

Ibn Ammar, who had played the long game, had won (as the Sevillian kingdom did not have that amount of wheat either) and tried to reach an agreement with the Castilian to find a way out of his inability to obtain that amount of wheat. He proposed that, in order to save his honour, he could replace all that wheat by withdrawing all his troops from the lands of Seville and sending them against the Taifas of Badajoz, Murcia and Granada, which were not vassals of the kingdom of Seville. And, although Alfonso VI did not agree at all with this solution, he had to accept it in order to wash his honour. He did so, however, after asking for a double tribute in that year, which Ibn Ammar accepted immediately. In this subtle and intelligent way, Ibn Ammar managed, single-handedly and without causing a single death among his troops, to make the fearsome Christian army retreat to lands beyond the territorial limits of Seville.

Sevillian Infantry: This soldier wears a helmet, made in two parts and with a nasal, which covers half of his face, and a mail shirt under his clothes. On his helmet, he has a scarf tied as a turban. He carries shield, spear and sword. We can see how military clothing in Al-Andalus had many more similarities with that used in southern Europe (north of the Iberian Peninsula) than that worn in North Africa. (Artwork by Giorgio Albertini © Helion & Company 2025)

El Cid Campeador: This Castilian knight wears the typical clothing of a warlord of the time, a helmet with a nasal, full mail with 'verdugo' head covering, sleeves and leggings. El Cid, whose name was Rodrigo Díaz de Vivar, had throughout his life two famous swords, the one called 'Tizona' (the one in the image) and 'Colada'. He also carries a 'kite-shaped' shield. (Artwork by Giorgio Albertini © Helion & Company 2025)

Sevillian Archer: This Sevillian archer is lucky to have a short-sleeved mail shirt, a protection that not all archers had. He does not wear a helmet, and, as a weapon, has a composite bow of the Arabic type and a sword typical of the infantry. Archers tended to position themselves in the rear of the army, from where they could shoot arrows with less danger to themselves. (Artwork by Giorgio Albertini © Helion & Company 2025)

Sevillian Light Cavalry: This Sevillian horseman of Berber origin (like many of the troops of the Kingdom of Seville) wears simple clothes, only a tunic with a turban, showing certain similarities to the clothes used by the Almoravids. As his primary armament, he carries a compound bow and has a typical cavalry sword. (Artwork by Giorgio Albertini © Helion & Company 2025)

Al Mutamid and Almoravid Heavy Cavalry: The Sevillian King is dressed in a long-sleeved mail shirt, and an iron helmet (made in two halves), decorated with a silk scarf. He wears a cape on his shoulders, trousers and high boots. The clothes of such an important personage were of a higher quality than most of his soldiers.
This North African rider carries a spear with a sword at his waist as his main weapon. In addition, he carries a further two spears in his left hand, where he also carries a small and light circular shield decorated with three tassels. This lightweight equipment gave him good mobility, although he was not well suited to hand-to-hand fighting. (Artwork by Giorgio Albertini © Helion & Company 2025)

Almoravid Infantry: This infantryman bases his armament on his spear and the sword at his belt. The circular tasselled shield he carries is small, although the men in the front line in combat may have used larger shields. Tactically, these infantry formed a tight body, presenting a front of spears that was very difficult to attack and that were supported by the arrows of their archers located in the rear. (Artwork by Giorgio Albertini © Helion & Company 2025)

Sevillian Heavy Cavalry: Heavy cavalry was the main weapon in the Sevillian army. This rider wears a full mail shirt under his clothes and has a helmet decorated with a turban. As armament, he carries a spear with a ribbon attached, and a sword hung on a cross belt from his right shoulder. As defensive equipment, in addition to his mails shirt, he has a large circular shield. (Artwork by Giorgio Albertini © Helion & Company 2025)

Almoravid Light Cavalry: This rider, who has just dismounted from his horse, wears a simple tunic and a turban. As armament, he carries three spears for use from the horse and a small circular shield. The Almoravid light cavalry was one of the main offensive elements of their army. (Artwork by Giorgio Albertini © Helion & Company 2025)

THE RISE AND FALL OF THE KINGDOM: 1069-1091

Al Mutamid had much to thank Ibn Ammar for as a politician, but he thanked him even more as a friend, showering him with all kinds of goods. For the monarch, the memories of his friend in the palaces of Silves remained in his memory, as these verses by the Sevillian king show:

Hello, Abu Bakr, greet my Silves inns. Ask them if they long for the days of love as I do. Greet the palace of the Barandas from a lad ever eager to be there. Den of lions and delicious maidens, what dens and what women's halls, what delightful nights in their shadows with girls with generous buttocks and slender waists! White and brown, piercing my soul like white swords and brown spears. That playful night at the levee, with that wench with the bracelet that meandered like the river. She took off her cloak, a willow branch her body, like the bud bursting into blossom. She poured me wine from her glances, from her glass; sometimes from her mouth. The touch of his lute bewitched me; as if I heard the strumming of swords on enemy necks.

Remains of the wall corresponding to the Caliphate Alcázar of Córdoba. This important city of Al-Andalus had to be taken by Sevillian troops on two occasions, each time with a son of the Sevillian king as governor. (Author's collection)

But the harassment to which the kingdom of Seville was subjected by Alfonso VI did not prevent the taifa from trying to continue to increase its extension at the expense of its neighbours. Thus, following the conquest of Córdoba (which would belong to the Sevillian kingdom until the end of the latter in 1091), Al Mutamid, taking advantage of the absolute weakness of the Toledo taifa, took all the territory of this kingdom that lay south of the River Guadiana as far as the Guadalquivir. It was during this period of advance towards the north and east of the Sevillian kingdom that cities of such importance as Baeza (Bayyasa) and Úbeda (Ubbadat al Arab) were taken, as well as part of the territory that had belonged to the former kingdom of Jaén (whose capital, as mentioned above, was taken in 1074). This territory had previously belonged to the Zirids of Granada, having subsequently been taken by the Taifa of Toledo, which was now crumbling by the day. It would remain under Sevillian control in the years to come, albeit with some revolts, such as that of Baeza in 1084, which left it in virtual independence from the kingdom of Seville.

But, in its progress towards the east, an old enemy would once again cross its path: the Zirid kingdom of Granada.

The Zirid Kingdom of Granada, A Tough Rival in the East

The expansionist policy of the Sevillian kingdom was the guiding light for Al Mutamid, since, in the face of the economic pressure from the Castilian-Leonese kingdom, it was necessary to obtain new inflows of wealth. Since to the south and west the situation had been completely controlled except

THE FALL OF MOORISH SEVILLE 1023-1091

View of a section of the city walls of Ronda, which after many vicissitudes became part of the kingdom of Seville. (Author's collection)

for the Taifa of Badajoz (which, due to its military and economic potential, as well as its vast territorial extension, had not fallen prey to Sevillian power), the Sevillian king began to exert greater pressure towards the east, where his lands were neighbouring those of the king of Granada, Abdalá. This king, of Berber origin, had managed to consolidate, not without considerable difficulty, his dominion over lands that today would partially correspond to those of Granada, Málaga, Jaén and Almería. Obviously, friction between the two kingdoms occurred on numerous occasions with varying degrees of intensity throughout the reign of Al Mutamid, such as the capture of Estepa in Seville by the Granadan Kabbab. Many of these clashes are reflected in the memoirs that the Zirid monarch of Granada wrote, in which we can see how the figure of Ibn Ammar (and his eagerness to reign over some territory) is blamed for a large part of the bad relations between the Sevillians and the Granadans.

The reality is that there were generally no major military clashes between the two kingdoms, but rather everything was done through various moves by each side, like a game of chess. And, as we have already mentioned, there was a third guest with a great deal to say in these clashes: the kingdom of Castile and León.

As the kingdom of Castile and León became more powerful, it was able to demand parias from new kingdoms. This was the case with the kingdom of Granada, which up to this point had kept its distance from the parias, but in 1074 (possibly) Pedro Ansúrez, King Alfonso VI's ambassador, went to demand the tribute from Abdalá. However, the Granadan, seeing himself safe because of the distance from the Christian kingdom and the existence of Muslim kingdoms between the two (specifically the Toledan kingdom of Al-Mamun), rejected the untempting 'offer' that he had been made.

The ambassador, with the Granadan refusal, returned to his homeland, but, on the way back, near the town of Priego, Ibn Ammar from Seville was waiting for him. The latter was aware of the ambassador's presence in Granada. After meeting with him and learning of Abdalá's refusal, he saw an unbeatable situation for his own gain. So he told Ansúrez that, if Abdalá refused to pay him 20,000 dinars (which was what the Castilians-Leonese had asked for), he himself would give them 50,000 dinars if they agreed to a deal in which the kingdom of Granada would pass to Ibn Ammar and Al Mutamid while all the wealth of the kingdom would go to the Christians.

The Castilian had the clear idea that obtaining the maximum amount of Andalusian money took precedence over the possession of more or less territory. (Why take care of the cow if you can have all its milk without any further effort?) Thus, after agreeing on the interests of each of the parties,

THE RISE AND FALL OF THE KINGDOM: 1069–1091

they agreed that the first measure necessary to take over the kingdom of Granada would be to build a castle in a strategic location that would allow them to harass and disturb the normal life of the kingdom of Granada. A Granadan traitor by the name of Ben Adha, who was familiar with the defensive positions of the Granadans, indicated the fortification of Belillos as the best place to tighten the grip on the Granadan kingdom. A rocky hill was chosen from which the defence of the fortress would be relatively easy to maintain, as well as an open door in the Granadan defences already in the interior of its territory; evidently, Ben Adha knew perfectly the topography of this area in the Eastern Mountains of the Zirid kingdom. Once the town was taken, it was necessary to build a fortress as soon as possible to defend against possible attacks by the Granadans. The labour was provided by the Castilians, after Ibn Ammar had previously 'hired' them, backed by gold from Seville, which enabled him to complete the fortress in a short time. The fact that the work was carried out by Castilians meant that the fortress was built with characteristics and innovations that were clearly more typical of Castile than of the Andalusian style. The garrison that would remain in the castle, according to the pact 'sealed' in Priego between Ibn Ammar and Pedro Ansúrez, would be made up of Sevillian troops that could eventually be reinforced by a Castilian army sent by King Alfonso VI. Al Mutamid himself was present at Belillos to observe the progress of the works, as well as to demonstrate the military power of Seville in the form of a parade within Granada's own territory.

State of the house after the restoration work. (Photograph by Fernando Alda, used with the permission of Cristina Vargas Lorenzo from her article 'La recuperación del palacio primitivo del Alcázar de Sevilla')

From Belillos, the Sevillians were to penetrate into the fertile plains of Granada, systematically destroying crops and felling trees to create a situation of terror and instability in the Zirid kingdom that would eventually lead to the collapse of Abdalá's power and its final surrender. As agreed at Priego and as mentioned above, the kingdom of Granada would pass into the hands of the Sevillian taifa, and Granada would be ruled by Ibn Ammar; in return, all the treasures of Granada would pass into the hands of King Alfonso VI.

As mentioned above, the work was completed in a short time, and the fortress was well garrisoned and provisioned, in anticipation of possible Zirid attacks. These attacks were not long in coming, for, as soon as Al Mutamid had withdrawn from Belillos in the direction of his kingdom and the Christian army and workers had also withdrawn in search of their lands, King Abdalá, aware of the seriousness of the situation, tried to take control of the fortress with a Granadan army recruited for the occasion. But the good defence of Seville and the solidity of the fortress prevented him from succeeding. And, although he thought of besieging the fortress to force it to surrender by hunger and thirst, he could see that, despite his constant vigilance, Belillos continued to receive supplies from outside with some regularity. Abdalá had to return to Granada with his head down because of his repeated failures to take the fortress.

From Belillos, as planned by Ibn Ammar at the time, a multitude of attacks were carried out on the Granadan plain, which greatly interrupted the daily activities of the local population. This incessant pressure from the kingdom of Seville on the kingdom of Granada led (as is usually the case whenever problems arise) to voices discordant with Abdalá's mandate. These were increasingly important and from families with greater influence in Granada.

This whole situation made Abdalá reconsider the good and bad that a lord or vassal alliance with the kingdom of Castile and León would bring. So, since the troops from Belillos were constantly harassing the lands of Granada and he had no means of expelling them from there, what better than to have the Christians on his side? So it was that Abdalá agreed to hand over the sum that he had refused Pedro Ansúrez some time before.

The taifa king of Toledo, a great collaborator of the Castilian-Leonese king, acted as mediator so that the payment of the Granada money could be made as soon as possible.

When the king of Granada finally bought the support of the Christians, the event of the capture of the Sevillian city of Córdoba by Al-Mamun of Toledo, allied with the omnipresent in all matters concerning internal Andalusian affairs, King Alfonso VI, took place. Immediately after hearing the news and faced with the possibility of being isolated beyond enemy lines, the garrison of Belillos abandoned the fortress, which after a short wait was taken by the Granadan army, now without any effort.

But things did not stay like that, because, when Ibn Ammar made a pact with the Christians for the fight against Granada and the construction of the fortress of Belillos, many debts were still outstanding. And of course, these were Ibn Ammar's debts to the Christians (who, as we can see, were always betting on the winning horse, with their tactic of making each and every one of the Muslim kingdoms of the peninsula poorer and weaker), which greatly compromised the Sevillian kingdom and even more so after the fall of Córdoba in 1075.

That was why Ibn Ammar was the first person interested in the continuation of hostilities between the kingdom of Seville and the kingdom of Granada, and he was constantly striving to prevent any kind of rapprochement between Kings Abdalá and Al Mutamid in one way or another and even more so now with the pressure that the Castilian-Leonese kingdom was exerting against both of them. Once again, Ibn Ammar contacted Alfonso VI, to try to bring him into favour in the conflict with Granada. He successfully tried to convince the Christian monarch how profitable it would be for both of them if Abdalá were to fall and be replaced by Ibn Ammar (who had increasingly hidden separatist intentions with respect to the kingdom of Seville) while all the wealth of the deposed monarch would pass to Alfonso VI. It was clear to the latter that, if there was to be any beneficiary in all this plot, it would be him. In one fell swoop, he would further impoverish two Muslim kingdoms while

Epigraph commemorating the erection of the minaret of the mosque where the church of San Juan de la Palma stands today between November and December 1085, sponsored by the Sevillian Queen Itimad. (Author's collection)

it was Ibn Ammar's men who would die in the fighting and not Christians. The idea of weakening a kingdom more and more, as he was doing with Toledo, would at some point bear fruit, which would be none other than the fall into Alfonso VI's hands of an entire kingdom without the need to have fought.

Ibn Ammar and Alfonso VI together set out on the journey to the kingdom of Granada, with the aim of putting even more pressure on the Zirid. They let him know by a messenger of their imminent arrival and that it was advisable for him to go to meet them and receive them. When Abdalá learned of Ibn Ammar's presence in the Christian expedition, he could only fear the worst, given the former's knowledge of the pacts that the latter had made during the Belillos incident. And, although Alfonso VI dressed the visit up as a renewal of the treaties previously signed with Abdalá, the latter remained doubtful about the malicious intentions of both men.

Faced with the dilemma of whether to go out to meet Alfonso VI or not, Abdalá finally opted for the least bad option, which was to go to meet him. The meeting took place on the outskirts of the city of Granada, and there, the 'dealer of the two decks' Alfonso VI, after groping him and listening to Abdalá's pleas, agreed to reach an agreement with the latter, in which he would pay him 30,000 meticals, thus renewing the pact of mutual aid between the two kingdoms. One of the tricks used by Abdalá was to convince Alfonso VI that, if he weakened Granada, it would be to the benefit of Seville and that, if Seville acquired so much power, it would possibly reject the Christian claims for parias.

Once the agreement between Castile and León and Granada had been renewed, Ibn Ammar found out what had happened and asked Alfonso VI for an audience to make him reconsider the matter. But Alfonso VI, more given to the certain fact (the 30,000 meticals) than the uncertain one (the conquest of Granada by Seville), reproached the Sevillian for having spoken so badly of Abdalá when he was really a man of great judgement. Despite this, and at Ibn Ammar's insistence, he managed to get Alfonso VI's approval for the exchange of towns between the two kingdoms. Thus, Estepa (Istabba), recently conquered by Granada, and Castro del Río (Qastruh) would pass back to Seville, while Alcalá la Real (Qalat Astalir) and Bédmar (Matmar) would be given in exchange.

Furthermore, due to Ibn Ammar's insistence on the towns of Qastro and Martos (in the possession of Granada and the key to the city of Jaén), Alfonso obliged the Granadan to hand over Martos to the Sevillians, while Qastro would pass to the Granadans, but after being exchanged for a castle in the border area of Alfonso VI's territories called Al Matmar (which, although it belonged to the kingdom of Toledo, Alfonso VI's total influence over it made him speak of this settlement as his own). Abdalá was evidently forced to accept this unfavourable barter, despite his refusal to do so.

Low-scale aggression would continue between the two kingdoms in the years to come, although the figure of Ibn Ammar would disappear from the turbulent relations between them. Ibn Ammar soon forgot his illusion of reigning in Granada in exchange for a new objective, which would be to reign in the kingdom of Murcia, as we shall see below.

Furthermore, the fall of the Taifa of Toledo at the hands of King Alfonso VI was the trigger that alerted the other taifa kingdoms to the danger posed by the Castilian-Leonese kingdom.

Access to the Mediterranean: Murcia

After the reconquest of the lands of Córdoba, the failure to take the Zirid kingdom of Granada and the new acquisition of the southernmost lands of the kingdom of Toledo, new prospects opened up for the advance of the Sevillian army. Al Mutamid, advised by Ibn Ammar (some sources tell us that part of the Murcian population was interested in changing their lord and contacted Al Mutamid), set his sights on the kingdom of Murcia, which would allow the Sevillian kingdom access to the Mediterranean Sea. It would be the Sevillian vizier who would be in charge of seizing these lands in eastern Spain. At that time, the lord of Murcia was called Abú Abderramán Ben Tahir and was independent of the kingdom of Valencia (to which it had belonged until recently), although he had few troops at his service. Evidently, the situation was very favourable, and this was taken advantage of by Ibn Ammar, who, with the excuse of visiting the count of Barcelona, Ramón Berenguer II, passed through Murcia on his way in the first half of the year 1078. There, he took the opportunity to make contact with some of the city's nobles who were critical of Ben Tahir's rule. After buying the will of several important families in Murcia, he moved to Catalonia, where he offered 10,000 dinars to Count Ramón for conquering the kingdom of Murcia together with his troops for Seville. The Christian kingdoms, eager for riches from the south of the peninsula, were always ready to interfere

THE RISE AND FALL OF THE KINGDOM: 1069–1091

Beautiful image of the castle of Lorca, which was one of the most important and faithful possessions of the kingdom of Seville in the Levantine territory. The kingdom of Seville came to be bathed by the Atlantic waters in the Algarve and by the Mediterranean waters in Murcia. (Open source)

in all the internal affairs between the taifas that they could. Count Ramón therefore accepted but asked for a guarantee that the agreement would be fulfilled. Ibn Ammar, faced with this condition offered by the Christians, dared to leave the son of Al Mutamid himself as the Catalan's hostage, all of this of course behind the back of the Sevillian monarch (who would never have accepted to put his son as a guarantee). Thus, Rachid, Al Mutamid's son, was held hostage by the Catalans, while Ibn Ammar hoped that he would get the money in time so that, when Al Mutamid found out, he would have his son back.

Al Mutamid, unaware of the reality of the secret pact that Ibn Ammar had made, sent his army to the lands of Murcia, where he joined forces with the Catalan allies. There, the days went by with multiple attacks on the Murcian troops. But time went by, and the Catalan count began to suspect that what had been agreed with Ibn Ammar might remain a dead letter, so he arrested the vizier, and the hitherto 'guest' Rachid became a prisoner as well. Evidently, the personal guard of both men tried to prevent their capture at first and, after failing to do so, to try to free them both at a later stage. But these troops were very few in number and were unable to achieve their objectives, and they beat a retreat in the direction of the Guadiana Menor, through which they knew that King Al Mutamid was on his way to the lands of Murcia to finish the campaign to capture the small principality.

It was in this area that the fugitives finally encountered the bulk of the Sevillian troops. It was two of the fugitives who were instructed by Ibn Ammar to give the news to the Sevillian monarch that met with him. In this conversation, Al Mutamid realised what his vizier was up to and that his son was a prisoner of the Christians because of Ibn Ammar's wrongdoing. Ibn Ammar's men reassured the king and asked him not to do anything to try to free them, as Ibn Ammar himself, by negotiating and talking with Count Ramón, would soon resolve the misunderstanding between the two parties.

Blind with rage, Al Mutamid ordered his troops to head for Jaén, to reorganise his ideas and decide on the next move. This was to immediately load the chains onto the nephew of Count Ramón, who, because of the alliance that had existed between the two sides, rode alongside the Sevillian king. It was not more than 10 days before Ibn Ammar, freed from his captors, arrived in the vicinity of Jaén, where he knew that Al Mutamid was temporarily residing.

But the vizier, who knew the king very well, was aware of the harm that the capture of his son had done him; he did not have the necessary courage to appear before him. To communicate with Al Mutamid, he decided to use verses that would bring him closer to the now distant Al Mutamid. They go like this:

Should I believe my presentiments
or listen to the advice of my companions?
Shall I carry out my plan
or shall I remain here with my escort?
When I obey the impulses of my heart,
I advance sure to see my friend's arms open to receive me:
But when I reflect,
I turn back.
Friendship drags me forward,
but the memory of the fault I have committed
pulls me back.
How strange are the decrees of fate!
Who would have foretold me that a day would come
when it would be more pleasant for me to be far from you than near you?
I fear you because you have the right to take my life;
I hope, because I love you with all my heart.
Have pity on him whose unswerving adherence you know,
Whose merit has no other merit than to love thee sincerely.
I have done nothing that can furnish weapons against me to the envious,
nothing to prove negligence or presumption on my part;
But thou thyself hast exposed me to a dreadful calamity,
Thou hast made my sword mouldy.
It is true, if I remembered thy many benefits,
Which have been to me what rain is to the branches of trees,
I would not let myself be thus consumed by horrible torments and I would not say,
What has happened, has happened because of me.
On my knees I implore your mercy,
I beseech you to forgive me,
but even if I had to experience near you the harsh North wind,
I would nevertheless exclaim:
O sweet breeze to my heart!

THE RISE AND FALL OF THE KINGDOM: 1069-1091

Impressive view of the castle of Mértola with the town at its feet. This taifa kingdom fell under the rule of Seville in 1044. (Open source)

Al Mutamid, after listening to his vizier's poem, was moved by the memory of his old friendship with Ibn Ammar, the many moments they had lived together and the great affection they had for each other; he felt unable to retaliate or take action against Ibn Ammar. The truth is that this friendship that existed between the two, though once true and real, was now being exploited by Ibn Ammar (after self-serving mortification in his poem) at the expense of the naïve poetic manner in which Al Mutamid often dealt with personal matters. So, after reading Ibn Ammar's poem, he responded to him in kind, composing a poem for the occasion, in which he said:

> Come take your place by my side!
> Come without fear,
> for goodness awaits you and not reproof.
> Come convinced that I love you too much to be able to afflict you;
> You know that nothing pleases me more
> than to see you cheerful and happy.
> When you come here
> you will find me as always,
> Ready to forgive the sinner,
> clement to my friends.
> I will treat you with kindness, as before,
> and I will forgive you your fault, if there has been fault;
> For the Eternal has not given me a hard heart.
> and I am not accustomed to forget an ancient and sacred friendship.

As we can see, it was not difficult for Ibn Ammar to conveniently bring Al Mutamid's interests closer to his own, as the great schemer that he was. And there were still many intrigues ahead of him during the conquest of Murcia, as we shall see later on.

After the vizier learned of his lord and master's reply, he now dared to come to his presence. There, he agreed with Al Mutamid to offer the Catalan count the promised 10,000 dinars and the life of his imprisoned nephew, in exchange for his son Rachid. But the Catalan, having seen his interests damaged, demanded three times the amount initially agreed. As Al Mutamid wanted to put an end to the whole messy affair as soon as possible, he tried to raise that amount of money. But it was not possible, so he devised a ruse to get it. He minted new dinars but not in the usual proportions of gold. They were minted in much lower proportions and in a way that was not noticeable at first glance.

The deception lasted until shortly after Rachid was handed over to his father in exchange for the rigged ducats, although it was too late to 'protest' to Al Mutamid about the deception. In the end, both parties were satisfied, at least for the time being, and the Sevillian king was once again able to return to his lands.

Once both Al Mutamid and Ibn Ammar arrived in Seville, the former left the latter a powerful army with which to continue the attempt to conquer Murcia. Leaving the army in the hands of the vizier shows that the confidence that Al Mutamid once had in his vizier was completely renewed. Perhaps this was influenced by Ibn Ammar's reports to the Sevillian monarch of recent contacts with Murcian nobles who wished to see the 'liberation' of the Murcian kingdom by Sevillian troops soon.

Ibn Ammar left Seville with the troops for Córdoba at the end of 1078 or perhaps the beginning of 1079, where he stopped to pick up more troops and continued on to the castle of Baldj (Vilches? possibly in the vicinity of Vélez Rubio), where he made friends with its governor, by the name of Ben

Image of the castle of Silves with the city at its feet. This taifa kingdom was captured between 1053 and 1054 by the Sevillian armies under the command of Prince Al Mutamid when he was only 13 years old. (Open source by Lacobrigo)

THE RISE AND FALL OF THE KINGDOM: 1069–1091

Rachic or Ibn Rachic. After telling him of his mission, the governor decided to accompany him to Murcia.

The most powerful Sevillian army corps headed towards Murcia, which they besieged; meanwhile, another army corps headed towards the town of Mula, which they took in a short time. This town was not taken at random by the Sevillians, as many of the supplies that were needed in the capital of Murcia to resist the siege passed through it. Ibn Ammar thought that, if food supplies were scarce, resistance would become laxer day by day, as indeed it did.

He had the idea of leaving his recent friend Ben Rachic as governor of the city of Mula, leaving him a garrison in which some of the powerful Seville cavalry stood out.

Ibn Ammar, after leaving Mula in good custody and Murcia in a deadly siege, returned to Seville to give the latest news of the Murcian adventure to King Al Mutamid.

Shortly after arriving in Seville, Al Mutamid and Ibn Ammar received news from the Murcian front that gave them very good prospects. Hunger was raging in the city of Murcia, and it is well known that this weapon is very powerful and can affect anyone. Discontent was growing among the population, who began to look favourably on being under Sevillian control. After all, who cares about one king or another? What mattered to them was to get on with their lives as best they could. The nobles who had secretly colluded with Ibn Ammar and his men took full advantage of this situation. Thus, supported by a group of treacherous nobles, the gates of the city were opened to the besieging Sevillian army. During Ibn Ammar's absence, Ben Rachic was the supreme commander of the troops, and he was in charge of taking possession of the city. For their part, the Murcian rebels themselves were responsible for capturing the legitimate Murcian ruler, Ben Tahir, imprisoning him in his own palace. The year was 1078–1079, and the Murcian pearl formed part of the necklace that Seville placed around its neck. In the same campaign, the city of Cartagena was also won for the Sevillian king.

When the long-awaited news of the capture of the longed-for Murcia arrived, Ibn Ammar, full of joy, requested permission from his king to go and take 'official' possession of the city. Al Mutamid, delighted by the extension of his territory with the fertile lands of Murcia, did not hesitate for a moment, letting his friend Ibn Ammar leave.

The vizier decided to enter in the most triumphant manner into the new lands acquired for the Sevillian kingdom, so he gathered around 200 mules and horses both from the royal stables and on loan from various friends. Each of these animals he loaded with precious fabrics and other riches and marched towards the lands of Murcia with his army on a triumphal march. In each town he passed through, he left some of the gifts they were carrying so that the citizens of those towns felt more united to the kingdom of Seville, incarnated in the person of its vizier.

The entry into the city of Murcia was triumphal, as in the rest of the towns of the newly conquered kingdom of Murcia. And, although at

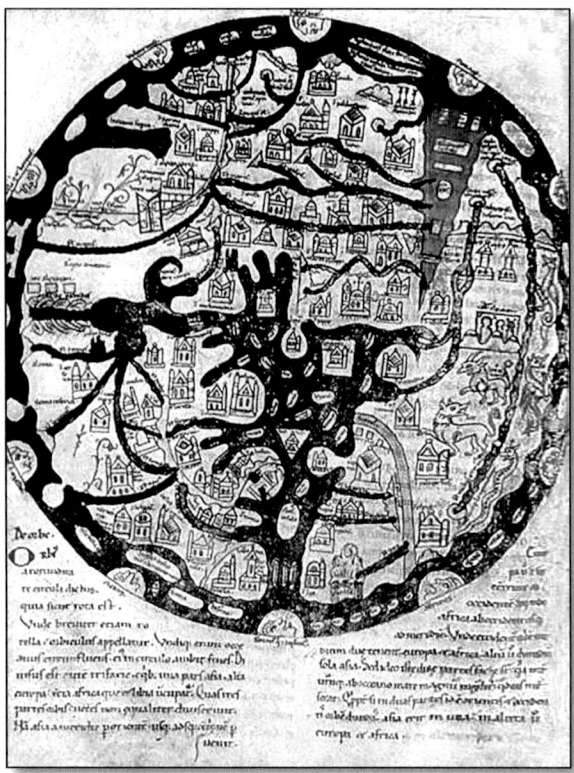

World map made in the eleventh century and copied from the work of Saint Isidore of Seville. The 'return' of the saint's body to Ferdinand I by Al Mutadid took place in 1063. (Open source)

first it seemed logical to show such a display of gifts and congratulations to the new subjects (keeping the population happy is vital for a happy government), something strange was brewing. Ibn Ammar had the permission of Al Mutamid to govern that part of the kingdom of Seville, but, more and more each day, this government was becoming more and more independent of the directives coming from Seville. Ibn Ammar treated himself as a true king and behaved as such, to the point that, when he carried out any important act, he did not do so in the name of Al Mutamid but rather said, 'So be it, God willing', clearly ignoring his faithful friend and lord.

This behaviour was nothing more than a revolt that Ibn Ammar was determined to conceal in order to avoid the punishment of Al Mutamid. The latter had his loyal men in Murcia who informed him of the real situation of excision to which the easternmost part of the Sevillian kingdom was being subjected. But, rather than being enraged, as the occasion possibly required, Al Mutamid was overcome by a feeling of sadness, of betrayal, not of the vizier of his kingdom but of a friend whom, as we have seen, he deeply appreciated (it has even been said that they became lovers during their stay in the Algarve; although this is an unproven fact, what is certain is that they were bound by a strong friendship). Here, the poetic and romantic Al Mutamid again defeated the political Al Mutamid, and what troubled him was the thought that perhaps he had been deceived for many years by his 'friend' from his younger years. It is true that Al Mutamid was aware of how the man they had brought out of nowhere had become one of the leading and richest representatives of the kingdom; it is true that he had always shown great interest in climbing higher and higher, commanding more troops, controlling more land. But Al Mutamid thought Ibn Ammar did it largely to please himself, to try to emulate his lord.

The reality is that Ibn Ammar may not have planned such a rebellion but that it gradually got out of hand, until alarm bells rang in the Sevillian royal palace. Once that moment arrived, Al Mutamid became convinced that Ibn Ammar may never have been as deep and devoted a friend to him as he himself felt towards him. He therefore sent official messengers to Murcia to meet with Ibn Ammar and, reprimanding him for his actions, to clarify the murky situation that was emerging in the Sevillian city regarding the future of Murcia.

Perhaps it was at this point that Ibn Ammar realised how far he had come and how far he himself was distancing the ancient kingdom of Murcia from Seville's control. As it had worked on other occasions, he decided to

THE RISE AND FALL OF THE KINGDOM: 1069-1091

win back the will of Al Mutamid with a new poem that would explain to him his situation in Murcia while trying to 'touch' the heartstrings of the Sevillian king. The verses are as follows:

> No, you deceive yourself when you say that the vicissitudes of fortune have changed me!
> The love I have for Chams, my old mother, is less strong than the love I feel for you.
> My dear friend, how is it possible that your goodness does not light up my life with its rays!
> As the lightning lightens the darkness of the night?
> How is it possible that not a tender word comes to comfort me, like a sweet breeze?
> Oh, I suspect that some infamous people I know have tried to destroy our tender friendship!
> Thus do you withdraw your hand from me, after a friendship of twenty-five years of fulfilled happiness, spent without your having had the slightest complaint against me, without your having made me guilty of any wrongdoing, do you thus withdraw your hand from me, leaving me a prisoner in the clutches of fate? Am I anything else to you but an obedient and submissive slave? Reflect a moment, do not be hasty; he who is too hasty, falls; while he who walks circumspectly reaches the end of his journey; Ah, you will remember me when the bonds of friendship that united us are broken and you are left with nothing but self-interested and false friends. You will look for me when none of those around you can give you good advice and I am not there; I who knew how to sharpen the wits of others.

It is true that, with the friendship that Al Mutamid, above all, had professed for a quarter of a century to Ibn Ammar and the important services that the latter had performed for the kingdom of Seville (let us remember the incident of the chess game without going any further), possibly the waters would have returned to their course, and the king would have forgiven the vizier after his beautiful and complacent verses. But, unlike Al Mutamid's pardon to Ibn Ammar in Jaén, in this case, the two individuals were separated by many days of travel on horseback (the journey to Córdoba from Seville alone represented three days, without baggage or impediments). And the replies from one and the other would not cross paths so easily; furthermore, there were many courtiers who had a good dose of hatred and envy for the figure of the vizier, so they 'contaminated' the possible pardon that the king would grant again to his friend, with the need to restrain the dissident Ibn Ammar. Perhaps it was these facts or perhaps not, but what is certain is that, on this occasion, there was no pardon for Ibn Ammar. The anti-Ibn Ammar courtiers such as the powerful Abu Becr Ben Zaidun (the most influential man in that period at the Sevillian court) had triumphed. It was only a matter of time before Ibn Ammar and all his power were swallowed up by an Al Mutamid with mixed feelings towards him.

But, when Ibn Ammar 'technically' separated from the Sevillian kingdom, it became a small independent kingdom again, with few resources and very powerful enemies, including Ben Abdalaziz, prince of Valencia and friend of the deposed Ben Tahir, in addition to Al Mutamid. The Valencian pressured Ibn Ammar to hand over the still-captive Ben Tahir to him, also letting the Sevillian monarch know. The latter, from distant Seville, ordered the release of the captive and his handover to Ben Abdalaziz, mainly so as not to disturb his relations with the powerful Valencian kingdom. But Ibn Ammar, once again, acted on his own, refusing the release, possibly for fear of the actions that the latter might take against him once he was released. However, he could do little when, aided by some of Ben Abdalaziz's men, Ben Tahir was freed from the fortress of Monteagudo, where he was being held captive.

This escape infuriated Ibn Ammar, charging his hurtful words against the Valencian prince who had collaborated in the escape. He wrote one of his hurtful and well-measured verses in which he tried to pit the Valencian people against their prince, little less than inciting a popular revolt, with the threat of charging with his troops in case this did not happen. The truth is that Ibn Ammar's disastrous conduct in Murcia did not make many people happy, as his haughtiness and his former fondness for easy living, parties and wine did not help his new people to take any liking to him.

When Al Mutamid became aware of these verses, he threw his hands up in the air, as he was provoking a powerful taifa, with whom relations, despite the conquest of Murcia, were not bad. The paradox was that, as Murcia was 'officially' part of the Sevillian taifa, this could mean open warfare at a great distance from the metropolis. And, as usual, he responded to Ibn Ammar's verses with others in which he reminded him of his low and humble origins that had grown only at the expense of others.

As is logical, this war of verses provoked insult or jubilation depending on the side, for Al Mutamid's reply was praised by the Valencian prince while it touched Ibn Ammar to the core (not in vain, Al Mutamid knew him well and knew where every word that came out of his sharp pen could hurt him most). So, to Al Mutamid's offensive missive, Ibn Ammar hastened to produce other verses in which he clearly and effectively insulted both the Abbadid family and Queen Itimad herself. And, although at first he decided not to make them public because of their hurtfulness, it so happened that, when he told them in private to a group of friends, one of whom was Jewish and was a confidant of the prince of Valencia, he obtained a copy for his master, who took it upon himself to make them known to Al Mutamid after sending them by messenger pigeon. The verses that Ibn Ammar composed in a fit of hatred for Al Mutamid and his family are as follows:

> Thou hast chosen from among the daughters of the populace that slave whom Romic, her master, would gladly have exchanged for a year-old camel. She hath cast into the world debauched sons, chubby

little men who shame her. Al Mutamid, I will sully your honour, I will tear the veils that cover your crookedness, I will tear them to shreds. Yes, emulator of the ancient heroes, yes, you have defended your villages, but you knew that your women were cheating on you and you indulged them.

Al Mutamid's reception of these verses only radicalised his stance against his formerly dear friend Ibn Ammar. He could forgive offences against his person, but he would never do so about what he loved most in the whole world: his family. To publicly insult his wife, children and other women in such a felonious manner sullied the honour of the Sevillian king, and that stain would only be removed when Ibn Ammar paid for his constant betrayals of the Sevillian with his life.

But the enemies of the weak increased day by day and surrounded Ibn Ammar. So, living in Murcia with all the pleasures at his feet, he began to abandon the government of the city. This was taken advantage of by his friend of convenience Ben Rachic, who, in cahoots with the prince of Valencia, managed to incite the garrison defending the city of Murcia to demand the money owed to them while he lived surrounded by wealth and luxury. The surprised Ibn Ammar, under the threat of being sent to Al Mutamid in chains and unable to pay his soldiers, immediately fled the city, as he was unable to cope with the mutiny.

From then on, Ibn Ammar began a journey to different courts where he could offer his services. He first went to the court of Castile and León, offering himself to King Alfonso VI in the city of León, who rejected him because of the obscurity of his activities. Subsequently, he served the lords of Zaragoza, Lleida and Zaragoza again. While on one of the missions entrusted to him by Mutamin of Zaragoza, Ibn Ammar was captured by the lord of the fortress of Segura, Ben Soail. The latter decided to sell him to the highest bidder (let us not forget the many enemies he had made during his eventful life), who was none other than Al Mutamid himself, who took advantage of the situation to take possession of the fortress in exchange for a good sum of money.

After paying the ransom, which included treasure and horses demanded by Ben Soail, and once in the hands of the Sevillian troops under the command of Radi Bila (son of Al Mutamid), he was taken to Córdoba loaded with chains, a city he arrived in on 7 November 1084 and where the king himself would go to meet him. The troops were instructed by the king not to neglect for a single second the guarding of this much desired captive. Ibn Ammar's entry was prepared with special hatred, as he entered on the back of a beast of burden, carrying two sacks of straw and loaded with the chains that imprisoned him; furthermore, an appeal had been made to the population not to miss the 'spectacle'. In this way, Al Mutamid mortified the pride of Ibn Ammar, who, on his way through the city of Córdoba on his way to Murcia, had caused the Cordoban nobles to kiss his hand or his clothes. Once the old friends met again, Al Mutamid reprimanded him for the thousand causes that had been forged since he went to take possession of the city of Murcia, how he had brought him out of poverty to give him wealth and power, how he returned the trust he had placed in him, but the one that had hurt him the most, he left for the end. We refer to the verses vilifying the family of Al Mutamid, which Ibn Ammar recognised as his own. Attempting to employ the technique of self-incrimination, he was again claiming that Al Mutamid's piety favoured him: 'I have wronged you, I have offended you gravely, but forgive me!' But the Sevillian was inflexible with him. He could not allow the insult to his family, so he agreed to leave him locked up in the dungeons. Soon after, he was transferred along the Guadalquivir basin to the city of Seville, where he made a 'triumphal' entry similar to the one he had made in the old caliphate capital.

Ibn Ammar's presence had not gone unnoticed by the people, who made all kinds of jokes against the former strongman of the kingdom. Ibn Ammar's imprisonment was prolonged over time, in such a way that he himself sensed that it was only a punishment that would soon come to an end and a happy one for him: forgiveness by the king. To this end, he did not cease to compose verses praising the figure of the Sevillian and his family. But the king, perhaps tired of the many verses he addressed to him, decided to forbid him to be given paper and ink to write on. But Ibn Ammar gambled everything on one card, requesting paper and ink for one last time for a final verse. He sent it to the king, who barely accepted it without changing his mind about Ibn Ammar's captivity. The two men met again, and Al Mutamid's way of expressing himself conveyed to Ibn Ammar the certainty (according to him) that the king would soon pardon him. This filled the prisoner Ibn Ammar with joy, and, whoever he spoke to, he let him know that the king would pardon him. Even with one of the two sheets of paper he had been given to write, he sent a letter to Rachid, a son of Al Mutamid, letting him know the good news for him. Not surprisingly, the forthcoming release and reinstatement to his former posts did not please many of the courtiers who had taken a clear stand against Ibn Ammar, including the powerful Abu Becr Ben Zaidun. If he returned, they could now be the ones persecuted by the vizier. The situation left no room for error, so he met with the king and made him aware of his uncertainty about Ibn Ammar's early release. Al Mutamid was surprised at the strength of the rumour. The once transigent monarch was overcome with anger; he could not allow Ibn Ammar's continued disdain and mockery of him.

Al Mutamid enquired what had become of the two sheets of paper he had given to Ibn Ammar to write on; one was for the poem, but where had the other gone? Had it been sent to someone asking for help? Although at first he tried to conceal it, Ibn Ammar eventually told that he had used it to send a missive to Prince Rachid. The knowledge of the contents of this letter, confirming Ibn Ammar's pardon, blinded the king with anger, so he took an axe that he found on hand (this axe had been a present from King Alfonso VI to Ibn Ammar, who had later given it to Al Mutamid) and went to the dungeons looking for the captive. Once he found him, Ibn Ammar was paralysed by the look of death that Al Mutamid was wearing, and, seeing that his fate might be sealed, he threw himself at the feet of the monarch begging for forgiveness. But, in a fit of hatred and revenge, Al Mutamid struck the edge of his axe several times against the chained Ibn Ammar, causing his death. These events took place between 1086 and 1087, and, despite their importance, they were soon dwarfed by the onslaught from the north of the battle-hardened Castilian-Leonese troops, although these will be recounted a little later.

In the end, Ibn Ammar's risky ruses had failed partly because of the disillusionment that Al Mutamid felt for his old friend, partly because of the plots and intrigues that were hatched from within the royal palace itself so that he would never be released. This was probably the end of Ibn Ammar in one way or another, for, even if he could one day obtain the king's pardon, he would never obtain it from many other influential figures at court, such as the fearsome Ben Zaidun, who would sooner or later have been responsible for more or less rightly incriminating the king's favourite.

Ibn Ammar's death had important repercussions in many of the kingdoms of the Iberian Peninsula; not in vain had he been in many of them, leaving behind him many enemies.

Now, the lord of Murcia was Ben Rachic, who immediately recognised the sovereignty of Al Mutamid, who to a certain extent followed in Ibn Ammar's footsteps, since, although belonging to the kingdom of Seville, Murcia acted and was managed as a semi-independent kingdom, with the occasional episode of sedition. The tense situations that arose from 1085 onwards in the Sevillian kingdom and therefore in the taifa universe of the Iberian Peninsula meant that Al Mutamid was unable to exercise his sovereignty in the city of Murcia with complete freedom of force. In fact, coins minted in Murcia with the name of Al Mutamid have been preserved for the years 478, 480, 481, 482 and 484 of the Hegira, which would correspond to the years from 1085 to 1090 in our calendar. What is known from the accounts is that the town of Lorca remained loyal to the Sevillian king until the end, without any tricks or plots against him.

El Cid and Seville

It was the year 1079, in the middle of summer, when an event of some significance took place in the Sevillian kingdom, at the hands of a man of such importance for the history of Spain as Rodrigo Díaz de Vivar, El Cid Campeador. Following the Castilian-Leonese policy of 'squeezing' the Muslim kingdoms with the parias, King Alfonso VI sent ambassadors of tax collectors to the kingdoms of Granada and Seville to collect the annual parias. The group that set out for Granada was led by Count García Ordóñez of Castile (the new royal lieutenant and governor of La Rioja), accompanied by Count Fortún Sánchez (a nobleman from Alava and son-in-law of the king of Navarre), Lope Sánchez, brother of the former, and Diego Pérez, a notable of Castile – all of them accompanied by their escort troops, mainly made up of León and to a lesser extent Aragonese, Navarrese and Castilians. The retinue on its way to Seville was led by Rodrigo; it had left Burgos

THE FALL OF MOORISH SEVILLE 1023–1091

Statue in homage to El Cid Campeador in the Prado de San Sebastián, the work of Mrs Huntington. Its pedestal commemorates El Cid's help to Al Mutamid in defeating the Granada troops at the Battle of Cabra. (Open source by Charles V of Habsburg)

accompanied by an escort of between 100 and 150 lances of Castilian origin. After several weeks on the road, they finally reached the city of Seville. There, as was customary with Castilian tax collectors, they were received with a multitude of honours. The Castilians were housed in the summer fortress of Al Mutamid, which was located near the Barqueta Gate (in what today would correspond to the area where the convent of San Clemente is located). They stayed there for several days with all kinds of praise from the Seville garrison, until one day news arrived that troops from Granada and Murcia accompanied by Christian troops (from León, Aragon and Navarre) were rioting in the lands of Al Mutamid. Specifically, they were ravaging the regions of Lucena and Cabra and had even taken control of the latter town.

This peculiar alliance of Christians and Muslims was no more than the Christian embassy sent to collect the parias in Granada, who, after having been hospitably received by the king of Granada, had been convinced by the latter that there were some lands that belonged to him and that the belligerent Al Mutamid had taken them away from him. Since the payment of the parias meant that Castile and León would support any of his vassals, Count García was ready to help him, once he had collected the parias for that year, which consisted of 40 kilos of gold, in the form of 10,000 dinars (an Andalusian coin weighing about four grams, also known as mizcal or metical). It is possible that this was not the only cause that incited the Christians to help Granada in its interminable conflict against Seville, and possibly there were good 'prizes' in riches for those who helped in this mission.

In this way, Count García and the other nobles who accompanied him, after accepting King Abdalá's order, joined their troops with those of Granada and some troops from the region of Murcia. Marching together at the head of this large coalition army, they advanced towards the kingdom of Seville with the intention of ravaging and taking the lands and fortresses in the geographical area of Cabra.

As we said, after hearing this news from the Sevillian king, Rodrigo had to listen to and accept the latter's request for help to confront the powerful enemy army. Al Mutamid based his arguments for asking Rodrigo for help in a similar way to Abdalá had done with Count García; that is, he demanded the defence and protection that he was obliged to provide as a representative of King Alfonso VI, who held them as vassals through the collection of parias.

Although it is obviously difficult to know the reality, it is true that it is said that the phrase that Al Mutamid said to Rodrigo would be similar to this: 'Your king sends you to collect parias from me while others, whom he has also sent for a similar purpose, run over my lands and burn them and

THE RISE AND FALL OF THE KINGDOM: 1069–1091

Wall of Granada from the Zirid period. During the eleventh century, the Zirid kingdom of Granada was one of the fiercest rivals of the kingdom of Seville. (Open source by Pepepitos)

plunder them together with my enemy, the king of Granada. If my gold is worth as much as Abdalá's, you should do something for my kingdom.'

Rodrigo, after weighing up the situation and accepting the arguments of the Sevillian monarch, agreed to what the latter so urgently requested. By the very nature of his mission in Seville, the Castilian troops were obliged to provide him with defence and protection, and this was exactly the case. Therefore, after alerting his men and having Sevillian troops join him, he marched with the coalition army towards Córdoba to confront the invading troops. Knowing of the existence of Christian troops commanded by his own King Alfonso VI and the important leaders of this expedition, he tried to warn them with the intention of reaching an 'amicable' arrangement out of the reverence and respect due to King Alfonso VI and a tributary of his king and to get them to retrace their steps towards the lands of the king of Granada.

Count García and King Abdalá took no notice whatsoever of the warning given to them by the young Castilian knight. What is more, due to the high rank of the ambassadors led by Count García, and knowing how few troops the Sevillians could bring and the even lesser numbers of Rodrigo, they belittled him, mocking him. The 'Granadan' troops were made up of the four Christian mesnadas (corresponding to some 400 knights), some 700 Muslim horsemen and around 3,500 footmen from Granada and Murcia, making a total of 1,100 knights and 3,500 infantrymen. On the 'Sevillian' side, the troops were led by Rodrigo's mesnada (about 100–150 cavalrymen), 400 Sevillian horsemen and about 2,000 Sevillian infantrymen, making a total of approximately 500 cavalrymen and 2,000 infantrymen. In this situation, we can see that the number of troops that the Sevillian taifa could 'raise' for an emergency situation was not very numerous.

Given the number of troops that made up the two armies, we can better understand the reason for Count García's arrogance towards Rodrigo.

What happened next was inevitable; thus, in the lands of Córdoba, Muslims from Seville and Castile confronted Muslims from Granada and Castile, in order to favour the interests of one or the other. The *Historia Roderici* tells of this confrontation that took place in the lands between Doña Mencía and Cabra, which has come to be known as the Battle of Cabra:

> Rodrigo hearing that the Grenadians had arrived at Cabra ... quickly went out to meet the attackers with his entire army ... the fighting between the two intermingled armies lasted from mid-morning until the hour of noon. The army of the King of Granada suffered a tremendous slaughter, both of Mohammedans and Christians, until they were all defeated and fled before Rodrigo.

As the account tells us, the confrontation, which lasted more than three hours, ended with a full-scale defeat of the coalition of Granadan–Leonese troops.

Although there is not a great deal of information on this battle, the cause of the Sevillian victory should be attributed to a large extent to the good work of Rodrigo and his men in the combat. Possibly, knowing his numerical inferiority, he played the trick of a massive charge with all his cavalry towards the centre of the enemy formation, achieving relative numerical superiority in that area. In this way, and after controlling this combat zone, he turned against the enemy troops that had been left behind him with new cavalry charges (the tactic used here has come to be known as the 'Castilian tornado'), while his infantry went to this zone to protect the cavalry's movements. Both Castilians and Leonese were troops very accustomed to combat, so, despite the blow dealt by the Castilians–Sevillians to the Leonese–Granadans, the latter still continued with their initial formation. But the Muslim troops from Granada and Murcia, faced with the bloodshed that had been generated, opted to disappear from the battlefield, cowardly fleeing. First, the cavalry troops fled, and later (mainly because of the speed) the infantry. The result was that the Leonese were massacred by the Castilians and Sevillians, until they finally opted to surrender. In this way, the main men of the Leonese embassy were captured, although we will leave it to the *Historia Roderici* to tell us again the end of this battle:

> In this battle, Count García Ordoñez, Lope Sánchez and Diego Pérez were captured along with many of their soldiers. Once the victory was won, Rodrigo Díaz held them captive for three days; he then stripped them of their tents and other belongings and allowed them to go free.

THE RISE AND FALL OF THE KINGDOM: 1069–1091

Count García, because of his contemptuous treatment of Rodrigo's warning to avoid combat between Christians, was given the greatest humiliation. This consisted of grabbing the count by the beard and taking him from the battlefield to the camp. According to the chronicles, Rodrigo carried a lock of this beard with him for many years as a souvenir of that victory.

As we have seen, once the battle was over and the prisoners captured, Rodrigo was only willing to hold the Christians for three days, leaving them at liberty, although after making them promise not to take up arms again against Castile or any of its allies or vassals. This was because Rodrigo had to return to Seville to collect the parias from Al Mutamid, and he did not want to find himself in the position of having to leave the Christians prisoners in the Abbadid capital. Thus, with their early release, he was playing a double game, as he 'lowered the Leonese's spirits' but was not playing into the hands of the Sevillians (with the possibility of asking for ransoms of any kind in the future). What happened with the Muslim prisoners is another matter, as they were indeed taken captive to Seville and delivered personally by Rodrigo to Al Mutamid so that the latter could voluntarily choose to obtain a ransom for them or simply punish them as a 'warning to sailors' for the kingdom of Granada.

Walls of the Alcazaba Cadima, seat of the Zirid king of the Taifa of Granada. This kingdom became, for a short period in the eleventh century, both an ally and an enemy of the kingdom of Seville. (Open source by Pepepitos)

At the same time that the defeated troops were making their way back to the Castilian-Leonese court, Rodrigo returned with a triumphant appearance in command of the Sevillian–Castilian troops to the capital of the Abbadid kingdom. After a march of two or three days, he reached the walls of Seville, entering the city through the gate of Córdoba or Bab Qurtuba (today one of the few gates of Muslim origin that still exists, with important changes, integrated into the Church of San Hermenegildo in the Ronda de Capuchinos). The scene could perfectly well have been as follows:

THE FALL OF MOORISH SEVILLE 1023-1091

Rodrigo leading the party, accompanied by the men of his mesnadas with banners and raised lances, followed by the Sevillian horsemen and by the prisoners from Granada and Murcia and a mule herd carrying the many riches that the Granadans had taken from the lands of Seville, and closing the triumphal retinue were the Sevillian infantry. They made their way from the gate of Córdoba to the Royal Alcázar, being the object of all kinds of praise from the happy Sevillian population along the way. It was here and as a result of the Battle of Cabra that Rodrigo began to be known by the nickname of El Cid Campeador, derived from 'Cide al mansur' ('victorious lord' in Arabic) and Campidoctor (derived from the Latin indicating his wisdom in battle) or, as it was transferred to Arabic, 'Cide al Kambayatur'.

Once in the Royal Alcázar, Al Mutamid thanked him warmly. He offered all kinds of gifts to him, his men and to Alfonso VI on the occasion of such a complete victory and behaviour of the Castilians, when their pact required it.

A few days later, El Cid and his spearmen marched towards Castile with the parias of the kingdom of Seville and a multitude of gifts that Seville had offered them as homage. And, although the return was triumphant, the welcome in Castile was one of great indifference on the part of Alfonso VI. This was possibly due to the fact that, although El Cid had accomplished the mission with complete success, he had humiliated a nobleman of great power at court, Count García, whom he had held prisoner for three days. Although the count had possibly acted out of a desire for riches rather than for the name of Castile, without giving any importance to the fact that the kingdom of Seville was protected by his own King Alfonso VI and that at that moment there was an embassy from him to collect the parias in his capital, King Alfonso VI could not have been indisposed against him, since he represented the highest nobility of the kingdom and it was rather difficult to hold him responsible for any wrongdoing. It is to some extent surprising that Count García, despite knowing of the existence of El Cid's letter inviting him to withdraw to the lands of Granada, went ahead with his attacks in the area of Cabra, ignoring the treaties between the Castilian-Leonese and Sevillian kingdoms and, at the same time, confronting fellow countrymen who were there to do the same thing he was supposed to do in Granada. The consequence, as we have said, was that, although the victory at Cabra of El Cid and the subsequent incident with Count García (despite nobly fulfilling his embassy in accordance with the rules of medieval vassalage) were not given much publicity, El Cid was pushed into a series of events that ended with his banishment from the kingdom of Castile and León. This victory came at the cost of the lifelong enmity of Count García Ordóñez, who was too powerful for El Cid and too close to King Alfonso VI. He did not cease in his intention to distance El Cid more and more from his own king with all kinds of trickery.

As a reminder of these almost millenary events, fortunately in Seville, there is a famous monument known as 'the horse' in the Prado de San Sebastián, which represents El Cid in a defiant attitude, created by the American artist Mrs Hungtinton and given by her to the city of Seville in

1929. On its pedestal, on one of the faces is engraved this sentence of thanks from the Sevillian people for his victory as an ally of Seville against the king of Granada. Exactly, it reads:

> Seville, golden court of the poet King Motamid, hosted Mio Cid, ambassador of Alfonso VI, and saw him return victorious from the king of Granada.

It is beautiful to see how, despite the fact that these events are unknown to many Sevillians, Seville's gratitude to El Cid for his help in such a delicate situation still persists. It is a beautiful and poetic gesture that a people, who coined the name of El Cid, which Rodrigo Díaz de Vivar has carried and will carry with him forever, still remember him.

Peace with Granada

Monaite Gate of Granada. This was the main gate of the Alcazaba of Granada during the Zirid period (eleventh century) and the entrance to the palace of the rulers of Granada. (Open source)

The truth is that, as the memoirs of the Zirid monarch of Granada state, as soon as Ibn Ammar disappeared from the Sevillian government, after his disastrous activity in the kingdom of Murcia, the good understanding between Abdalá and Al Mutamid became more evident day by day. Trade relations between the two increased, and normality on the borders between the two kingdoms became a daily occurrence. This peace, so desired by both, allowed them to know each other's vision of the Christian sword hanging over their heads. This was the common enemy, as it was gradually undermining the power of the Muslim kingdoms while leaving their coffers at zero.

Because of the growing weakness of both kingdoms, they agreed that it was necessary to join forces in partnership to negotiate as one voice against the Christians.

Despite the good relations between the kingdoms of Seville and Granada, it is true that there were certain problems in specific places. The most notable of these was caused by Kabbab (the same man who had taken the town of Estepa for Granada some time before), who, although he theoretically showed his submission to Abdalá, in reality acted independently, managing the lands under his command (Antequera and Estepona) as his own. Knowing the peace that existed between the two kingdoms, Kabbab continued to carry out military actions against Sevillian territories, on his own account. Abdalá, aware of the matter, urged him to abide by the peace treaty without fail. Evidently, Kabbab's interests were different, and he did not follow the orders of 'his' monarch.

Abdalá, after hearing many complaints from Al Mutamid about the affronts Kabbab was inflicting on them, agreed to draw up a plan to put an end to his dangerous activities. The Granadan explained to the Sevillian that it would be of no use if he attacked Kabbab if he tried to flee and managed to take refuge in Sevillian territory. Al Mutamid understood the importance of closing this wound in the Sevillian–Granadan peace treaty, so he agreed to Abdalá's requests.

Remains of the Puerta de los tableros Gate in Granada. This gate and bridge, built in the eleventh century during the Zirid rule of Granada, allowed communication between the old Alcazaba in the Albaicín district and the new Alcazaba of the Alhambra. (Open source)

Abdalá pressed his troops into the territory controlled by Kabbab, who, after seeing himself in danger of falling into the hands of the Granadan, offered both towns to the Sevillian king Al Mutamid by messengers. In this way, he would keep his position, only changing the master. But the trick backfired, as Al Mutamid, faithful to his pact with Abdalá, sent him the traitor's letter, confirming the non-interference of his troops in this internal Granadan affair. Thus, Kabbab finally had to surrender and was subsequently pardoned because of the value of a man like him in the Granadan army. So the waters returned to their course again, and peace took hold of the borders between the two kingdoms.

The goodwill between the two monarchs soon had positive repercussions for the kingdom of Seville, since, faced with a revolt in the Sevillian town of Baeza, the rebels offered themselves to the king of Granada, who, also loyal to his new ally, sent him the letter of the traitors and did not interfere in the matter. The rebellion was therefore put down without any further problems, due to its absolute lack of external support.

At the same time as the events in Antequera and Estepona, another Granadan, Ben Tagnaur, who was of the same lineage as Kabbab (and with whom he had made an agreement to help in case either of them was attacked), also maintained a high degree of independence in Yarisa. Once again, Abdalá had to put his troops on the march to confront his traitors. He had previously informed Al Mutamid of this fact, the latter offering his help as an intermediary as well as offering him troops if necessary. After a siege lasting more than six months, he managed to capture the enclave with a tremendous drain on his troops and coffers. Finally, Ben Tagnaur was punished by being crucified with his brother, who at that time held a high position in the kingdom of Granada, although he was found guilty of treason for supporting his brother.

Anecdotes from the Reign of Al Mutamid

The name of Al Mutamid has been linked to many anecdotes that occurred during his reign. In this section, we will recall two of them as good examples of the 'poetic–romantic' character of the Sevillian king: the Grey Hawk and the nocturnal encounter he had with a Sevillian sheikh.

There had always been highwaymen in the lands of Al-Andalus, although, during the reign of Al Mutamid, there was one who stood out above the rest. He called himself the Grey Hawk and terrorised several regions of Seville, as well as many of the roads leading to the capital. After many attempts, the Sevillian troops finally managed to capture the bandit.

Spanish postage stamp with the effigy of the third king of the Taifa of Seville during the eleventh century: Al Mutamid. He is certainly the best known of the Seville monarchs today, although he has been largely ignored within the city of Seville itself. (Open source)

As was customary at the time, he was condemned to die on the cross in a public act on the outskirts of the city. It is said that, while on the cross, the bandit attracted the attention of one of those present, who was at the time a cloth merchant. Despite his pitiful state, he persuaded the merchant to go and collect a large amount of money he had accumulated from his crimes and hand it over to his wife. This treasure was in a grotto that his wife, who was now a widow, could not access; hence, the bandit had asked him for help.

The merchant, who saw the opportunity to get his hands on a good sum of money after accepting the commission, went to the grotto. As soon as he took hold of the rope and began to descend into the cave, the Hawk's wife cut the rope (as her husband had instructed) and let the merchant fall into the deepest part of the cave. Having eliminated the merchant, the woman stole his donkey and his goods and made her way to Seville, where she sold

THE FALL OF MOORISH SEVILLE 1023-1091

Images of two twinned arches studied in recent years by Miguel Ángel Tabales Rodríguez's team in the vicinity of the Patio de Banderas in Seville, everything of which seems to indicate that they correspond to the legendary palace of the Abbadid kings. (Image by Fernando Alda, used with the permission of Cristina Vargas Lorenzo from her article 'La recuperación del palacio primitivo del Alcázar de Sevilla', *Arqueología de la Arquitectura*, 16 (2019), p.e089, DOI 10.3989/arq.arqt.2019.011)

them for a substantial sum of dinars. The Hawk had struck his last blow even though he was crucified and close to death.

The merchant began to shout, but, as it was siesta time and it was very hot, no one was passing by, and the woman was able to escape. Finally, the merchant was able to get out of the cave after some peasants heard his cries from inside the cave. He immediately went to the capital, where he reported the robbery to the Sevillian authorities. When this story reached the ears of Al Mutamid, he could do no less than order the thief to be taken down from the cross and brought to him, where he asked him how it was possible that he had committed a new misdeed in his situation. The Hawk, proud of his 'profession' replied that, if the king knew the delights of deceiving the people, he would leave his throne to devote himself to banditry.

Al Mutamid, delighted to hear the Hawk's reply, censured him, laughing at his impudence. He then offered him freedom and a good placement if he was able to give up banditry. The Hawk said that, if that was the only way to escape death, he would gladly accept. Al Mutamid, true to his word, granted him his freedom, releasing him from his old charges with the justice system and offered him a position in the royal guard, which the Hawk evidently accepted.

This anecdote from the reign of Al Mutamid once again highlights the romanticism and generosity that the king undoubtedly lavished, as well as the value that he placed on cunning and mischief, qualities that have always been associated with the Andalusian way of being.

The other anecdote that is remembered of Al Mutamid, in which his cheerful and unselfish character can again be appreciated, is the one he had with a sheikh who was famous for his witticisms, his grace and his eccentricities. The king, who since his youth had been in the habit of going through the streets of the city at night, disguised or undisguised, with some of his closest servants (as happened with Ibn Ammar when he met Itimad), on one of his 'outings' passed in front of the sheikh's door. As they were in the mood to continue their amusement, the king had them knock on the man's door so that he could entertain them with his graces. After knocking, a voice answered asking who was knocking at his door at that hour. Al Mutamid replied, 'a man who wishes you to light his lamp'. The sheikh, not knowing who it was, did not hesitate to tell them that he would not open the door even to Al Mutamid himself at that hour.

THE RISE AND FALL OF THE KINGDOM: 1069-1091

Hypothetical reconstruction of the Islamic palace of the Abbadid kings in the vicinity of the Patio de Banderas in Seville. (Reconstruction by Jesús García Carpallo based on Miguel Ángel Tabales Rodríguez and Cristina Vargas Lorenzo, used with the permission of Cristina Vargas Lorenzo from her article 'La recuperación del palacio primitivo del Alcázar de Sevilla')

The king revealed his identity to him through the door, and the sheikh's reply was that what he would receive from him would be a thousand slaps. On hearing this, the king and his companions at night laughed, and Al Mutamid himself decided to go elsewhere.

The next day, the sheikh received the sum of a thousand dirhems at his house with a message from the king telling him that he would give him one for each of the slaps he said he was going to give him.

Castilian-Leonese Pressure on the Kingdom of Seville

This was between 1082 and 1085, possibly the most fruitful years for the Castilian-Leonese cause. Continuing with its tactic of gradually exhausting the different Muslim kingdoms with the parias–razias binomial, Castile and León once again turned its desires towards the lands of the extensive Sevillian taifa, once its dominion over the border Taifa of Toledo was becoming clearer. King Alfonso VI, taking advantage of the death of one of his paria collectors in the kingdom of Seville, named Ben Salib and of Jewish descent, by Al Mutamid and the subsequent imprisonment of his companions, gave the Castilian the opportunity he had been seeking to obtain more benefits from the Sevillian taifa. The death of the Jew had been motivated by the fact that, when the Sevillian embassy went to the agreed place to deliver the 'taxes', under the command of the well-known Abu Becr Ben Zaidun, they proceeded to the verification of the money by the Castilian-Leonese ambassadors. In fact, it was becoming increasingly difficult to obtain such large sums of money, so, in some cases, the coins were not pure gold but had undergone alloys that lowered their grade (it is not known for certain whether Al Mutamid was simply unable to collect the amount agreed for payment or whether it was due to minor border conflicts with the kingdom of Almería that prevented the money from being collected). The Jew Ben Salib, arrogantly, as the Castilian-Leonese envoys were wont to behave towards their vassal states, said, 'Do you think me foolish enough to take this counterfeit coin? I take nothing but pure gold and next year I will need

THE FALL OF MOORISH SEVILLE 1023-1091

cities'. When Al Mutamid heard of Ben Salib's reaction, he made him come to him in the company of the rest of the Christian retinue. Once the Jew was in his presence, he ordered him to be crucified and the others sent to the dungeons. Although the Jew begged for his freedom in exchange for gold, Al Mutamid did not agree to forgive the one who dared to offend him with such haughtiness. Alfonso VI, having learned of the events, swore that he would take revenge for the events that had taken place in the heart of the kingdom of Seville, so he began by requesting the release of those imprisoned (which according to some sources could number up to 500 people), which he obtained in exchange for handing over the square of Almodovar. But, although this may seem a positive development for the integrity of the kingdom of Seville, it was no more than a mirage, since, immediately after securing the release of his men, the Castilian king ordered his troops to cross the border back into the kingdom of Seville and begin attacking various towns. The increasingly powerful Castilian-Leonese army sacked and burned any town in its path, entering Seville from the lands of the king of Badajoz and passing on to the Algarve, harassing Beja and Niebla, later sacking the rich Seville Aljarafe and laying siege for three days to the city of Seville itself from Triana, establishing its royal camp in front of the palace of the Sevillian king (this event occurred between 1081 and 1082, very possibly in 1082). The Sevillians Alfonso VI encountered on his way were either killed or seized and sold as slaves.

According to some chronicles, after demonstrating his power in the very faces of the Sevillian royal family, Alfonso VI led his troops southwards, ravaging the region of Sidonia and reaching Tarifa, where, putting his horse in the water, he said that he had reached the last border of what would become his Castilian-Leonese kingdom. This is a good example of the immense power of the Castilian-Leonese troops against any taifa kingdom in Al-Andalus, as they could move around the enemy kingdom from one side to the other and even besiege the capital of the kingdom without receiving any response from the other side.

Twin arches of the Islamic palace of the Abbadid kings in the vicinity of the Patio de Banderas in Seville. (Used with the permission of Cristina Vargas Lorenzo from her article 'La recuperación del palacio primitivo del Alcázar de Sevilla')

THE RISE AND FALL OF THE KINGDOM: 1069–1091

This incursion by the Christian army demonstrated to the Sevillians (and also to the other taifas, who saw themselves reflected in the mirror of what had happened in the kingdom of Seville) that their position of weakness was destined for the conquest of their lands, unless they somehow managed to obtain troops that could stand up to the increasingly well-prepared Christian armies.

The wealth, culture and knowledge that resided in Muslim Iberia would be of no use if there were no men willing to defend it. And it was the taifas themselves, ancestrally pitted against each other, who were the first to have done nothing up to that point to stem the fearsome tide that would presumably wipe out every Islamic kingdom on the peninsula in a short space of time.

It is interesting to make a final note on the subject of the coins of the kingdom of Seville, which according to Magdalena Valor were minted between 1043–1044 and 1085–1086. Sevillian coins were characterised by their beauty, fine workmanship and law. We can well understand the Jew Ben Salib when he detected that the supposed quality of the Seville coinage was not the quality of the coins he had been given.

The coins used in the period were dinar (gold), dirhem (silver) and felus (bronze), although in many cases they were minted with various alloys, which reduced their purity.

As the number of territories under the rule of Seville increased, several mints produced Abbadid coins: Seville, Murcia, Al-Andalus and Córdoba.

The issue of coins with their mint of origin and with the names of high-ranking figures of the time served to further legitimise the various taifa kings and, in this case, the king of Seville. In fact, the first coin considered to be from the kingdom of Seville, dated 1041–1042, is a dinar bearing the names of the founder of the Abbadid dynasty together with Caliph Hixam II. Furthermore, it was customary for not only the name of the king to appear on the coin but also that of the heir to the throne.

As a curiosity, it is worth noting that the coins minted by the kingdom of Seville did not incorporate the name of the city until 1072–1073, having previously been identified as Al-Andalus.

Statue of King Alfonso VI in Toledo, the 'scourge' of the Andalusian taifa kingdoms. This king encouraged the collection of parias even from kingdoms with which he had no physical border, such as Seville and Granada. (Open source by Francisco Javier Martín Fernández)

THE FALL OF MOORISH SEVILLE 1023-1091

Hypothetical reconstruction of the communication between the Islamic palace of the Abbadid kings and the towers of the first enclosure of the alcázar. (Reconstruction by Jesús García Carpallo based on Miguel Ángel Tabales Rodríguez and Cristina Vargas Lorenzo, used with the permission of Cristina Vargas Lorenzo from her article 'La recuperación del palacio primitivo del Alcázar de Sevilla')

Fall of Toledo to Alfonso VI

In May 1085, an event took place that affected all the taifa kingdoms of the Iberian Peninsula in one way or another: the fall of Toledo, capital of the taifa of the same name and former capital of the Visigothic kingdom prior to the arrival of the Muslims on the Iberian Peninsula, into the hands of King Alfonso VI. In addition to the symbolism of it, its capture had another added element, since the kingdom of Toledo was the ideal platform for new campaigns against the other Islamic kingdoms of the peninsula; Alfonso VI could now follow and intervene in the life of the taifas to the south of his kingdom much more easily.

The situation of complete dependence of the kingdom of Castile and León on the kingdom of Toledo was becoming more evident day by day. The king of Toledo, Yahya al-Qadir, was not nearly as good a ruler as his predecessor, his grandfather Ismail Di l Nun. In fact, his accession to power coincided with the loss of the city of Córdoba to Al Mutamid, as described above. To the north, the Taifa of Zaragoza dominated the lands of Santáver (the birthplace of the ruling family of Toledo); to the west, Al Mutawakkil of Badajoz was constantly engaged in border clashes, and the city of Cuenca was besieged by Aragonese troops belonging to Sancho Ramírez. As we can see, the whole kingdom was in trouble, but, in spite of this, the main problem was the poor governing qualities of al-Qadir, who was more concerned with women and the life of luxury than with saving his ailing kingdom. The people of Toledo themselves, faced with the critical situation of their kingdom, were very much aware of the wear and tear that the turbulent political situation of the country was bringing them; they even considered the only way out to be a hypothetical surrender of the kingdom to Alfonso VI of Castile and León.

It was this extreme situation that led to a pact between Kings Alfonso VI and al-Qadir on 6 May 1085, whereby the latter would hand over the city to

THE RISE AND FALL OF THE KINGDOM: 1069–1091

Tile in Seville's Plaza de España depicting the capture of Toledo in 1085 by King Alfonso VI. After this event, the unstable balance between Christians and Muslims in Al-Andalus was definitively broken. (Open source by Charles V of Habsburg)

the former in 19 days. The surrender would be peaceful and unopposed by the dwindling forces of Toledo.

The pact had several clauses, the first of which was to allow the aforementioned 19 days to elapse before the Christians entered the city so that all those Toledans who did not wish to be under Castilian control would have time to collect their belongings and go wherever they wished. Furthermore, the surrender would not be limited to the city of Toledo but would cover the whole of its territory. Alfonso VI also agreed to place al-Qadir as a puppet king in the Taifa of Valencia, which at the time was also controlled by Castile.

So it was that, on 25 May 1085, with all the pomp and circumstance required, King Alfonso VI entered the capital; Toledo once again belonged to a Christian kingdom after more than 300 years. From then on, he could call himself 'Emperor of all Spain' (imperator totius Hispaniae) or 'the ruler of the men of the two religions', as he put it in his letters from then on. Seven years of permanent harassment of the kingdom of Toledo by the Castilians were behind him, harassment that, although it may seem absurd, had already been agreed between the two monarchs, in order to hasten the already well-known end of the Taifa of Toledo.

The weary population of Toledo that had remained in the city, thanks to the al-Qadir agreement, did not have to pay more tribute to their new

THE FALL OF MOORISH SEVILLE 1023-1091

Side view of the hypothetical reconstruction of the Islamic palace of the Abbadid kings in the vicinity of the Patio de Banderas in Seville. (Reconstruction by Jesús García Carpallo based on Miguel Ángel Tabales Rodríguez and Cristina Vargas Lorenzo, used with the permission of Cristina Vargas Lorenzo from her article 'La recuperación del palacio primitivo del Alcázar de Sevilla')

masters than they had previously paid to their own king, and they were able to keep (at least temporarily) their main mosque.

After the conquest of the capital, the troops of King Alfonso VI made multiple incursions in different directions in the lands of Toledo, in order to parade their banners and demonstrate their dominion over these lands.

The conquest of the city and its kingdom was sung in verse by the Toledan archbishop and chronicler Don Rodrigo Ximénez de Rada as follows:

> The secured Castile laid siege to its Toledo
> setting up camps for seven years and blocking its entrances.
> Although perched on the rocks and enormously populated.
> Surrounded by the Tagus, full of the best things,
> overcome by lack of food she surrendered to her undefeated foe.
> Applaud him Medinaceli, Talavera, Coimbra,
> Avila, Segovia, Salamanca and Sepulveda,
> Coria, Coca, Cuéllar, Iscar, Medina, Canales,
> Olmos and Olmedo, Madrid, Atienza and Riba,
> Osma with Guadalajara, Valeránica, Mora,
> Escalona, Hita, Consuegra, Maqueda, Buitrago,
> May they sing of their victor forever and ever:
> Alfonso, may your triumphs resound above the stars.

But the fall of the kingdom of Toledo was expected, and, despite the pact between al-Qadir and Alfonso VI, in which it was said that the entire kingdom of Toledo would pass to Castile and León, this was not exactly what happened. The Sevillian King Al Mutamid was very astute, as he had his troops ready to enter Toledo as soon as he heard of the fall of the capital. In this way, the Sevillian vanguards entered deep into the territory of the extinct kingdom of Toledo, taking control of many squares and castles, apparently even occupying the city of Cuenca (Kunka). This obviously brought Al Mutamid back into conflict with King Alfonso VI. The distance of these lands from the capital of the Sevillian kingdom and the difficulties that the latter had whenever they encountered the Castilians marked the short duration of these lands under Sevillian rule.

Later on, we will learn how all these large tracts of land were handed over without a fight by the kingdom of Seville to King Alfonso VI.

In short, the fall of Toledo was only the first drop in the storm that would rage over the taifa kingdoms. Thus, Valencia was controlled by El Cid to keep al-Qadir on the throne, the lordship of Albarracín became a vassal of Alfonso VI, Zaragoza was besieged immediately after the conquest of Toledo became effective, the castle of Aledo (in the heart of the Murcian lands belonging to the king of Seville) was controlled by the Christian warlord García Jiménez, while, in the vega of Granada and in the lands of Almería, incursions by Christian troops became routine, with little response from the Muslims. The situation had suddenly become untenable, since, at least when the kingdom of Toledo existed, despite its dependence on Castile, it still allowed a safe distance to the southern taifas such as Seville; now, Seville's borders bordered directly on the Christian ones.

First Request for Help from the Almoravids

The fall of the kingdom of Toledo in 1085, although taken advantage of by the Sevillians to extend their dominions as far as the city of Cuenca (occupying part of the present-day provinces of Ciudad Real and Cuenca), set alarm bells ringing among the taifas in the south of the peninsula. The threat embodied in the kingdom of Castile and León was gradually reaching each and every one of the places in Al-Andalus, where they were at ease and had a substantial influence on both their internal and external policy.

Moreover, the kingdom of Alfonso VI now bordered the kingdom of Seville, so the Castilian-Leonese king would not only be satisfied with the collection of tribute but would also demand lands (specifically those that had been annexed by the Sevillians after the fall of Toledo) in exchange for not conquering Córdoba.

The common people realised that their scant troops could do little against King Alfonso VI and his army, and so some groups of people began to appear who proclaimed the need to abandon their lands for safer places. The same feeling was felt in Seville, Granada and Badajoz, as they all knew that their parias served to keep the Christian roller rolling over the Iberian Muslim territory.

There might have been a chance if the integrity of Al-Andalus had been maintained, but so many years of estrangement and fighting between the different taifas had finally exhausted them. Now faced with a common and unfaithful enemy, the taifas moved closer together to form a common front, although it was of little use to unite their dwindling and tired troops against the powerful King Alfonso VI.

Events on the Iberian Peninsula moved so quickly after the capture of Toledo that an immediate response was needed in Al-Andalus. And this was not long in coming, thanks to the sovereigns of Granada, Badajoz and

THE FALL OF MOORISH SEVILLE 1023-1091

Seville (led by the latter), who decided that it was vital for the survival of their kingdoms to obtain external military support. It was clear that they were not going to find the support they needed on the peninsula, as there were no possible allies who could really tip the balance in favour of the Muslims. During this period of history, a fundamentalist Muslim empire had been forming in North Africa (present-day Morocco), known as the Almoravids. They were chosen for various reasons, such as their proximity, the important fact that they professed the same Islamic religion and, above all, because they possessed an emerging military power on a par with that of the Castilians. After a first attempt to attract the Almoravids to the 'Iberian problem' by the lord of Málaga, which failed, Al Mutamid of Seville, Abdalá of Granada and Al Mutawakkil of Badajoz, plus some others, agreed in a joint plenary session to go to North Africa to request the help of Yusuf ben Tasufin, leader of the Almoravids.

Because of their important role during this period in the history of Al-Andalus, we give a brief biographical sketch of both Al Mutawakkil and Abdalá.

Walls of the citadel of Mérida on the banks of the River Guadiana. The kingdom of Badajoz was the atavistic enemy of the kingdom of Seville, despite which they would end up collaborating against the Christian enemy. (Author's collection)

Like Abdalá in Granada and Al Mutamid in Seville, Omar Al Mutawakkil al Allah (meaning 'the one who trusts in God alone') was the last king of the Taifa of Badajoz. He occupied the throne from 1072 to 1094 and was therefore a contemporary of the aforementioned rulers of Seville and Granada. Given the same political circumstances experienced in the other taifas, the kingdom of Badajoz was immersed for most of the reign of Al Mutawakkil in continuous clashes, whether against the Seville, Córdoba, Toledo or Castile and Leon.

Abdalá ben Buluggin occupied the throne of Granada between 1073 and 1090. His reign had certain similarities with that of Al Mutamid, as he

THE RISE AND FALL OF THE KINGDOM: 1069–1091

had to bear the heavy burden of the parias to be paid to the king of Castile and León, Alfonso VI. For most of his reign, Granada and Seville were in open conflict, with numerous border disputes. Abdalá, in his memoirs, acknowledged that the misunderstanding between the two kings was largely due to the Machiavellian actions of Ibn Ammar, who was after his kingdom. In any case, the capture of Córdoba in Seville by the Toledans of Al-Mamun helped to reduce the intensity of the conflict between the two taifas.

Returning to the attempt to bring the Almoravids closer to Andalusian interests, there was a majority opinion in favour of obtaining their help, although there were doubts on the part of some monarchs about the behaviour of the Africans in their kingdoms or the intentions they might have once on the peninsula. But there was no room for doubts or suspicions, it was necessary, and the people demanded a change in the defeatist and vassal dynamic that the taifa kingdoms were accumulating. As we have already mentioned, the population was very anxious about the course of events and looked favourably on the arrival of foreign aid, especially thanks to the proclamations made in their favour by the alfaqids (who ensured the proper observance of Islamic rules). After all, the North African neighbours were seen as religious puritans who would save Al-Andalus not only materially but also morally. It is well known that the Islamism of the taifa period was far from extreme, as the population had become much more flexible in following their religion on a day-to-day basis. Without going any further, the production of grapes to make wine took up an endless amount of Andalusian crops, when wine was not allowed to be consumed by a good Muslim. This low morality should, the alfaqids thought, disappear in the face of the fundamentalism professed by the North Africans.

Walls of the citadel of Badajoz, where the taifa kings of Badajoz resided until they were overthrown by the Almoravids. (Open source by ICorbacho)

THE FALL OF MOORISH SEVILLE 1023-1091

It is said, although it is not possible to know for certain whether the event was real or not but it does make clear Al Mutamid's position in the call for help to the Almoravids, that he told his son Al Rasid, 'I do not want posterity to accuse me of having been responsible for Al-Andalus becoming the prow of the infidels; I do not want my name to be cursed in the almimbars. And if I have to choose, I would rather be a camel driver in Africa than a swineherd in Castile'. It is quite possible that this phrase was never uttered by the Sevillian king, although it does indicate the great differences that existed between the Almoravids and the Andalusian taifas, despite the fact that they professed the same religion. The decision was made, and the die was cast. Only fate would determine whether it was the right decision or not.

Yusuf ben Tasufin had been emir of the Almoravid empire since 1070, and, in the same year, he founded the new capital of his empire: Marrakesh. From 1073, he began to use the title of Emir of the Muslims (since he was only below the caliph of Baghdad), and, by 1084, he had conquered the entire western Maghreb and was very close to Al-Andalus, from which he was separated only by the Strait of Gibraltar. The Almoravids had declared jihad in the lands of North Africa, which led to the conversion to Islam of the entire population of that area, and they appeared to the Andalusians as a hope because they were co-religionists and possessed a very powerful and powerful army.

An Andalusian embassy composed of Abé Ishaq ben Muqana (cadi of Granada), Ben Zaidun (vizier of Seville), Ubayd Allah ben Adham (cadi of Córdoba) and possibly Ben Al Qasira (khatib of the Sevillian kingdom) travelled to North Africa (specifically to the city of Ceuta) to meet with Yusuf at the end of August 1085 (some sources question whether Al Mutamid himself came in person as part of this embassy or whether this embassy even took place a year earlier, although it seems unlikely). There, they reported on the urgent situation in the peninsular lands due to the growing thrust of the Christian troops, who only three months earlier had conquered the capital of the Toledan kingdom. To ensure the 'correct' help from the Almoravids, they limited their presence on the peninsula to the time necessary to defeat the Christians, and they would only act as auxiliaries to the Andalusians. Yusuf, for one reason or another, agreed to help the Andalusians, possibly with the intention of getting first-hand knowledge of what was happening in Al-Andalus. He evidently became aware of the many dissensions between the different taifas, and so, as was the case with King Alfonso VI of Castile and León, he considered it of great interest to take advantage of these 'troubled waters' for his own benefit.

The Almoravids and the taifas agreed that the North African troops would land in Al-Andalus via Algeciras, to which Yusuf agreed but, to ensure the correct arrival of the troops on the peninsula, demanded that Algeciras in Seville be ceded to him as a base of operations. This allowed for an Almoravid 'bridgehead' on the peninsula, for which the Sevillian vizier excused himself by saying that he had no authority for such action. Faced with the possibility of entering the Iberian Peninsula 'amicably' and gaining

THE RISE AND FALL OF THE KINGDOM: 1069-1091

control of such an important enclave in the Strait of Gibraltar, Yusuf wasted no time in sending several ambassadors to Seville to meet with Al Mutamid, including Ben Al Ahsan and Cadi Abd Al Malik.

Al Mutamid showed his courtesy and detained the North African embassy for many days in Seville, possibly because of the difficult decision he had to make. In the end, the Sevillian king had to accept the imperative need for Almoravid support in Al-Andalus, and so he allowed them to return with the missive in which he accepted the surrender of Algeciras. However, he made it conditional on the Almoravids waiting 30 days before they could vacate it completely. Despite the Sevillian missive announcing the surrender of Algeciras after 30 days, Yusuf, seconded by his alfaqids, decided to move on to European lands immediately after the departure of the Andalusian embassy, beginning to show that, although he had come to help as an auxiliary force, in reality he felt he had the right to act with complete freedom. To this end, he routed the bulk of his troops towards the city of Ceuta, from where he would embark to reach Algeciras. Only a year had passed since the Muslim loss of Toledo in 1086, and everything was about to change on the peninsula. Nothing would ever be the same again.

Before turning to the decisive participation of the Andalusian–Almoravid army that confronted the Castilian-Leonese troops in the Battle of Zalaca, we will give a brief overview of the general characteristics of the Almoravid and Andalusian military formations.

The Almoravids

The Almoravids are known as soldier-monks who came from nomadic groups originating from the Lamtuna tribe of the Sinhaya confederation, who lived in the Sahara. Their main occupation was cattle-breeding in the areas corresponding to the western Sahara. Due to persistent attacks by their enemies from both the north (the Zanatas) and the south (the blacks), they were grouped together in a smaller strip of territory, which gave them greater unity, as opposed to the greater dispersion they had had up to that time.

In 1036, an Islamic religious man named Abdallah Ben Yasin, who had studied for seven years in Al-Andalus, wanted to reform the Islam of the Sinhaya by making it more rigorous, but he was not accepted by the Sinhaya, who forced him to leave their lands. After his expulsion, he had no alternative but to take refuge in a Ribat or Convent-Fortress on the island of Tidra off the Sinhaya coast with a small group of followers. From that moment on, the number of disciples who joined them increased significantly, as this Ribat was considered to be a holy place where

Image of a Tuareg taken in 2003 looking very similar to what the Almoravids must have looked like when they conquered a large part of Al-Andalus at the end of the eleventh century. (Open source by Jean Louis Gonterre)

THE FALL OF MOORISH SEVILLE 1023-1091

the purification of the individual and a model formation of the good Muslim was achieved. In this way, the number of followers, as we have already mentioned, was increasing like wildfire, and so was the military potential that these monk-soldiers were acquiring. It was there that these men definitively acquired the name 'Almoravids', from the Arabic name 'Al-Murabitum' (meaning 'men of the ribat').

The men trained there, both militarily and religiously, behaved like true fanatics who interpreted the suras of the Koran with great rigour, considering as infidels many of their co-religionists who did not follow their religion to such an extreme. This confrontation was much greater if the people they faced were not Muslims, as was the case with the Christians, against whom they unleashed a veritable 'holy war', obviously with strong religious implications.

Although co-religionists of the Andalusians, the appearance of the North Africans was completely different. The way they dressed was very distinctive, very similar in appearance to the current Tuareg desert dwellers (who are descendants of those tribes), austere and determined because on many occasions they only let their eyes be seen (in Al-Andalus, they were called the veiled ones, because of this way of dressing). The veil was so important for the men that they never took it off under the condemnation of being looked down upon by their friends and relatives.

Abdallah Ben Yasin considered it absolutely necessary for his belief to spread throughout the world, and his world began in the Maghreb. Despite his good qualities as a preacher, Ben Yasin was not a military strategist, so he looked for another man who could execute the military designs that destiny had in store for the Almoravids. That man's name was Abu Bakr, who, in 1058, seized the city of Sigilmasa, which was the key to gold control and gave them, apart from the military power they already had, an important economic power to feed the powerful army that was gaining men day by day. At the beginning, these were mainly Berber contingents from the Lantuna tribe, although, as their area of influence expanded, Berbers from the Jazula, Zanata and Masmuda tribes also swelled their ranks, as well as black sub-Saharans (mainly from slave labour or prisoners of war); in time, many mercenary formations from as far away as the Anatolian peninsula would join them.

The borderlands between the kingdoms of Seville and Badajoz were silent witnesses to many clashes between the armies of the two kingdoms, which did not result in the definitive victory of either. These kingdoms went from being enemies to collaborators before finally being at loggerheads again. (Open source)

Their military formations were characterised by a large number of camel troops (who dismounted from their mounts to fight and acted as traditional infantry) and a smaller number on horseback (mainly from the assimilated tribes of the northern Sahara who had a greater tradition of horse riding), mainly armed with pikes, spears, swords and javelins; there was also an increasing number of archers in their ranks. In general, the Almoravid armies favoured light infantry and cavalry over heavier troops, which meant that one of the main tactics of their cavalry consisted of a succession of attacks and retreats.

Other elements that the Almoravids took very much into account in their military actions were flags and drums. The flags, as well as making the appearance of their military formations more impressive, were used by the Almoravid generals to control their troops from a distance, thus facilitating their movements. The drums fulfilled a simpler mission, since, in addition to accompanying the marches of the soldiers, when used in large numbers, they often caused panic among their opponents, mainly in cavalry formations that were disintegrated when the horses fled in stampede.

At that time, the Almoravid army was ready to take control of the Maghreb, and it was a nephew of Abu Bakr, named Yusuf ben Tasufin, who began the conquest of the territory of present-day Morocco, founding the new capital of his nascent empire in 1070: Marrakech. The culmination of the conquests in the area of present-day Morocco culminated in 1077 with the conquest of Tangiers and in 1084 with the conquest of the present-day Spanish city of Ceuta, which at that time enjoyed a certain degree of autonomy. It was at this moment of maximum economic, territorial and military power that Yusuf ben Tasufin met the Andalusian embassy that asked him for help in confronting the powerful 'infidel' army of Alfonso VI.

Yusuf's forces included a non-Berber personal guard of about 500 mounted men (including Arabs, Europeans and Turks alike) and about 2,000 black sub-Saharan cavalrymen. This personal guard, in addition to protecting their leader, also played an important role in combat; they were men specially chosen for their skill in battle. Moreover, such large formations of sub-Saharan blacks (mainly from the area of present-day Senegal) had a rather negative effect on the morale of the opposing troops.

In general, it can be concluded that the Almoravid troops were made up of true professionals in the art of war, accompanied by many more men who joined them wherever they went (the latter with a variable military level were usually used as a shock force against the enemy formations, preceding the intervention of the Almoravid troops themselves), who acted like a roller due to their huge number of men and combat skills.

The Armies of the Sevillian Taifa

The Sevillian army can be considered one of the most important of all the taifas of the peninsula, but, when it came to facing such qualified rivals as the Castilian-Leonese troops or the Almoravid formations, they were definitely not on a par with them, and it was difficult for them to face them openly with any prospect of victory. In general, the taifa kingdoms had a limited number of warriors of their own, as they corresponded to a markedly demilitarised society and therefore mercenaries and slaves were the majority of their members.

THE FALL OF MOORISH SEVILLE 1023-1091

Detail of the Bayeaux tapestry showing clothing and weapons similar to those used by Christian troops and some Andalusian troops during the eleventh century. (Open source)

It should be borne in mind that, in general, the taifas did not have sufficient military power to confront the powerful Christian troops, which led to the payment of parias. So the role of the Sevillian army could be likened to that of a lion for its Muslim neighbours and a mouse for the Christians and Almoravids.

Evidently, Al Mutamid knew the faults and virtues of his troops, so, despite continuing to pursue an expansionist policy at the expense of other taifas (Toledo, Granada, Badajoz and Murcia), he agreed to continue with the parias towards the Castilians inherited from his father. He knew that it was possible to grow but without openly confronting the Castilians. Despite Al Mutamid's intentions to avoid clashes with the Castilian-Leonese troops, Alfonso VI's aggressiveness towards the various taifas provoked many small-scale clashes between the two armies.

During the time of the taifas and in particular of Al Mutamid, it was not the most common way of settling conflicts by means of specific massive battles, but it was preferred to strike the enemy in depth in order to return soon to one's own lands. Moreover, as most of the war missions consisted of the capture of one town or another, siege operations were the most frequent.

As we have already mentioned, the Sevillian troops were made up of Arab-Andalusians, Berbers (mainly from the Berber taifa troops conquered by the Sevillian kingdom in previous years) and mercenaries of different origins (from black Africans to Christians and North Africans).

Mercenaries can quite possibly be considered the backbone of the kingdom's military forces, although their numbers were not necessarily very large. This is due to the fact that they were professional troops accustomed

THE RISE AND FALL OF THE KINGDOM: 1069–1091

to fighting. As we have already mentioned, the mercenaries could have different origins, but the majority were of Berber origin (the Tanyiyyun). Others in smaller numbers were Christian (Frankish saqalib).

The taifas did not have warrior elites in the style of the Christian kingdoms, but they did have many 'mercenary' troops. The appearance of the Arab and Andalusian formations must not have differed much from the Castilian formations of the time (chain mail, helmets, footwear), being more similar to these than to those of the North Africans. Evidently, there was no real uniformity in the dress of the warriors of the Sevillian taifa, ranging from those who resembled the 'Christian' appearance of the Andalusians to those who looked more like the Almoravids than the Berbers in the Sevillian army. Abdalá himself, king of Granada, commented in his text that the Almoravids found it difficult even to differentiate the Andalusians from their Christian enemies because of their similarity in dress and weaponry.

Their cavalry formations (mainly light cavalry, although to a lesser extent they also had heavy cavalry in the style of the Christian kingdoms of the north), archer formations and Andalusian infantry were very important. The weaponry was the usual of the period, consisting mainly of swords, daggers and spears.

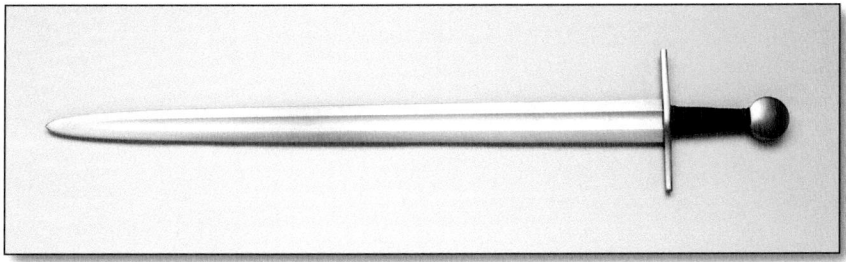

Oakeshott X model sword used in the eleventh century. Swords of this type were possibly used by Christians and some Andalusian troops in the Battle of Zalaca. Although they could be used to attack with their point, they were more often used for striking. (Open source by Soren Niedziella)

The Andalusian light cavalry was characterised by the fact that the riders used short stirrups and bent legs, which allowed greater control over the horse, great mobility and speed. On the not so positive side was the fact that it was not a cavalry suitable for clashes against well-formed infantry units or against the heavy cavalry of the Christians. These facts determined that their main mechanism of attack consisted in harassing the enemy at a suitable distance from the enemy.

One fact that was decisive in the future of the armies in Al-Andalus was due to the change in their composition that, although it began to take shape in the early days of the emirate-caliphate, intensified during the rule of Alhaken II. We are referring to the mass recruitment of Berber mercenaries who ended up predominating over the hitherto core of the Andalusian army, who were the descendants of the Baladis and Syrians who had arrived during the conquest of Visigothic Hispania and later. This meant that most

THE FALL OF MOORISH SEVILLE 1023-1091

of the Andalusian armies were based on 'foreign' Berber troops. In the case of the kingdom of Seville, even though it was an Arab taifa, it also had to include Berber troops in its armies (like those of the annexed taifas of the Berber crescent), which in some cases, such as the Seville attack on Málaga, did not behave with loyalty to their king.

In summary, it can be considered that the taifa army of Seville was quite hardy, although a step below that of the Castilians and Almoravids. Moreover, the vast extension of the kingdom of Seville made it more difficult to assemble numerically important formations, except in the areas close to the capital of the kingdom. It was therefore necessary to plug many holes with very few fingers, and this was a determining factor when it came to having to face much more numerous and battle-hardened troops during the era of the reign of Al Mutamid.

Among his poetic compositions, the Sevillian monarch also dedicated several to war themes, highlighting the bravery of his men. One of them, dedicated to one of his champions, emphasises the chivalrous character of this man, named Abu Sinan. This verse reads as follows:

> How excellent is Abu Sinan the wise-hearted knight!
> Men fierce as lions fear him,
> But singers love him with passion.
> He torments enemies with bravery,
> Enamours fair women with his beauty.

Another verse in which Al Mutamid mixed love and war is the following, which he also dedicated to one of his knights of unknown name:

> He fought with his eyes,
> With the sword,
> With the spear,
> Pray to men, brave lions.
> Pray to women, beautiful gazelles.

As was the case in the rest of Al-Andalus, it is worth recalling the main missions that were entrusted to the troops. They can be summarised in three types of action: sieges of towns, cavalcades and, to a lesser extent, pitched battles.

Sieges were the most common way in which an Andalusian army tried to capture a town. In this type of combat, the aim was to starve and thirst the enemy while devastating the surrounding area. The assault with its corresponding direct attack on an enemy town would involve too many casualties among the assailants to be generally discarded. An example of this type of tactic was the siege of Aledo, in which the combined Muslim troops laid siege to the town for a period of four months, with only minor hand-to-hand fighting provoked by small sorties by the defenders.

The cavalcades (also known as algaras or algazúas) were possibly the procedure most commonly used by the armies of Seville and Andalusia in general. It consisted of the use of a fighting force with a certain degree of mobility to attack, devastate and plunder areas usually bordering the Sevillian kingdom. Combats of this type are commented on dozens of times in this text and did not have the purpose of conquest, although they did allow the deterioration of an enemy area, facilitating a subsequent annexation of the territory by purely attrition of the rival. Although it cannot be quantified, it is true that the Sevillian army was not so numerous (even in its period of greatest power) that it could afford actions involving a large number of men without destroying large areas of its territory. However, this type of action facilitated the use of small armies, and the results obtained in the event of triumph were always interesting, while in the event of failure they would never represent a major 'blow' for the Sevillian kingdom.

The pitched battles, although possibly in our minds as the main way of waging war during the ancient historical period, were actually the least desirable, and we can practically only speak of one in the historical context of our text: the Battle of Zalaca, which we will discuss in the next section. The unwillingness to engage in such a battle was obvious. Thousands of men facing off against thousands of men on the opposing side could, in the event of defeat, mean such a major setback for the army and the kingdom that it was preferable not to engage in such a battle.

As a final note on the Sevillian armies, it is important to highlight the Sevillian navy. Inherited from the former caliphate navy, Seville had some docks for the manufacture of warships, to which it would add those of the Taifa of Saltés and Huelva after its conquest.

Although we do not know the number of ships in the Seville arsenal, during this period, warships used both sails and oars. The types of ships used were called sambuk (with two masts), baghia and ghaja (with three masts). Having inherited the ships of the caliphate fleet, the warship was the galley, and the cabbos were the transport ships. The commander-in-chief of the fleet, as during the caliphate period, was the amir al-bahr or lord of the sea, while each ship was commanded by a caid.

The navy's function was generally limited to the control and protection of the coasts of the kingdom, although we know of its use in combat on at least two occasions. The first of these was during the attempted conquest of Málaga from Seville under the command of a young Al Mutamid, still heir to the throne, in which the Seville ships anchored in the port of the city of Málaga to tighten the siege even further. The second case involved the use of the remains of the Sevillian fleet in the defence of the city of Seville from the river during the final attack that the Almoravids unleashed on the capital of the kingdom. Accounts tell how the Sevillian ships were set on fire in what was to be the beginning of the attackers' control of the river, which would later prove decisive in completely isolating the city.

Another known use of the Sevillian fleet was to transport the Almoravids from North Africa to the Iberian Peninsula when they were 'called' by various taifa kings to help them fight the Castilians.

THE FALL OF MOORISH SEVILLE 1023-1091

Battle of Zalaca

Yusuf's arrival in Algeciras was marked by the haste of the Almoravid emperor, as he suspected, thanks to the alfaqids, that his call for help from the Andalusians was nothing more than a strategy devised by Al Mutamid to put pressure on King Alfonso VI and force him to sign new peace treaties more advantageous for the Iberian Muslims. Thus, while the Almoravids would protect them from the Christians, it would be the Christians themselves who would protect them from the Almoravids' desire for conquest. Whether this is true or not, the reality is that large numbers of well-prepared troops quickly arrived in Algeciras. There, with this imposing army backing him up, General Dawud ben Aisa again demanded the square of Algeciras, which was under the command of a son of Al Mutamid, by the name of Al Radi. He immediately sent a messenger to Seville to inform his father of the situation. In addition, other Almoravid messengers left for Seville with a message from Yusuf, in which he 'generously' said that he forgave Al Mutamid the expenses incurred for the provisioning of his galleys and the food supplies of his soldiers. Al Mutamid, faced with the fait accompli, could do no more than authorise his son to cede the square and

Old engraving depicting the Battle of Zalaca in 1086, where the Andalusians and their Almoravid allies won an important victory against the kingdom of Castile and León, although it could not be used in subsequent years to swing the balance of power on the Iberian Peninsula back to the Muslim side. (Open source)

THE RISE AND FALL OF THE KINGDOM: 1069–1091

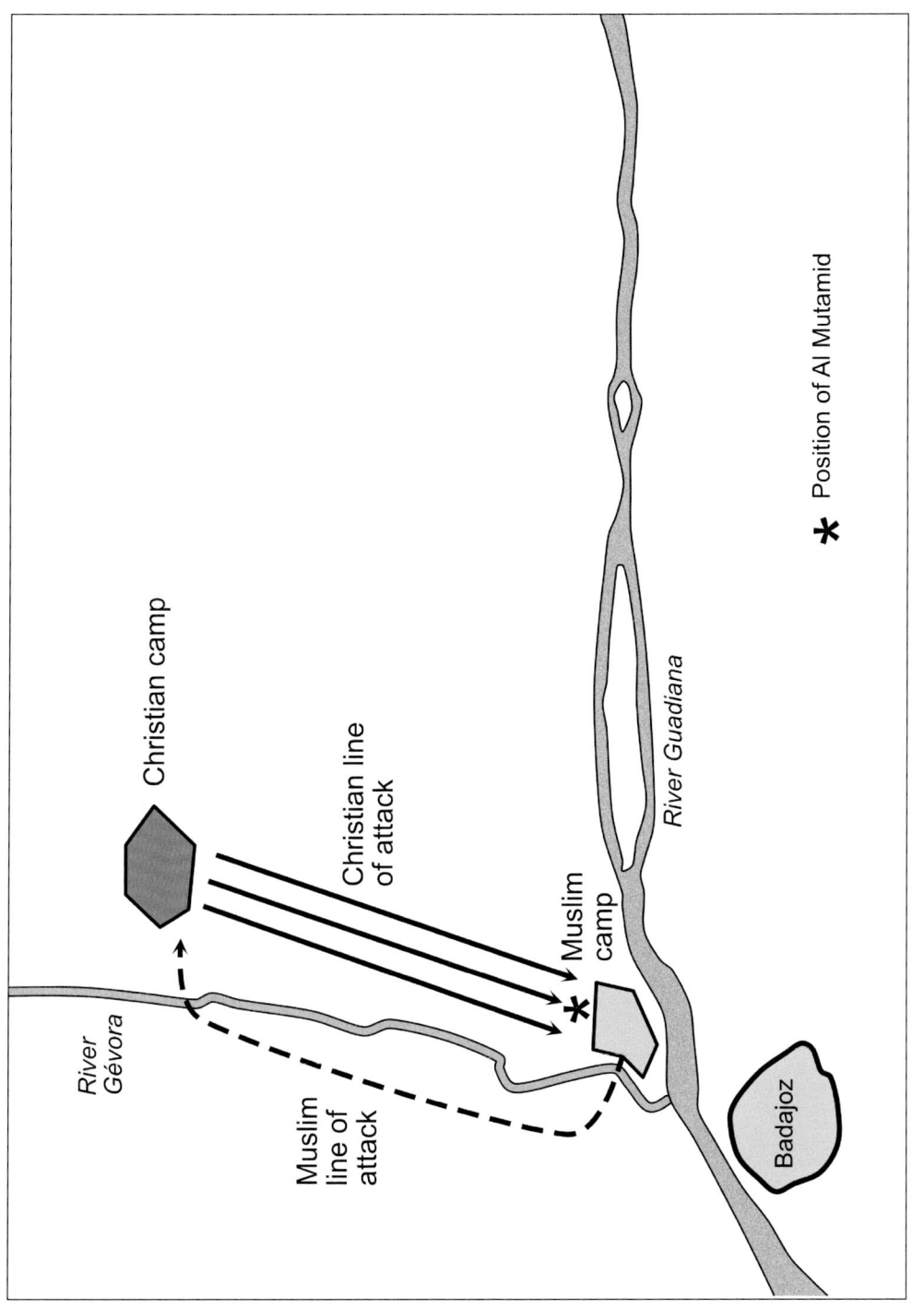

Battle of Zalaca, 23 October 1086. (Map drawn by the author)
GREEN AREA: MUSLIM CAMP
GREEN LINE: MUSLIM ATTACK LINE
RED ZONE: CHRISTIAN CAMP
RED LINE: CHRISTIAN ATTACK LINE

leave with his troops for the fortress of Ronda. In this way, the Almoravids had won their first place on the European continent.

What is certain is that this mutual distrust between the taifa kings and Yusuf led to an underhand confrontation between the two sides. The puritanical Almoravids really saw the Andalusians as infidels, as they easily flouted many of the precepts of the Koran, which really did not help at all for a complete understanding between these fortunate allies.

Once the advance party of the Almoravid army sent to the peninsula had settled in Algeciras, Emperor Yusuf came in person, and work was immediately set in motion to improve the fortifications of the fortress. While the work was in progress, Yusuf returned to Ceuta, where he felt safer, waiting for the work to be completed. Once the work was completed, the bulk of the Almoravid army led by Yusuf set off for Seville.

Al Mutamid heard of Yusuf's departure and immediately went with an escort of his own and the main leaders of the kingdom to meet them.

Once the two formations met, Al Mutamid rushed towards Yusuf to kiss his hand as a sign of respect, but Yusuf, wanting to show himself as an ally and friend, prevented him from doing so and then shook him in an affectionate embrace. There, he was presented with a number of gifts from the entire North African army.

After the meeting, both monarchs headed back to Seville, camping nearby. The arrival of the Almoravids in the capital of the kingdom was triumphant due to the great welcome they received from the population eager to free themselves from the yoke of the parias.

The pact that had been concluded in Ceuta stipulated that the Andalusian troops would join the Almoravids in the campaign against the Christians and that Yusuf would not harass any of the taifa kingdoms through which he passed nor would he listen to any Andalusian subject who wanted to provoke any disturbance in Al-Andalus.

After passing through Seville, the bulk of the Sevillian army joined the joint army. A week later, after leaving the lands of Seville, they headed towards the lands of Badajoz, making a first stopover of three days in the city of Artuxa (present-day Ecija). Following their route towards the northwest, they arrived at Jerez de los Caballeros (Yarisa), where they were joined by Abdalá from Granada (with an escort of 300 horsemen) and his brother Temín from Málaga (with 200 horsemen) as well as a son of Motacín from Almería who came with another cavalry regiment. They were joined by the troops of Al Mutawakkil from Badajoz.

They continued their journey towards Badajoz, always with the same disposition since the great military column had passed through Seville, Al Mutamid heading the Andalusian column and immediately after it the Almoravid column with Yusuf at its head. Although to avoid possible clashes or confrontations between the two armies, they agreed that the Andalusians would walk half a day ahead of the Africans so that, where the Andalusians camped in the morning, the Almoravids would camp in the afternoon. The last stop before reaching Badajoz was the town of Zafra, from where, after a pause, they finally reached the capital. About three months had passed since the original column had left Algeciras, and evidently, despite appearances, the relationship between the Africans and the peninsulars was not good, with the former being very arrogant towards the latter. So what was going to be an 'element' of help to the Andalusians had set the Almoravids up as the leaders of the column, being the ones who would give the orders and would not accept them from the taifas.

Once regrouped and suitably supplied in Badajoz, the different detachments of the taifa kingdoms and the Almoravids, once again forming a large column, set off towards the lands of Toledo, possibly in search of the Alcántara Bridge over the Tagus; by now, the Muslims were aware that the Christian army was close by. But so close were the Christian armies that they could not advance very far because, in the vicinity of the capital of the kingdom of Badajoz, they encountered the powerful army that Alfonso VI had brought back from an interrupted siege of the city of Zaragoza that he was carrying out when the Almoravids landed on the peninsula. The place known as Zalaca, Zallaqa or Zalaqa (by the Muslims) or Sagrajas or Sacralías (by the Christians) would be the scene of a bloody struggle for power on the Iberian Peninsula. The most recent studies believe that the site of the battle was located in the territory to the north of the mouth of the River Gévora in the Guadiana, on the right bank of the Gévora and next to the hill of Santa Engracia.

The Christian army, under the command of King Alfonso VI, had been formed with some haste, as, after the capture of Toledo, they had headed towards Zaragoza, which they besieged. It was during this siege that news arrived of the Almoravid landing at Algeciras, so, leaving the attack on Zaragoza for another, more favourable occasion, the Christian army headed southwest. This army included almost all the best of the peninsular Christians, including Álvar Fañez de Minaya, Count García Ramírez, Count García Ordóñez (El Cid's rival at the Battle of Cabra) and the Infantes de Carrión, as well as many knights from what is now France. Not among them, however, was perhaps the most important Castilian figure of the time: El Cid. It turned out that the disputes between Alfonso VI and Rodrigo Díaz as a result of the Battle of Cabra and the tares created by Count García Ordóñez against the Burgos native led to the banishment of El Cid, who was then in the kingdom of Valencia fighting on his own account.

Alfonso VI's idea was not to wait for the Muslim army to advance, preferring to advance into enemy territory and confront them there. The Christian victory would, on the one hand, put a stop to the African islands and, on the other, prevent a union between the armies of the different taifas, as was happening. Knowing the movements of the Almoravids and the Andalusians through his network of spies, he was aware of the presence of the Muslim army in Badajoz, and so Alfonso VI and his men set off hastily towards Badajoz so that (as we have already mentioned), when the Muslim army left Badajoz, a few kilometres later, they met up with the Christian army.

THE FALL OF MOORISH SEVILLE 1023-1091

Capital of the Royal Palace of Estella from the twelfth century showing a battle between a Christian knight with an elongated shield and an inscribed cross against a Muslim horseman carrying a buckler. Although it does not correspond to the eleventh century, the clothing and appearance of both warriors should be very similar to that of the Battle of Zalaca. (Open source by Mattana)

It was October 1086, and Alfonso VI had decided to gamble the near future of the Iberian Peninsula on a single battle in order to put a stop to the Muslims. As it is reasonable to think, the Castilian king did not attack without making a proper study of the situation, and, given the advanced stage of the year, in the hypothetical case of a defeat, it would be difficult for the Muslims to exploit their victory, as the harsh winter in the central peninsula would prevent it.

On the other hand, the taifa kings and Yusuf had also decided (possibly more by Yusuf's decision than by the others) that they would wait for the Christian army in front of the city of Badajoz so that, if they were defeated, they would have asylum and a fortress there. What can be seen from the tactics of both sides is the fear that both sides had of each other, although perhaps the Muslims were more cautious (mainly the Almoravids, who were completely distrustful of the Andalusians, whom they saw as having no fighting capacity).

It did not take Alfonso VI long to send a message to the Muslims and specifically to Yusuf, in which he said, 'Here I am, I have come to meet you, and you, on the other hand, stay and hide in the vicinity of the city'. After this letter, Yusuf decided to advance his troops slightly, crossing the Guadiana, although without losing the saving walls of the city of Badajoz as a reference point; the Christians occupied some hills to the north of the Guadiana, some nine kilometres from this river and one kilometre from the River Gévora; one army was therefore some five kilometres away from the other. Yusuf, with this wait for the enemy and sheltered in the walls of Badajoz, could gauge the potential of his army against the Christians with a view to future combats, but, in case of defeat, he could always take refuge in the powerful walls of the city. Both sovereigns, following old traditions in pitched battles, agreed to fix the meeting of their weapons for a specific

THE RISE AND FALL OF THE KINGDOM: 1069–1091

day. It was Thursday, 22 October 1086, and Alfonso VI proposed a date to the Muslims as follows: 'Tomorrow Friday is your feast day and Sunday is ours; I propose that the battle should take place the day after tomorrow, Saturday'. After learning of this 'pact', Al Mutamid warned Yusuf of how unreliable Alfonso VI was, for he had known him for a long time and had always proved it to him. As a result of his wise warning, Al Mutamid only got a certain contempt from Yusuf, who did not heed his words at all.

Before going on to describe the events of the battle, we will briefly comment on the disposition of both armies so that we can get a better idea of what happened in Extremadura.

On the Muslim side, Yusuf, after proclaiming himself leader of the joint army (without any possibility of complaints from the Andalusians), set up his camp at the back of the Guadiana and with the city of Badajoz guarding their backs. Between them and the Christian army, there was flat terrain that would serve to make the most of the cavalry troops (mainly light) that the Muslim army had. The number of troops is very difficult to know for certain, although there are studies that put the number at around 6,000 Andalusians (of which around 5,000 would be infantry troops and the rest light cavalry) and on the Almoravid side around 4,000 or 5,000 (of which around 2,000 would be light cavalry and the rest infantry). Evidently, these approximately 10,000 men did not have the same combat value, as the fierce North African troops were far superior to the Andalusian ones, although, as we shall see, not in all cases.

On the Christian side, the figures that have come down to us are also disparate and unreliable in many cases, although, after the 'recruiting' that King Alfonso VI did in his many possessions, the contingents that were presented for combat could exceed 1,000 knights (although in the Christian case the cavalry was mainly heavy, much more powerful than the light Muslim cavalry) and 4,000 or 5,000 infantrymen. This would make a total of at least 6,500 men, a lower figure than the Muslim one, although it was considered valid by Alfonso VI, due to its great fighting capacity, supposedly greater tactical ability and superior number of heavy cavalry. We must not forget that the Christian cavalry was more experienced and much better armed for hand-to-hand combat than the Almoravids or the armies of the taifas.

The disposition of the Muslim troops was motivated by the distrust that Yusuf felt towards the Andalusians, from whom he expected them to flee at any moment (an absurd thought, since they were the ones who had requested his help, but that was the situation in the Muslim camp).

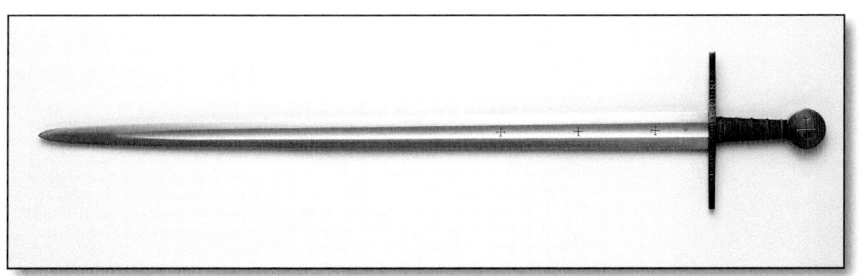

Oakeshott XI model sword used in the late eleventh century. Swords of this type were possibly used by Christians and some Andalusian troops at the Battle of Zalaca. Although they could be used to attack with their point, they were more often used for striking. (Open source by Soren Niedziella)

145

THE FALL OF MOORISH SEVILLE 1023-1091

So, according to the Muslim chronicles, after a dream, Yusuf changed the disposition of his troops inside the camp, possibly to keep the Andalusians, who were physically separated from their African allies, under more control.

As dawn broke on 23 October 1086, King Al Mutamid of Seville, who was praying the dawn prayer, heard news of movements in the Christian camp. He had been unable to sleep because of his great distrust of the Christians (and the pact that Yusuf had accepted from Alfonso VI to fight the battle on Saturday, 24 October), as well as their proximity. This distrust was very useful for the Muslims because, although the date of the following day had been 'agreed' for the battle, the Christians tried to surprise the confident Muslims because the two armies were so close to each other. But Al Mutamid, who was an 'old fox' and was used to dealing with Alfonso VI, was not at ease. That was why he took special care to place observers, specifically some Sevillian cavalry units, ahead of his own lines, who were finally the ones who detected the surprise attack that the first Christian troops made on the Muslim camp, specifically on the area occupied by the Andalusians under the command of the Sevillian king. The Almoravids were well protected to the rear and did not notice any enemy movement, as they were confident that the battle would be fought the following day.

The situation became very difficult because, although the Christian attack was quickly noticed, the Christians were already so close that they inflicted heavy casualties on the Andalusians. Al Mutamid quickly requested help from the Almoravids to avert the danger of the destruction of the Andalusian troops. But Yusuf behaved as he was, as a traitor to the Andalusians, since he intentionally delayed the help requested by Al Mutamid, leaving them as cannon fodder at the feet of the Christian cavalry. The words he is said to have said are quite indicative of the 'friend' that the Andalusians had sought out to confront the Christians: 'What do I have to do with these people being slaughtered? They are all enemies.'

Thus, we find the surprised Andalusians, commanded by the Sevillian Al Mutamid, fighting in an inferior position against the overwhelming Christians. It is quite possible that the Andalusian troops were not completely overwhelmed in the initial attack thanks to the fact that the Sevillian lookouts were able to raise the alarm, but even so the Christians, led by Alvar Fáñez and García Ramírez, went on to overwhelm any Andalusian who came their way, causing chaos and death among them. Once the clash between the Castilians-Leonese and the Andalusians had taken place, the victory seemed to have been won by the Christians.

It would have been close for the former, as the Andalusian troops could have been annihilated, but this did not happen thanks to the good work of the Sevillian king in combat. Al Mutamid, as we know, had been fighting and leading armies since he was a child, and he was not prepared to give up in this battle that could be decisive for the fate of Al-Andalus, so, despite not receiving the requested Almoravid reinforcements, he knew how to lead his troops, instilling them with courage and bravery. Al Mutamid suffered several wounds in the line of battle (the most severe were to his face and hands), but this did not prevent him from continuing to fight, ready to die in combat if that was his destiny. Some of the Andalusian troops (not those from Seville who were around their king) who began to leave the battlefield as soon as the battle began started to return to the battlefield thanks to the attitude that Al Mutamid showed in combat. In this sense, Al Mutamid wrote some verses to his son Abu Hisan, who accompanied him in this campaign:

> I thought for a moment of escape,
> but firmly I returned to the fight,
> For when I looked at you, my son,
> I was ashamed to flee.

It was only when the Sevillians, supported by men from the other taifas, managed to stabilise the front line with difficulty that an Almoravid infantry unit and another unit of Berber cavalry under the command of Syr came to their aid. At that moment, however, the wounded Al Mutamid noticed that the Christians were no longer pushing as hard as they had been, and it did not take him long to see why.

Yusuf, who, as we can see, considered the Andalusians and the Christians to be almost equal enemies, after having used the Andalusians as bait, took advantage of the disorder created in the Christian ranks by the fight against the taifa troops and the long distance between them and his camp to attack the unguarded Christian camp with the bulk of his cavalry. His Almoravid troops had been hidden during the Christian attack, with the vegetation on the banks of the River Gévora and after surrounding the hill of Santa Engracia.

Yusuf himself stated in a letter about this battle and about this particular event that he came out 'from behind a ravine like a whirlwind of flames with all my forces, mounted on pointed Arab steeds'.

When the Christians noticed the encircling manoeuvre, they sent the bulk of their troops towards their camp (hence Al Mutamid noticed a lesser push against his reduced troops) and turned towards it, but now they only found the Almoravid light cavalry that, after having destroyed the Christian garrison that remained in their camp and razed it to the ground, was now turning against the Christian rearguard. The fighting that followed was very fierce, with the Christian camp being taken repeatedly by both sides. But, in the end, the Christian troops were 'caught in the crossfire', with Yusuf on one side and Al Mutamid on the other, and the Christians were gradually whittled down. The final coup de grâce was delivered by Yusuf's black guards, who approached where Alfonso VI was fighting, and it is said that they even managed to wound him with a dagger in the thigh. The fighting, which had begun at dawn, was still going on at dusk, and it was only when night fell that it ended with a great victory for the allied Muslim contingent. The Christian cavalry fled towards the camp, which at least freed them from the pressure of the Almoravid infantry, who could not move at the same speed. Despite the complicated situation, the Christian troops managed to organise themselves sufficiently to avoid a disbandment that would make it easier to be massacred and to retreat in an orderly fashion, making the enemy advance more difficult.

The Almoravids unsuccessfully attempted to capture the Christian king, who with some 300 knights took refuge in a nearby mountain. Due to the difficult access to this position by the Almoravids, Alfonso VI could not be captured. During the retreat, there were a greater number of Christian casualties, including important figures such as the Galician Count Don Rodrigo Muñoz and the Asturian Don Vela Ovéguez, as well as the shameful escapes of Count García Ordóñez and the Infantes de Carrión. Alfonso VI, wounded, was forced to take flight with some 500 of his knights, crossing the Tagus at the Alcántara Bridge as far as Coria, some 150 kilometres from Zalaca, and from there he set off for the city of Toledo. King Alfonso VI's contempt for the men of the taifas, which he extended to the Almoravids, played heavily against him in this battle, and he was punished for it.

The Almoravids, instead of pursuing with their cavalry the Christians who fled with their king, preferred to devote themselves to the easier task of exterminating all the wounded Christians left on the battlefield and cutting off their heads, which they piled up to form a kind of altar. Referring to the altars made from the heads of the Christians, the chronicler Ben Al-Kardabus explained the actions of the Africans:

> … the Muslims hastened to cut off the heads of the polytheists and built with them minarets like those in the courtyards of the mosques, and from the top of them the muezzins for three days carried out the call to prayer. Then all those Muslims who had remained unharmed returned to the camp. This incomparable victory took place on Friday the 10th of Rajab in the year 481 (23rd of October 1086 in our calendar). With it the throat of the Peninsula breathed a sigh of relief and because of it many regions were affirmed …

The diminished Andalusians, seeing these scenes, realised that their brothers in Islam had little sympathy for them, as they had been left to their own devices and used as bait for the Christians. Important figures in the Andalusian scene such as the Zirid Prince Maksan and Abu Rafi Al Fadl (eldest son of the courtier of Cordoban origin Ben Hazm) had been killed in the battle. Moreover, their savage behaviour towards the wounded and prisoners definitely showed them what kind of allies they had sought. But who was going to complain about that to the Africans? Nobody, since the joy of victory and the fear of the much diminished Andalusian troops against the much less worn-out Almoravids did not give room for much more.

Evidently, the Almoravids were doubly happy with the triumph, as they had not only automatically put a stop to Alfonso VI's invasion, subjecting him to a heavy blow, but also allowed the cream of the Andalusian troops to be annihilated (this would prevent them from being able to defend

THE RISE AND FALL OF THE KINGDOM: 1069–1091

themselves against the Christians in the future, and they would therefore be forced to resort to the Almoravids again). Yusuf's move obviously worked out perfectly.

Al Mutamid composed some verses to Yusuf after the victorious battle, in which, as the occasion demanded and despite the events that took place in the battle, the Seville native flattered the North African. These verses read as follows:

> Blessed be your raid;
> May it bring swift victory,
> By Allah, what a sword is yours!
> It is a pestilence to those of the cross.
> No doubt, the Day of the Well will have a twin brother.

After the battle, the logical thing to do would have been to advance with the allied army to take advantage of the little defence that the Christian lands now had (especially the recently conquered Toledo or the town of Coria), but Yusuf, after learning of the death of one of his sons in Ceuta (possibly ill as a result of a previous revolt in his lands), decided to return to Africa but not before leaving Al Mutamid a detachment of some 3,000 men to guard and at the same time watch over the taifa lands, under the command of his Lieutenant Muhamad Ben al Hay. So what could have been a great victory for Al-Andalus, because of Yusuf's decision, remained a mere victory, from which the Christians would not take long to recover.

On his return to Africa, Emir Yusuf passed through Seville, where he gathered in council the various kings and princes of the taifas who had taken part in the battle and ordered them to work together from that moment on, since the Christians would only attack again if they saw the disunity that had existed until then. And, although they all agreed and promised to work together, Temin, the prince of Málaga (brother of the king of Granada), quickly asked him for help against his brother. And, although Yusuf overlooked it, it was clear that it was very difficult for all the southern taifas to 'row' in the same direction. Yusuf, after sharing with the Andalusians the satisfaction of this victory in their holy war, adopted the title of Amir al-Muslimin wa Nasir al-Din (Emir of the Muslims and Defender of the Religion) and set out for occupied Algeciras and then on to North Africa.

The important and courageous performance of the Sevillian king, seconded by his troops, is noteworthy. Although they did not have the same potential as the Almoravids in this battle, they were far from being inferior to the Africans. The problem of the Sevillian troops was based more on their numbers than on their combat value, as they had demonstrated on many occasions when facing rivals with armies of similar size to their own. Another problem arose when the army in front was a Castilian-Leonese army, normally superior in numbers and much more experienced in hundreds of battles. It is an observable fact that, when the taifas united, they achieved a different result to when they acted on their own (always of course with North African support), and that was the only possibility of continuing to resist the Christian thrust. However, as we shall see later, the enemy was not only to the north but also to the south.

In conclusion, it can be considered that Zalaca was not a decisive battle either in terms of the number of casualties on both sides or in terms of territories conquered. Despite this, it did allow Yusuf to meet the Castilian-Leonese troops in person, whom he would face again just a few years later, defeating them once again at Uclés, managing to halt the Christian advance and even reconquering such important places as Coria and Valencia and even taking Toledo by storm.

Problems in Murcia and the Disastrous Campaign of Aledo

After the Battle of Zalaca, the taifa kingdoms that had taken part in it were temporarily freed from the tax they had to pay to Castile and León. This situation was short-lived, however, as, in little more than a year, Alfonso VI had recovered from the setback he had received and, in the absence of the Almoravids on the peninsula and the reappearance of discord between the different taifas, he once again took control of the peninsular war.

Thus, the Muslim population in general, which had seen how it had been freed from paying the paria tax to the Christians (albeit replaced by an Almoravid religious tax, albeit of a lesser amount) and was once again able to get back on its feet, once again found itself faced with the harsh reality of its manifest weakness in the face of Castilian-Leonese power.

The area where Alfonso VI again interfered in the life of the Muslims was in the east (perhaps fleeing from the area of the kingdoms of Badajoz and Seville, which he now knew to be more capable and emboldened to defend themselves), relying mainly on an enclave that the Christians possessed halfway between the Seville towns of Lorca and Murcia, within the territory of the Sevillian kingdom. From Aledo (Alit), where large Castilian contingents were garrisoned, multiple raids were carried out that paralysed the normal functioning of supplies to both capitals, as well as to Almería itself. This fortress was taken by the Christians in the spring of 1085, and it is calculated that it could hold a garrison of up to 12,000 men if necessary. With the capture of Aledo, the Castilian-Leonese, under the command of the noble knight García Jiménez, managed to weaken the Muslim power, creating great unease among the Muslims. From that date onwards, they carried out raids in Muslim territory with audacious punitive expeditions in the orchard lands of Murcia and Orihuela, coming to dominate the valley of the Guadalentín and controlling the main communication routes. But it was after Al Mutamid's defection from vassalage to the Christians that Aledo received orders to exert greater pressure on the adjoining territories, which belonged to the Abbadid kingdom.

THE RISE AND FALL OF THE KINGDOM: 1069–1091

Ancient representation of the Andalusian and Almoravid siege against the fortress of Aledo in 1089, which ended in a resounding Muslim failure that was to have disastrous consequences for the various Andalusian taifas in the years to come. (Open source)

As early as 1088, there were reports of various Christian riots in the Levantine lands, a situation that was of particular concern to Al Mutamid, lord of some lands in that area.

After the Battle of Zalaca, a reinforced Al Mutamid, aware of the incursions into his territory from the fortress of Aledo, tried to settle all the problems that still existed in his Murcian territory, for, although it was true that the Christians were ravaging his lands, it was also true that, as we saw earlier, Ben Rachic (regent of Murcia), despite having sworn allegiance to the Sevillian king, behaved like a king independent of Seville. Taking advantage of the presence of the 3,000 Almoravids with him, Al Mutamid saw the opportunity to harass the rebel and depose him, placing in his place his son Al Radi (the one who had had to abandon Algeciras so that the Almoravids could take it over). So Al Radi set off for Murcia with the Almoravid Syr's men and troops from Seville, totalling between 1,500 and 2,000 men. We do not know why, but Al Radi gave his father excuses for not continuing at the head of the military column, and it was his brother Al Motadd who took command. From Aledo, the well-prepared Castilians, aware of his presence, sent 300–500 men (mainly heavy cavalry) against the allied column. In the confrontation that took place near Lorca, we do not really know how it happened, but we do know the result, which was nothing more than a flagrant defeat for the Muslims, who shamefully ended up on the run.

After this unsuccessful attempt to control Aledo, Al Mutamid decided to embark for North Africa to meet with Yusuf and thus obtain the help of the entire Almoravid army. Leaving Seville, he reached the mouth of the River Sebu at the Marmora, which was where the Almoravid emir resided at the time. There, he informed him of the new and increasingly powerful Christian attacks and the need for Aledo to be taken. He took the opportunity, of course, to discuss the issue of Ben Rachic, although this remained in the background (since Yusuf, despite his intentions to conquer Al-Andalus, tried to keep out of supporting one Muslim leader over another).

The agreement reached was that Yusuf and his army would return to the peninsula, joining the 3,000 men they had left in the Sevillian kingdom. In addition, the troops of the various taifa kingdoms (as at the time of the day of Zalaca) would prepare for this campaign in support of the Almoravids.

It was the spring of 1089, and, once again, Emir Yusuf arrived on the peninsula with his army. From Algeciras, where military forces from Seville were waiting for him under the command of their king, they set off towards the border between the kingdom of Seville and Granada, where Abdalá was waiting for them with his troops to join the army. After being joined on the way by troops from Almería, they headed towards Aledo, which they immediately besieged. The allied army was made up of the following kings and their respective troops: Emir Yusuf, Al Mutamid of Seville, Abdalá of Granada, Al Mutasin of Almería, Ben Rachic of Murcia and Temin of Málaga.

Although morale was good at the beginning, the situation gradually stagnated, and a thousand and one problems began to arise in those who maintained the siege.

The number of besieged troops was approximately 2,000 infantry and 1,000 cavalry, and they had enough food, water and ammunition to hold out for a long time. In addition, they had the advantage that the rebel Ben Rachic, despite being on the Muslim side besieging Aledo (to gain points against Yusuf), on the other hand secretly supplied the Christians and even cut off the supply of food on several occasions to the besiegers (to gain points with Alfonso VI). In this way, the Christians resisted with few

Impressive view of the castle of Aledo. A coalition of troops from Granada, Seville, Murcia, Almería and Málaga together with the Almoravid army was unable to capture it during a siege that lasted four months. (Open source)

difficulties, as the clashes between the Muslims were of direct benefit to them.

The siege of the fortress was carried out as perfectly as possible, both in terms of men and equipment. Each of the taifa kings participated in the best possible way with his men, depending both on their numbers and their knowledge of warfare. Frontal attacks were carried out every day, in order to give the besieged no respite; these were carried out alternately by each of the sides that made up the coalition of Muslim troops. In addition, almajeneques and crossbows were built in front of the areas that were considered most vulnerable, with a greater capacity for this type of combat. Despite the good will, however, it was all to no avail, as the Christians held out without much wear and tear. Due to their great resistance, the Muslims decided to maintain the siege until the Christian enclave surrendered by starvation.

It also happened that, in the besiegers' camp, there were groups of people who tried to get closer to Yusuf in order to obtain more privileges. One of these groups were the religious alfaqids, who were closer to the ideas of the religious orthodoxy maintained by the Almoravids than by the various taifa kings (whom they hated for being free thinkers, friends of the arts, friends of wine poetry and quite unconcerned with religion). If they approached the African correctly, in the event that they were to retain power in Al-Andalus (as would actually happen), they would be the ones on whom all political and religious influence would be placed. It was not only the alfaqids who were causing trouble in the siege camp at Aledo but also the common people, who, prompted by the words of the alfaqids, began to show clear signs of discontent towards their own kings. The cause was clear, since, in the face of the ostentatious and luxurious life that all the Andalusian Muslim courts led, it was the people who had to maintain them with increasingly burdensome taxes that were demanded without dissimulation in the face of the slightest pressure from the Christians.

All these rebellious movements against the taifa kings did not go unnoticed by Yusuf and his men. The African knew that, with little effort, a large part of the Andalusian population would side with him to overthrow their current kings. But the time had not yet come, although it was drawing nearer.

The Andalusian kings were faced with the choice of either putting up with the complaints against them or protesting; they opted for the latter, which in the end proved to be the most destructive.

Taking advantage of these troubled waters of all against all, the rebel and advantage player Ben Rachic began to make important approaches to the Almoravids, to whom he gave large sums of money, in order to gain their sympathy. His idea was to get Yusuf (unofficial lord and master of all Al-Andalus) to annul his agreement with Al Mutamid to return Murcia to the Sevillian.

Certain that his rapprochement with the Almoravids and above all with Syr had borne fruit, Ben Rachic allowed himself the insolence to publicly show his rebelliousness towards the Abbadid, as well as publicly belittling him (he even had the prayer said in Murcia in the name of Yusuf and not that of his master, Al Mutamid). Evidently, this conflict reached Yusuf, who had to decide between one and the other in order to give him the reason. After weighing the pros and cons of his decision, he came to the conclusion that he had even more to give to Al Mutamid than Ben Rachic. So he violently reproached Ben Rachic's publicly rebellious attitude towards Al Mutamid. Yusuf evidently knew of Ben Rachic's hidden dealings with the Christians and how he wanted to create confrontations with Al Mutamid, with the sole purpose of gaining complete independence and very possibly to throw himself into the hands of the Christians as a tributary. So, after a trial between the two leaders, conducted by the alfaqids (and the long hand of Yusuf), it was decided to declare Ben Rachic guilty of having rebelled against his master, Al Mutamid. The punishment was to hand him over to the Almoravid emir, who immediately handed him over to the Sevillian, laden with chains, but on the condition that he would not end his life. The latter handed him over to his son Al Radi, who interned him in the Sevillian camp, where he was kept for the duration of the siege.

It seemed that the Murcian problem would be solved, especially when the emir ordered the inhabitants of Murcia to recognise their lord Al Mutamid once again. But the anti-Sevillian population of Murcia refused the emir's proposal and took up a defensive position against any attempt by Sevillian troops to enter the city. Thus, the Murcian problem caused by Ben Rachic only mutated into a similar one, under Ben Rachic's lieutenant.

It seems that Al Radi was selected by Al Mutamid to take over the government of Murcia, but its inhabitants refused to accept him. Moreover, they even logistically supported the Christians of Aledo against their co-religionists.

Between assaults on the fortress and all kinds of complications among the besiegers, the days went by without the objective of taking the enclave being achieved. But the whole situation took a turn when informers brought the news that a Castilian army under the command of Alfonso VI was on its way to save the position of Aledo. This news came as a bitter blow to the besiegers, and the scheming Yusuf used it to end the siege, as his troops were tired and he was wary that the Murcian rebels would welcome the Christians and provide them with supplies, leaving the Muslims in inferior conditions.

Finally, the emir decided to return to Africa and thus ended the siege. The Andalusians also had to do the same and return to their own lands. In any case, the tears created during the siege between the different Andalusian kings would give rise to various disputes between them, such as Abdalá's dispute with his brother or that of Al Mutamid with Al Mutasin of Almería, the latter over the possession of fortresses in Sorbas (Surba) and other enclaves in the mountain range now converted into a border between the kingdoms of Seville and Almería. In all these cases, Yusuf did not try to act as a mediator but rather let them drag on, causing an even greater weakening of the already weak taifas.

These disputes with Al Mutamid remained frozen but resulted in the latter sending Yusuf information about private conversations he had with his Sevillian 'friend'. In these, an innocent Al Mutamid told the Almerian that Yusuf's presence in Al-Andalus would be limited to the time that he decided, since they were nothing more than beggars who were dying of hunger in their homeland and had been fed and well paid since they had been called, and that, when they had to be dispensed with, it would be done without any difficulty whatsoever. We do not know whether or not such arrogance on the part of the Sevillian was true, but what is clear is that Al Mutasin used these words to make Yusuf feel uneasy against Al Mutamid. When the African heard of this, he probably made the decision to wipe out all the taifas and take power in Al-Andalus, although this idea may well have been in his head since the Battle of Zalaca. In this way, the man who thought himself victorious in this mess, Al Mutasin, had only lit the fuse for what would become the Almoravid invasion.

At the end of 1088, it seems that the Sevillian king regained control of the situation in Murcia and took charge of its government thanks to the support of the caid of Lorca, Abul Hassan, who acted de facto as governor in Murcia. He possibly ruled in the name of Al Mutamid until the city fell to the Almoravids in the first half of October 1091.

The result of the siege of Aledo for four months (possibly between June and October 1089, although other sources place it in the autumn of 1088) was therefore of disastrous results for the Andalusians, as they only managed to increase the clashes between them, favouring on the one hand the return of the Castilian fiscal pressure and on the other hand becoming even more dependent on the decisions and troops of Yusuf. As we have said, after the Al Mutasin affair, Yusuf made the definitive decision to return to the peninsula but no longer to help the Andalusian kings but to take over their lands and incorporate them into the Almoravid empire. To facilitate this step, he had the confessed help of the alfaqids and cadis (those who stood to lose the most if the Christians finally triumphed), who allowed him to direct the will of the people in his favour, thus showing himself to be the saviour of good Muslim customs, rather than what he really was: an invader.

The Almoravid Invasion

As we have seen, the lands of Al-Andalus had become a breeding ground where Almoravid religious orthodoxy could easily take root in the face of Andalusian laxity or African military power in the face of the manifest weakness of our compatriots. In the face of this, all that was needed was a cause to motivate Yusuf's return to the peninsula. And this appeared in the form of new hostilities by Alfonso VI on all his borders and, above all, the return of the Taifa of Granada to the regime of parias and vassalage to Castile.

THE FALL OF MOORISH SEVILLE 1023-1091

Vault of a room belonging to the taifa palace in Seville. (Used with the permission of Cristina Vargas Lorenzo from her article 'La recuperación del palacio primitivo del Alcázar de Sevilla')

This situation had returned to Granada because of the critical situation that King Abdalá was experiencing. Since Yusuf's departure, Alfonso VI had once again put the right kind of pressure on the Granadan taifa to return to obeying its taxes. And, although the skilful Abdalá tried to remain faithful to the coalition with the Almoravids (who would never consent to vassalage of any kind to the Christians), he found himself materially between a rock (the figure of the Castilian 'ambassador' Alvar Fañez, who was in charge of the regions of Granada and Almería) and a hard place (the absence of Almoravid or any other taifa's help). Finally, after the threat of taking the city of Guadix, Abdalá had to submit to the payment of the parias, and, to minimise the negative effect that these would have on his already 'economically squeezed' people, he decided to pay them out of his own money. Even so, Abdalá tried to gain time in the negotiations in case Almoravid forces came to his aid again, although the delays caused by this wait were of little use.

As the Castilians did not spare even a dirham in economic matters, Abdalá had to start by paying the taxes that were overdue from the time of the Battle of Zalaca. These amounted to 30,000 meticals, which were offered to Alvar Fáñez. Once he had paid what was due, a new pact was signed to update the previously signed pact, which was broken shortly afterwards. In this pact, Alfonso VI undertook not to attack the territories of Granada or violate the clauses that constituted the pact. The Christian king also offered, if Abdalá considered it appropriate, to help him recover any territory that Al Mutamid had taken from him. In doing so, he was only trying once again, as well as making a good economic profit, to bring the taifas back into conflict with each other. He did not want a coalition of all of them to be repeated, due to the danger that this could pose at any given moment to the Castilian offensive. Abdalá, who evidently signed the obligatory treaty, considered it appropriate to reject this 'kind' offer from the Castilian. The leader of Granada had no intention whatsoever of getting involved in these internecine struggles between Muslims against Muslims in which there was always only one beneficiary: the Christians.

In the mutual distrust between the two monarchs, the Granadan monarch acknowledged that this pact would only cause problems in the long run with the Almoravids, to which Alfonso VI did not attach much importance either.

Abdalá, still maintaining some of the 'team' spirit that the various southern taifas had had just two years earlier, sent an emissary to Al Mutamid to inform him of the decision he had taken by force to return to paying tribute to Castile. He also sent a similar letter to Emir Yusuf, in

THE RISE AND FALL OF THE KINGDOM: 1069-1091

which he excused himself from his action because of the urgency with which the matter needed to be resolved, due to the suffocating pressure from the Castilian monarch.

Shortly afterwards, he received a reply from Emir Yusuf, accusing him of treason. The reply from the Sevillian king was not much better either, as, when he saw that after the pact the Sevillian lands were attacked and no longer the lands of Granada, Al Mutamid thought that Abdalá and Alfonso VI were acting in mutual agreement.

Al Mutamid was neither willing nor able to make any kind of incursion into the lands of Granada or even to try to stop the many blows by Castilian troops that were attacking the northern border of his kingdom. The reason was that his dwindling armies, once majestic, were basically composed of mercenary troops that were on difficult occasions (such as this one) rather difficult to handle.

Despite Abdalá's 'good intentions' not to get involved in any more conflicts with Muslims, he did have time in 1090 to meddle again in the already complicated affairs of Murcia. Obviously, as soon as Al Mutamid became aware of this, he was deeply angered but could do nothing more. Finally, the Murcian issue was abandoned by Abdalá because another even greater problem loomed over him: the emir was returning to the peninsula.

Image of the north wall of the present-day wall of the Royal Alcázar in Seville, where we can imagine what it would have looked like in the eleventh century, although it is obviously not exactly the same as at the time described in this text. (Author's collection)

Yusuf's intentions were to punish the emboldened Castilians as well as the traitor to the Muslim cause and the holy war, the Taifa of Granada. The Sevillian king, although he was worried about this new arrival of the Almoravids, naively thought that Yusuf would be content to prey on Granada. Yusuf easily managed to get the alfaqids to issue a fetua in which they decreed that the rulers of Granada and Málaga had lost their rights because of their many attacks.

On 10 June 1090, Yusuf crossed the strait again towards his stronghold of Algeciras and set off for Córdoba, where he was received with full honours by King Al Mutamid, with all kinds of gifts and riches to his satisfaction. In the meetings they held, Al Mutamid took a clear stance against the position of Abdalá of Granada, accusing him of maintaining pacts of collaboration with Alfonso VI. A messenger then left for Granada with a message from the emir to his king in which he said, 'come to meet me without delay'. Evidently, Abdalá, who feared the worst after learning that Al Mutamid had repeatedly accused him, made all sorts of excuses for not coming to meet the emir (long gone were the days when Yusuf's presence on the peninsula

THE FALL OF MOORISH SEVILLE 1023–1091

was enough of a lure for all the southern kings and princes to come as one to meet him; this confidence in the African had justifiably disappeared completely).

Immediately, Almoravid intelligence ensured the defection of Lucena in Granada to their cause, while Almoravid columns took over various castles.

The bulk of the Almoravid army set out to besiege the capital of Toledo, but the warning of the imminent arrival of reinforcements from Castile and León made the fearful Yusuf decide to leave the siege towards the end of August 1090 and return to the lands of Al-Andalus. There, he set out first for the capital of Granada, where he arrived in the first fortnight of September (he entered the Zirid capital on 10 September 1090). The African army laid siege to the city, preventing the entry and exit of people and impediments, so the discontent (largely generated by the alfaqids) spread to the entire population in a few days. A large part of the Granada garrison, which was of Berber origin, did not take kindly to the Almoravids taking over the city, after all, of the same ethnic group as themselves. The Maghrebi militia that guarded the city finally decided to go over to the Almoravid side, leaving Abdalá alone and forced to surrender to the emir. He was stripped of almost all his possessions except for some jewellery and 16,000 dinars, with which he left for a forced political exile in North Africa, passing through Algeciras to Ceuta and from there to Meknes (Miknasa).

After the fall of Granada, the Almoravid army, with Yusuf in command, headed for the Málaga possessions of Abdalá's brother Tamin, who was easily captured and imprisoned after little resistance. He also found himself in North Africa, even temporarily coinciding with his brother in Meknes.

Yusuf's next target was the Taifa of Almería, which, although it had not entered into pacts with Christians, was also the target of Almoravids determined to seize power over the whole of Al-Andalus. The king of

Image of the Seville Gate of Carmona. The taifa kingdom centralised in this town became a fierce rival to the Sevillian kingdom, with which it was in dispute for many years. (Open source)

Almería held his ground and, thanks to his loyal troops, managed to maintain control of the city despite the blockade to which it was subjected. The same did not happen with the rest of the castles and towns that made up the eastern taifa, since, as soon as the Almoravid forces arrived, they were not shy about automatically changing sides.

While all this was going on, Al Mutamid, who considered himself close to Yusuf, who had been faithful to him by not making a new pact with the Christians and who had given him all the help and information about his neighbours, was waiting for a reward from the emir. This was no more and no less (as the Sevillian king believed) than the city of Granada. In any case, Al Mutamid, who was not inclined to trust Yusuf, was hiding a card up his sleeve: if relations with the Almoravids worsened, he would fall back under the influence of Alfonso VI in order to keep his kingdom intact.

Al Mutamid, after seeing Yusuf's behaviour in Granada and Málaga, as well as the harassment of Almería, rightly feared that his kingdom would be next. But he had not yet given him any further cause to attack the Sevillian kingdom. But this arose when Yusuf sent a messenger who demanded the presence of Al Mutamid immediately. The Sevillian, who was on his way with Al Mutawakkil from Badajoz to congratulate Yusuf on his recent victories in Granada and Málaga, realised that he was being set up. So they declined the invitation, excusing themselves with the supposed incursion of Castilian troops into the interior of their respective countries; Al Mutamid set off for Córdoba, and Al Mutawakkil for his own lands. The latter was warned by the Sevillian with the words 'be safe, because you can see what has happened to the lord of Granada and what will happen to me tomorrow'. Despite this, they tried to contact other taifa kings in the northeast of the peninsula to warn them of the actions that Yusuf was taking in the south.

Having laid his cards on the table, Yusuf again sent messengers to Al Mutamid requesting him to come to his presence immediately. Al Mutamid's reply could not have been clearer or more diplomatic, for he told him:

> that was justified when you were our guest and you intended to campaign against the infidels. Then I was obliged to help you with my person and with all my goods. But now you are only a neighbour, like Badis and his grandson. You have, moreover, much more strength than I have, to do me harm with your troops. Therefore, it is not possible for me to go blindly into danger, for surely what you want is to take over my states, since Granada has no value for you, if the other territories of Al-Andalus are not added to it.

Yusuf also insisted that Al Mutamid join in the fight against the Christians, something that the Sevillian had to refuse, as he would be swarming with enemies.

The Abbadid was therefore forced to resist in each and every one of the fortresses that made up his extensive kingdom and even ordered the walls of the capital of the kingdom to be reinforced. However, as was feasible, many

THE FALL OF MOORISH SEVILLE 1023-1091

Panoramic view of the citadel of Almería, one of the taifa kingdoms that did not have a direct conflict of importance with the Taifa of Seville during the eleventh century. (Open source)

of these fortresses were passed over to the other side as soon as they were besieged, as their distance from the capital of Seville and the situation of the kingdom itself made it impossible for reinforcements to arrive that would allow a glimmer of hope of maintaining resistance against the Africans.

In order to give a veneer of legality to his infamous actions, Yusuf obtained new fetuas from the alfaqids in which they were especially dedicated to the remaining taifa kings still outside African oppression; they also had a special dedication to Itimad, wife of Al Mutamid, whom they accused of having dragged her husband into a whirlwind of pleasures and of being the main cause of the decadence in the cult. As we can see, Yusuf was gradually tying up the loose ends that would allow him to turn Al-Andalus into another province of the Almoravid empire.

Al Mutamid saw the situation as very difficult to maintain, so he decided on a double manoeuvre to ask Alfonso VI for help; on the one hand, he first sent a messenger requesting his help, and, on the other hand, he sent an official embassy headed by Zaida to hand over his daughter-in-law as a sign of goodwill with the added bonus of handing over the Sevillian territories that had previously belonged to the disappeared kingdom of Toledo and that were now very difficult for the Sevillians to defend. While the first envoy was rejected by Alfonso VI, who declined to help the Sevillian, Zaida's embassy was a complete success, although the latter will be discussed in more detail later.

Continuing with the total Almoravid offensive against the kingdom of Seville, this first passed through more distant towns such as Segura and Úbeda, to reach Almodóvar and finally the city of Córdoba, defended by a son of Al Mutamid, Fath Al Mamun. Although resistance was expected to be strong, the defections of a large part of the population made it impossible to defend the city effectively. According to the chronicles, 'Al Mamun, sword in hand, tried to fight his way through the enemy and traitors, but succumbed to his numbers'. This brief quote shows us not only that the enemy was the Almoravids but also that part of the population of Córdoba changed sides, making it easier for the North Africans to take the city. After the fall of the city on 26 March 1091, Al Mamun was captured and killed, his head cut off, nailed to a pike and paraded throughout the town and then throughout Al-Andalus (remember that a similar event happened to another son of Al Mutamid, Abbad, when the city of Córdoba fell under the control of the Taifa of Toledo).

The importance of Córdoba's resistance in order to defend Seville was made clear by Al Mutamid when he told his son Al Mamun, 'do not lose your courage, because death is more bearable than humiliation, and a sovereign should not leave his fortress except to go to his tomb'.

The fall of Córdoba, added to the death of his beloved son Al Mamun, dashed what little hope the monarch had of resisting the Africans.

It is at this point in history that the name of Zaida and the role she played in mediating between the kingdom of Seville and the kingdom of Castile and León appears in her own right. There are numerous versions of Zaida's origin and life, often intermingled with legends. According to experts in this field, it seems to be confirmed that Zaida was a daughter-in-law of Al Mutamid. Specifically, she was the wife of his son Fath Al Mamun, who ruled the city of Córdoba and who died in the defence of the city after the Almoravid invasion.

Apparently, Fath Al Mamun, knowing of the proximity of the Almoravid army to the city of Córdoba, decided to send his wife, Zaida, along with his fortune, 70 knights and family members to the Sevillian castle of Almodovar del Río, which was well fortified and equipped for a possible siege.

Accepting this fact as the most accurate, controversy arose once again after the fall of Córdoba to the Almoravids. One version indicates that Fath Al Mamun himself, seeing the straitened situation of the city in its defence against the Almoravids, would have opted after evacuating her from the city of Córdoba to send Zaida to the safe court of Toledo. In another version, it was Zaida herself who, after the death of her husband (knowing that the fate of the kingdom of Seville had already been decided), possibly following the advice of Al Mutamid, went to the court of Toledo. In this last embassy from the kingdom of Seville to Castile, Zaida acted as the bearer of a treaty proposed by Al Mutamid to King Alfonso VI in which the kingdom of Seville handed over a series of important towns on the northern border of the kingdom (which had recently been annexed to the now defunct kingdom of Toledo) such as Uclés, Consuegra, Mora, Alarcos, Ocaña, Oreja, Caracuel, Zorita, Huete, Cuenca and Amasatrigo in exchange for Castilian-Leonese aid to the Sevillian kingdom against the Almoravids (it is not really clear whether all these towns came under real or at least nominal Seville rule). The possibility of protecting these towns to the north of the Sevillian kingdom seemed utopian, as the entire Sevillian army was dedicated to fighting the North African invader, so, rather than lose them, Al Mutamid tried to make some benefit from them with this curious deal

THE FALL OF MOORISH SEVILLE 1023–1091

that Alfonso VI accepted, although, as we shall see later, it would not bear fruit in any positive way for the Sevillian kingdom.

As we have analysed, the situation of pacts in the kingdom of Seville underwent very important changes from 1085, when the Toledan kingdom fell. If at the beginning it was a vassal of King Alfonso VI, after the Almoravids were called in, relations with the Castilians were severed. Little more than a year elapsed after the Battle of Zalaca before Alfonso VI imposed new parias on the taifa kingdoms, and Seville, believing itself safe with the Almoravids, did not accept them, a case that, as we have seen, was not the same in Granada. But the policy of Yusuf, the emir of the Almoravids, in terms of his attitude towards the Andalusian taifas changed: they were no longer weak allies as they had been at the beginning but had become overnight succulent pieces to add to the mosaic that made up the Almoravid empire.

Al Mutamid, after seeing the situation in which Granada was placed against the Almoravids, realised that, whether he wanted to or not, this could also be his future.

For her part, Zaida, after arriving at the court of Toledo, became the concubine of Alfonso VI and was later baptised with the name 'Isabella'. They had a son born in 1093, named Sancho, who died at a very young age during the Battle of Uclés in 1108.

After the loss of Córdoba in March 1091, the next major settlement (in addition to several small fortifications) was the city of Carmona on 9 or 10 May 1091 under the army commanded by Syr. Its territory was bordered by those of Ecija, Setefilla, Seville and Morón and included in its boundaries villages and smaller towns, such as Marchena and Paradas (Marsana and Bardis).

The fall of Carmona was only the beginning of the siege of the city of Seville. Two Almoravid armies marched against the capital, attacking it, one from the east and the other from the west. The Guadalquivir with what remained of the Sevillian fleet separated the latter army from the city.

Al Mutamid's last remaining hope failed, which consisted of the help of Alfonso VI's troops against the Almoravids. This aid, forged in Zaida's embassy to the Castilian-Leonese court, consisted of an army sent by the Castilian king under the command of the well-known Alvar Fáñez, who on Friday, 7 September 1091, in the vicinity of Almodóvar in Córdoba, came up against an Almoravid army that was waiting for him and, after a bloody confrontation, succumbed to them. This Almoravid army was possibly made up of Zenetes, Gomares and Mazamudes troops with a large contingent of cavalry, all under the command of Ibrahim ben Ishak from Lamtuna. The Sevillian monarch's morale declined completely when he saw all was lost, leaving the defence of the city to his son Rachic.

This double game (of simultaneously supporting the Castilians-Leonese and Almoravids), which did not work for Al Mutamid, was also carried out by the king of Badajoz with identical results. Al Mutawakkil, trying to please his new master, Yusuf, attempted a risky manoeuvre to save himself and his kingdom. In this way, he helped the Almoravids with some troops

THE RISE AND FALL OF THE KINGDOM: 1069-1091

Miniature from the Beatus of Urgell depicting the capture of Jerusalem by King Nebuchadnezzar. The Beatus dates from the end of the tenth century and therefore represents weapons from that period. At the top are three foot soldiers (armed with spear, stone, and sword respectively and circular shields) and below are three horsemen (two armed with sword and one with bow). (Open source)

in the conquest of the city of Seville, while on the other hand he agreed with Alfonso VI a treaty of mutual aid in exchange for ceding the strongholds of Lisbon, Sintra and Santarem to the Christians. These cities passed to the Castilian kingdom in 1093, which caused great discontent among the population of the kingdom of Badajoz, who, by turning against their monarch, facilitated his fall into the hands of the Almoravid empire and his capture and subsequent execution on the charge of having collaborated with the Christians in around 1094.

If in Seville, with the Almoravid siege, the already desperate situation was not enough, part of the population was also moving dangerously close to the Almoravid position, repudiating the Abbadid family. Although Al Mutamid knew the names of many of the seditionists, he decided not to punish them as they deserved so as not to end his reign with such barbarity (after all, he was not only a warrior but also a poet). And it was his having kept them at liberty that caused them to breach the wall on Tuesday, 4 September, through which the Almoravid troops gained access. As soon as the news reached Al Mutamid's palace, he took his sword and, without taking a shield or armour, mounted a horse with his guard and went to the breach (apparently in the present-day area of the Puerta de Jérez, known in his time as Bab al-Faray or Puerta de la Bella Vista or Buenavista). The desperate defence against the increasingly abundant Almoravids seems to have had an effect, as the ardour and fierceness of their king in combat made the Sevillian troops give their best. They threw a dart at him that only grazed his clothes but that made the battle even more fierce. Finally, the enemy breakthrough was aborted, and the breach properly plugged, so the assailants retreated.

Assaults on the walls followed one after the other, all of which were met with a firm response from the Sevillian defenders. But a very serious event was about to happen that would cause the victory to fall on the African side. Possibly on the same day that Al Mutamid had been wounded, it happened that the Almoravid troops managed to set fire to the Sevillian fleet in the Guadalquivir so that the backbone on which the defence of the entire western flank was built fell. Alarm immediately spread among the population and the Sevillian defenders, who realised that the end was very near after the river was in the hands of the assailants (on the land side, the Almoravids were commanded by Hudayr; on the river side, they were commanded by Abu Hamama). As the once proud Abbadid fleet caught fire, many Sevillians jumped from the walls or looked for an exit from the city to swim across the river and escape from the 'mousetrap' that the capital of the kingdom had become.

Despite the critical situation, the Sevillian army managed to hold out behind its walls, but the balance finally tipped in favour of the Almoravids when, shortly afterwards, Yusuf's nephew, the aforementioned Syr, arrived with numerous reinforcements.

The siege reached its climax on 9 September 1091, when the troops under Syr's command again stormed the city walls. The first onslaughts were repulsed by the few troops that still remained in the city, but, finally, the large number of men that the Africans put into combat managed to force the walls and enter the city (some sources mention that some Sevillians betrayed their king by opening the Bab al-Faray Gate during the night to the Almoravids, who quickly entered the city). After the Almoravids passed through the streets of Seville, all that remained was death, looting, rape and despair for those who had not fled the capital. The Africans, accustomed to having practically nothing more than the clothes on their backs, found a city in which there were luxuries they did not even know existed. The Sevillians were stripped of their belongings, from riches to clothing, and the palaces of Al Mutamid were, of course, completely plundered.

After leaving only desolation in their wake, the Africans arrived at the castle-palace where Al Mutamid and a sparse garrison were stationed. Inside the castle, the scene could not have been more desolate, as women wept, men ran from place to place and friends pleaded with Al Mutamid to surrender and end the looting in the city. But a warrior like him was determined to fight to the end, for he had been on hundreds of military missions since he was 12 years old and his pulse would not tremble now. Due to the magnificent construction of the walls of the Royal Alcázar, General Syr was unable to take the fortress by force of arms.

Al Mutamid, finding the alcázar surrounded, attempted two exits through two gates located to the south of the city (possibly belonging to his own palace or to the wall, respectively, such as those of Al Farach and

THE RISE AND FALL OF THE KINGDOM: 1069-1091

Al Najil). On both occasions, the superiority of the Almoravids made itself felt, as both attempts were aborted.

Some verses by the Sevillian king reflected the moments of the entry of the Africans and his desire to be able to die in combat; they read as follows:

> When my tears had at last ceased to flow, and my torn heart was a little calmed: <Surrender, I was told, is the wisest course>. Alas, I answered, a poison would seem sweeter to me than to swallow such shame! Let the barbarians take my kingdom from me, and let not my soldiers forsake me: my courage and my dignity forsake me not. The day I fell upon my enemies I wanted no armour; I went forth to meet them with nothing but a tunic, and, expecting to meet death, I threw myself into the thick of the fight, but alas, my hour had not come.

For some reason (possibly some traitors were the cause), the palace gates were opened from the inside, and some Almoravid troops were able to advance through the palace. Hearing the sound of weapons in the courtyard of his residence, Al Mutamid threw himself and a few men to defend it. The Sevillians fought with such fury that they managed to repel the African soldiers. One of his companions, his son Malic, was killed in the battle. Al Mutamid's pain was greater than if he had been mortally wounded; the Sevillian monarch, on the other hand, was not even scratched. Once the Almoravids had been expelled from the courtyard, Al Mutamid returned to his quarters in dismay, even considering the possibility of suicide rather than surrendering to Yusuf's men. But, thinking that this would alienate him from Allah, he finally opted for the humiliation of surrender. And, although he initially tried to set some conditions for the surrender (he had sent his son Rachid the same night to meet with Syr but without success), in the end, it had to be unconditional. Once the decision was made, he gathered his family and close friends who were still with him in the palace and took leave of all of them one by one, thanking them for their loyalty, after which he surrendered with Rachid.

After they were captured, Syr made another demand: on pain of execution of Al Mutamid and his entire family, he would have to send envoys to his sons Al Radi and Al Motadd, who at the time ruled the cities of Ronda and Mértola, respectively.

Al Mutamid agreed to this demand and dispatched the messengers, who immediately left for Ronda and Mértola. He begged his sons to lay down their arms, as all was lost, but the lives of their imprisoned parents and siblings were still at stake. Itimad also took part in the writing, as she knew well the haughtiness of her sons and how difficult this could be for them.

Al Radi received the missive in his city of Ronda, which for some days had been guarded in the distance by an Almoravid army under the command of General Guerur, but they did not dare to attack because of the difficult access they had to besiege the city. Moreover, the city was well

THE FALL OF MOORISH SEVILLE 1023-1091

Again an image of the Cantigas where we see a Muslim detachment (with turbans) leaving their camp. Let us remember the importance of a good defense of the camps and the importance of their loss at the hands of enemy troops, as happened in the battle of Zalaca. (Open source)

prepared to withstand a siege for as long as necessary. Al Radi's decision, after a few days of deliberation, to surrender the city was all the harder. He agreed with Guerur that his people and troops would be respected, as well as his life. But, in surrendering the city, the traitor Guerur went back on his word, murdering Al Radi. The cause: the Sevillian's delay in replying to Al Mutamid's letter and of course eliminating the one he had unjustly plundered so that no one would discover that he had taken their wealth without the approval of Emir Yusuf. The freemen and soldiers of the garrison were not respected either, as they were executed once taken prisoner. Finally, Guerur seized the existing slaves in the city of Ronda and sent them as a gift to Yusuf.

Something similar happened in Mértola, but Al Motadd was quicker to decide than his brother. He surrendered the city in exchange for respecting their lives and property. In this case, the infamous Almoravids did not honour the pact either, although they limited themselves to plundering his property, respecting his life.

As for Al Mutamid, Itimad and the other members of his family who were imprisoned in Seville, they were loaded with chains and publicly paraded in such a pitiful state to a ship anchored on the banks of the Guadalquivir. Specifically, the ship was located where the Muelle de la Sal (Salt Quay) is today. The people who saw them passing through the streets and being pushed into the ship did not stop screaming and crying inconsolably.

In a few days in September 1091, a kingdom that had been a mirror in which the other taifa kingdoms looked at each other, a kingdom that managed to extend from the Atlantic Ocean to the Mediterranean Sea, a kingdom that managed to unite a large part of Al-Andalus under a single government; in short, a kingdom that, despite the convulsions of the century in which it was born and died, took the name of Seville to the highest point of the Muslim world on the peninsula, was extinguished forever.

8
Exile

Muelle de la Sal. This is where the royal family of Seville embarked, headed by Al Mutamid, for their exile in Africa. At this geographical point, the Taifa Kingdom of Seville can be considered to have ended but not the story of the royal family, who managed to save their lives. (Author's collection)

After the conquest of the capital of the Sevillian kingdom, we had left the royal family on a ship ready to set sail for North Africa, where they would all be held for life. The Arab historian Ben Al Labbana left us a testimony of what that sad moment was like for the whole city:

> The sky weeps in the evening and in the morning for the Ben Abbad, for the mountain whose base collapses and which owed the breeze to them.
> Traveller: the noblest of houses is uninhabited.
> Prepare the saddle and gather the remnants of provisions.
> In the valley, someone is waiting to live in it,
> but the servants have been lightened and the river crops have dried up.
> Yes, the Ben Abbads have been deprived of Seville.

As they once were of the land of Baghdad.
I can forget everything but that morning on the river,
When I saw them in the sailboats like dead men in their graves.
The people filled the two banks of the Guadalquivir
And watched in amazement those pearls floating on the foamy water.
The young women dropped their veils
and their faces appeared torn like shreds of tunic.
The time has come to say goodbye.
Shout men and women who would be prepared to serve as hostages.
The boats begin to sail as the cries accompany them.
Like the camel driver's song as the caravan sets out on its journey.
How many tears flowed that day on the water!
How many pieces of heart were carried away by those insensitive boats!

It is evident that, despite the unease of the population due to the complicated political situations with Al Mutamid, the people in general appreciated him, especially compared to the horde that had conquered them, one very distant both socially and religiously from the rather more cultured Sevillian population.

The ship's destination was the city of Tangier, where the royal family disembarked in a pitiful state, laden with chains. Despite this, they showed the gallantry and presence of mind they had always had. An example of this is when they docked in that city and were disembarked, the crowds crowded around to see them and insult them. Among them was a jester poet called Al Hosri, to whom Al Mutamid had once given a few coins for his performances. He composed several poems in honour of Al Mutamid (only one of which the king recognised as new), and, despite the deposed king's situation, he dared to mockingly ask him for alms or a gift for his work. The monarch, very calmly and demonstrating his greatness even in the worst circumstances, took out a bloody coin from inside his shoes. The coin, which was gold and worth 36 cequíes (kekis), was the only thing Al Mutamid had been able to take from his wealth, and he gave it to the insolent man. Handing it to him, he said, 'Take it, and take it back, and say that Al Mutamid never dismissed a poet without giving him a gift'. The wretched buffoon did not even thank him for the gift, leaving yet another token of his infamy.

They were then transferred to Meknes (possibly at the end of 1091), where they coincided at some point with the deposed King Abdalá of Granada. They stayed there for many months until Yusuf remembered them but only to transfer them to another prison-fortress (called Qalat Mahdi), in this case in Aghmat, some 30 kilometres south of Marrakesh.

During those long months, Al Mutamid did not cease to compose verses in which he recalled time and again his fortunate former life, his present miserable one, his beautiful city of Seville and in general a review of what his whole life had been like.

Other verses that reflect his state of mind are the following, which he sent to his son Rachid, also imprisoned with them, although with some difference pending between the two:

> I was the emulator of the beneficent rain,
> the lord of generosity, the protector of men,
> when my right hand lavished gifts on the day of the distribution of gifts,
> or took the lives of enemies in the day of battle,
> and when my left hand held the bridle that held the steed,
> frightened by the noise of the spears.
> But now I am in the power of captivity and misery,
> I resemble a sacred thing that has been desecrated,
> Like a bird whose wings have been clipped.
> I can no longer answer the plea of the oppressed, nor of the poor.
> The joy of my countenance, to which you were accustomed,
> Has changed to gloomy sadness;
> sorrows do not allow me to think of joys;
> Today all eyes turn away from me,
> when once they all sought me.

Despite being held well within the lands of the Almoravid empire, the Sevillians were not given any relief in their grief. Al Mutamid and his family lived in abject poverty (they received no financial support, as did the Zirid Abdalá of Granada). The king suffered more for his family, whom he adored and who were always with him, than for himself. Itimad and his daughters were forced to work as spinners to earn enough money to at least keep them from starving. Al Mutamid, who could not do any kind of trade (he was not allowed to), devoted himself to composing heart-rending verses in which he poured out the suffering he endured. He could not bear to see his family in such a situation, and so he wrote:

> I wept, watching a mob of partridges pass by me;
> they were free, they knew neither prison nor chains.
> It was not out of envy that I cried,
> but because I would have wanted to do what they did,
> Because then I could have gone where I wanted;
> My joy would not have faded,
> My heart would not be full of sorrow,
> I would not weep for the loss of my children.
> How happy they are, they are not separated from each other,
> none of them experience the pain of being away from their family,
> they do not spend the night as I do in horrible anguish,
> when I hear the bolts or the lock at the prison door creak.
> Alas, God preserve their grandchildren!
> mine lack water and shade!

THE FALL OF MOORISH SEVILLE 1023-1091

Some of Yusuf's other prisoners exiled in Aghmat became friends with the Sevillian, to whom they gave company and conversation. They were being released while Al Mutamid remained in his prison. To these departing prisoners, he also composed some of his verses:

> Why should my weeping never
> shall never run out of my tears
> that my withered cheeks
> constantly running?
> For the unhappy friend
> pray, my friends, to heaven
> and thank him because
> He delivered you from captivity.
> To hope for equal fortune,
> I dare not dream it.
> Who will break the chains
> That wound my limbs?
> They gird me like black serpents
> their iron links,
> And like the teeth of lions
> They crush my bones.
> But this present joy
> of my pain is consolation,
> your hearts beat
> with joy in your breast.
> Go, then, happy and free
> and praise God together
> for my constant unhappiness,
> for your good and contentment.

The memory of his beloved Seville, its palaces, its gardens, its women, was very present to Al Mutamid in several of his verses. He longed for them as if they were people who longed for him; all that was once light and joy had turned to shadows and sadness due to his confinement in North Africa:

> The deserted palaces of Seville
> for their princes groan,
> generous and sweet in peace,
> lions in battle.
> Of Zoraya the Alcazar laments;
> its sublime domes
> no longer from my sovereign largesse
> the dew they receive.
> The great Guadalquivir mourns my absence;
> the quintas and gardens,
> who looked at themselves in their liquid mirror,

EXILE

to opprobrium they surrender.
And I, who out of the torrent of my gifts
I made happiness to flow,
swept in a torrent of misfortunes,
From Libya to the centre I came.

While, from my absent land,
I am in Maghreb captive,
there in my beloved homeland
the empty throne mourns me;
my strong spear and my cutlass
are dressed in mourning.
The almimbars mourn me
out of compassion and affection.
Happiness, which smiles on others
has fled from me forever.
Alas! that of noble souls
envious and enemy
robbed me of crown and kingdom
Fate has vanished,
And filled with bitter sorrows
the bottom of my breast.
Of my deplorable fate
The heavens themselves are jealous.
So, free from chains,
To see again those places
leave me, where blissful
and respected I have lived;
to ride on the waves
of the calm Guadalquivir,
in the light of the stars
on a clear summer night;
in the shade of the leafy olive trees
of the leafy olive trees,
and hear the light whisper
of the gentle aura in the myrtles,
or among the green boughs
of the turtledove's moan.
If only my eyes could see again
the superb buildings
of al-Zahi and Zoraya,
by my love they moved,
they would shine with joy
the magnificent towers;
and al-Zahi would shelter me
in his enchanted enclosure,
as a bride receives

> to the sweet beloved owner.
> Impossible is so much happiness;
> to hope for it is delirium,
> and if it were not to hope in Allah
> and in His infinite power.

Living in abject poverty, with Itimad exhausted and his daughter Butayna unaccounted for, Al Mutamid managed to write his best poems to the lost time, to everything he had and would no longer possess, to his chains or to the ravens of Aghmat.

During Al Mutamid's captivity, he and his wife Itimad heard news of one of their daughters, whose fate they had not known since they had been imprisoned. It was Butayna, one of their youngest daughters, who had disappeared after being seized by the Almoravids when they took the city of Seville. It was only after some time that Al Mutamid and Itimad heard something of their daughter, as the latter received some verses that his daughter had composed, in which she recounted her adventures since her separation from her parents, which were circulated by word of mouth. In them, Butayna recounted how, after her capture, she had been sold as a concubine to a Sevillian merchant as a gift to his son. But, when the merchant's son wanted to have relations with her, she refused on the grounds of her royal lineage; she replied that she could never be his without marriage and always with her father's permission. The merchant agreed that Butayna's verses should be taken to Aghmat so that Al Mutamid could give his approval to such a marriage. The verses read as follows:

> Listen to my speech and heed my words,
> For conduct shows who is noble.
> Be not ignorant that I was a captive, but also that I am
> Daughter of a king descended from the Abbadies,
> A great king whose time has passed away
> So time is heading towards ruin.
> When God wanted to separate us
> And wanted to taste us, as viaticum,
> The taste of sadness,
> Hypocrisy rose up
> Against my father and in his own kingdom,
> And the separation that no one desired, drew near.
> I fled,
> I was seized by a man
> Who, in his actions, did not behave righteously,
> For he sold me as slaves are sold;
> But he has bound me to one who protects me from all things
> Except from adversity, and he wants me
> To marry me to his chaste son,
> Of good character,

who goes to you to ask your opinion to satisfy you,
you see the integrity of my conduct.
Would to God, my father, you would inform me
If hope my affection may hope,
And may Rumaikiya, the queen, with her favour,
May she ask for us prosperity and bliss.

The arrival of the verses in Aghmat brought immense joy to both Al Mutamid and Itimad, for they heard again of a daughter they had thought was gone forever. Moreover, they saw that, in the pitiful situation she had been thrust into, being sold into slavery, this marriage might be the least bad of Butayna's exits. Al Mutamid, despite the pain of not being able to see his daughter and protect her himself, signed a document giving his permission for the marriage to take place and writing to her, not without some resignation:

My daughter, be affectionate to him,
Time has decreed that you accept him.

The king watched his wife and daughters at work all day long, coming back with their beady eyes to embrace him at the end of the day. The queen and the Sevillian princesses walked barefoot through the mud of the streets, like beggars. But Itimad could never get used to such a hard life (even though she had been a hard-working slave in her early years; as they were in Aghmat, it was infinitely worse than being a slave in Seville) and fell ill. But the already appalling conditions were made worse when it came to finding someone to entrust the queen's care. Al Mutamid was rightly suspicious of some of those who offered themselves, until, as fate would have it, a former doctor at the Sevillian court by the name of Abu Ala Avenzoar was in North Africa. Al Mutamid wrote him a letter in which he begged him to attend to him, as he finally did. To this doctor, he sent the following verses, in which we can glimpse the despair that Al Mutamid was suffering:

Detail of the front of the column in the Royal Alcázar in Seville in memory of Al Mutamid. This is one of the few existing tributes in the city of Seville to one of its former kings, far surpassing those of his father and grandfather, which have been completely forgotten. (Author's collection)

Is not death preferable to life for a long-lived wretch?
for a wretched man of long misfortune?
If everyone wishes to find his love
I wish only to find death.

THE FALL OF MOORISH SEVILLE 1023-1091

Sadly, though, medical help was of little use, for Itimad died, and with her the mighty Al Mutamid felt himself dying too. He translated this grief into verses in which he mourns his sons Al Mamun and Al Radi:

> The turtledove cries at the sight of two lovers together in the nest,
> at dusk, because she has lost her beloved;
> She weeps without tears, while mine are more abundant than raindrops;
> her mourning, she discovers it, and prefers to keep her secret, without a whimper;
> But why should I not weep?
> Is my heart of stone?
> For even from stones rivers flow.
> She weeps for a single loved one she has lost,
> I mourn many of my own!
> my little son, my faithful friend,
> the one torn by misery, the other drowned by the sea;
> and those two stars, ornament of the world,
> who rest in their tombs,
> one in Córdoba, the other in Ronda.
> I would be guilty if I prevented my eyelids from weeping,
> For only resignation heals the soul;
> Tell the bright stars to weep with me
> For these two, who were like stars, shining stars.

Sometimes, Al Mutamid was distracted from his sad fate when he received a visit from a poet who, knowing of his whereabouts, decided to travel to Aghmat, or from a letter sent by a friend. The most loyal friend he had in his exile was Ben Labbana (the same who composed the verses for the embarkation of the royal family to Africa), who visited him on several occasions. He brought him recent news from the city of Seville, of how the people were very unhappy with their new masters and wanted the return of their true king, of subversive movements against the Almoravids and, most importantly, of the army that Abd Al Djabbar had formed in 1093 in the lands near Ronda to revolt the Sevillian people against the Almoravids. Al Djabbar was a son that Al Mutamid had had with another of his wives and had managed to stay in the peninsula. The cities of Algeciras and Arcos declared themselves for him, so the revolt began to have some chance of success. His small army was made up of a few notables, men who had managed to escape from their imprisonment in Málaga (around 1093) and supporters of the Abbadids who were unhappy with their new overlords and who, having a member of the royal family, immediately made him their king (in fact he came to reign in Arcos de la Frontera briefly). The year was 1095, and Al Djabbar's raids reached the vicinity of the city of Seville.

Al Mutamid was at first fearful that one of the few who had escaped from his family's captivity might suffer as they did, but then he saw it as a slight breeze of hope, for, if his son continued his triumphs, he might one day be able to return to his country. His verses in this regard are eloquent enough:

> Oh, I would like to know if I shall ever see my garden and my lake again!
> in that noble country where the olive trees grow,
> where the doves coo,
> where the birds make their sweet chirping sounds.

But Al Djabbar's luck ended when he was killed by an arrow during a fight against Almoravid troops in 1095 led by Syr, so Al Mutamid finally realised the improbability of getting out of there, and he showed his loss of illusion with verses like:

> Why in oblivion and in idleness
> my sword is already mildewing,
> though burning with a thirst for war,
> I always want to strip it bare?
> Why is the steel of my lance
> the steel of my lance
> without being dipped in the blood
> of the enemy bands?
> I will never ride any more
> on my steed of battle,
> which, the hard bridle clashing,
> with foam splashed.
> It will not obey my bridle
> nor, sensing the ambush,
> To warn me of danger,
> He will rise on his haunches.
> If the spear can't lance no one,
> Nor the cutlass pity,
> Though covered with reproach,
> though they lie roaring,
> Thou at least, O mother earth!
> Have pity on my misfortunes;
> give me rest in thy bosom,
> bury me in thy bosom.

Yusuf, who was aware of Al Mutamid's visits, ordered again to load him with chains so that there could be no attempt to escape from Aghmat and turn towards Al-Andalus. Al Mutamid's verses to his chains are well known:

THE FALL OF MOORISH SEVILLE 1023-1091

> My chain, do you not know that I have given myself to you?
> Why, then, do you not feel tender and pity?
> My blood was your drink and you have already eaten my flesh.
> Do not clench your bones.
> My son Abu Hasim, seeing me surrounded by you,
> turns away with a wounded heart.
> Have mercy on an innocent little boy who never feared that he would
> to come to implore you.
> Have mercy on his little sisters, who look like him and whom you have
> and whom you have made swallow poison and coliquintida.
> There are among them some who are already aware of it,
> and I fear that crying will blind them.
> But the others still do not understand anything and do not open their mouths
> open their mouths only to suckle.

In his solitude, with no one to talk to or share his feelings with, the Sevillian king expressed his state of mind, as in the following verses:

> Why should I wait for the return
> those happy hours,
> and for my wounds to heal
> and my pains cease?
> With my life misfortune
> has bound itself forever
> O palace of al-Zahi!
> O sumptuous banquets
> when at my table kings used to
> kings used to sit at my table!
> So pleasure and pain,
> so the evils and the goods
> the fabric of our life
> with various colours they weave,
> Till it cuts the cloth
> and hope cuts through death.

In 1095, shortly after Al Djabbar's death and at the age of 55, the suffering caused by the deaths of his wife and children, the situation of his family and his own physical exhaustion finally brought down Al Mutamid, who still had time to write his own epitaph:

> The clouds are mulling with everlasting weeping
> thy soft earth, O grave of exile
> that you cover the remains of King Ben Abbad.
> You keep with him three illustrious virtues:

science, mercy, clemency, congregated;
the fertile abundance that famines
came to extirpate, and water in drought.
You cover the one who fought undefeated
With sword, spear, and bow;
He who to the fierce lion was hard death;
the emulator of destiny in vengeance;
of the ocean in pouring out favours;
Of the moon in shining through shadows;
the head of the hall.
If true:
not without justice, with exact rigour,
a celestial design came to wound me.
But, until this corpse, I never knew
that a towering mountain could
could fit in trembling parihuelas.
What more do you want, O grave?
Be pious
With so much honour that to thy custody they
trust.
The roaring, frowning lightning,
When it swiftly crosses these contours,
For me, his brother - whose eternal rain of mercies
of mercies you restrain with your lute-
shall weep without consolation.
And the frost on thee soft tears, drop by drop,
will distil the eyes of the stars,
Who knew no better fate to give me.
The blessings of the Lord descend,
unsubmissive to number, incessant,
On him who rots thy hot bosom!

Back of the column in the Royal Alcázar in Seville in memory of Al Mutamid. Under this king, Seville reached its maximum territorial expansion, although never with the intention of re-establishing a state that would unify the whole of Al-Andalus but rather to further enlarge the Sevillian kingdom. (Author's collection)

Since that date, he has been lying in Aghmat, currently in a mausoleum next to his beloved wife Itimad and one of his sons (very close to where King Abdalá of Granada lies). It should be remembered that the heir to the Sevillian throne, Al Dawla, who was also held by the Almoravids, seems to have died in the same prison as his father, although several years later, around 1135–1136.

The historian Al Marrakushi wrote of the Sevillian monarch: 'If one wants to cite the examples of beauty generated by Al-Andalus from the time of the conquest to the present day, then Al Mutamid would be one of them, if not the greatest'. With him ended the Abbadid dynasty, which can be considered, despite the circumstances of the time, as the most brilliant of the taifa period and under which the arts and letters shone with a splendour such as our country had never experienced before.

THE FALL OF MOORISH SEVILLE 1023-1091

We can consider Al Mutamid the Muslim version of the idealised medieval Christian knight-king, in whom courage and bravery in combat were compatible with the most beautiful amorous deeds and manifest generosity, although with the difference that Al Mutamid really existed and was, if not by birth, a Sevillian at heart.

Together with numerous other historical events that took place in Seville, the tolerance and culture that Al Mutamid was able to give to his people left as a legacy the way of being of Seville and Andalusia: a cheerful, open, hospitable and wise people.

Al Mutamid's life, which went from a triumphant reign to a bitter exile in chains, has become legendary and is a good metaphor for the rise and fall of Al-Andalus. Despite his death, the figure of Al Mutamid, the warrior, the lover, the chivalrous, the generous, the poet, the romantic, will live on forever in the memory of his beloved city of Seville, even though many of its inhabitants are completely unaware of our Muslim past.

There is an Almotamid Street in Seville today, but I do not know of the existence of an Abul Qasim or Al Mutadid Street. Likewise, apart from the column erected in the courtyard of the Royal Alcázar in Seville

Of the many Muslim kings of the Iberian Peninsula, Al Mutamid is one of the few known to be buried with his wife Itimad and one of their daughters. Photograph of the tomb of the three in Agmat, Morocco. By Rui Ornelas (Creative Commons Attribution 2.0).

in homage to Al Mutamid, I am unaware of the existence of any plaques, statues or any kind of monument commemorating the only three kings of a Sevillian kingdom throughout history. Quite possibly because they are Muslim kingdoms, history seems to have given them the role of foreigners or strangers to our land, when, as always in the history of our 'bull skin', most of the population has been tied to the land for centuries and centuries, only changing the government or the dominant religion in each period of history. And Seville as a melting pot of civilisations is a good example of this; any Sevillian should accept and be proud of our Turdetan, Roman, Arab or Christian past.

This humble text serves to rescue at least a little from oblivion this 69-year period of time that saw the birth and death of a Hispanic kingdom, just like its Iberian contemporaries, both Muslim and Christian. The Taifa Kingdom of Seville achieved the greatest size and power that the capital of Seville would never achieve again, occupying a large part of the south, centre and east of the Iberian Peninsula in its period of greatest size. It also serves as a reminder of the three Sevillian kings, who, except for the last of them, who fortunately has continued to be remembered to a great extent for his poetry, have been largely forgotten by Seville and the Sevillians.

* Note: Most of the poetry presented from Al Mutamid comes from the works of Manuel Francisco Reina and Miguel José Hagerty.

A picture from the book of Alfonso X (Christian playing chess with Moor). The original source is the book Libro de los Juegos or Libros del Axedrez, Dados et Tablas of 1251 to 1282. This chess game would not differ much from the one narrated in our book between Ibn Ammar and King Alfonso. (Open source)

Appendix I

Chronology

Chronology of the most important events related to the Taifa Kingdom of Seville and some of the circumstances that led to its creation.

890: The emir of Córdoba, Abdullah, faces multiple revolts throughout the territory of Al-Andalus.

899: Agitation among the people of Seville against the power of Córdoba, led by the Banu Khaldun and Banu Hayyay families.

899 or 900 (Approximately): Kurayb Banu Khaldun succeeds in defeating the troops of the governor of the emir of Córdoba in alliance with troops from Mérida, Sidonia and Niebla in the fields of Tejada, Aznalcóllar and Gerena.

899–913: First stage of Seville's independence from the centralised power in Córdoba. Ibrahim Banu Hayyay is lord of the city of Seville.

913 (20 December): The Cordoban troops enter Seville in triumph. The first Muslim kingdom of Seville comes to an end.

1002 (August): Death of Almanzor in the town of Medinaceli after the riot over San Millán de la Cogolla. He is succeeded by his son Abd al-Malik.

1008: Death of Abd al-Malik. He is succeeded by his brother, Abderramán Sanchuelo.

1009 (January): Caliph Hixam II is forced to abdicate to Mohammed Al-Mahdi, who will rule under the name of Mohammed II. Beginning of the fitna.

1009: Battle of Alcolea, after which Suleiman is proclaimed the new caliph.

1010: Battle of Acabalbacar, after which Mohammed II regains control of the caliphate.

1013 (19 April): Suleiman enters Córdoba in blood and fire. Possible death of Hixam II.

1016: Ali ben Hammud proclaims himself the new caliph.

THE FALL OF MOORISH SEVILLE 1023-1091

1019: Abul Qasim is elected the new cadi of the city of Seville by decision of the caliph of Córdoba, following the death of his father, Ismail, succeeding him in the post.

1021–1022: Three new caliphs succeed each other.

1022: Popular revolt in Seville against the power of Córdoba.

1027: The last caliph of the Caliphate of Córdoba is elected; his name is Hixam III.

1027: Abul Qasim recognises Yahya ben Ali as caliph, preventing the sacking of the city of Seville. Meanwhile, Abul Qasim acts as king of the city of Seville. The Taifa Kingdom of Seville is born.

1030: Clash between troops from Seville and the kingdom of Badajoz in the lands of Beja. The prince of Badajoz, Muhammad ben Aftas, is captured.

1030 (Between March and April): Muhammad ben Aftas is returned to the king of Badajoz.

1031 (30 November): Hixam III is deposed. End of the caliphate.

1034: Betrayal by troops from the kingdom of Badajoz of the Sevillian troops commanded by Prince Ismail when they are attacked by surprise as they pass through the Sierra de la Estrella.

1036: Alliance of the Taifas of Carmona, Granada and Almería against the Taifa of Seville. Attacks on Ecija, Alcalá and Triana.

1039: New clashes between the Taifas of Carmona, Granada and Málaga against the Taifa of Seville.

1039 (December) or 1040 (January): Birth in the city of Beja of Al Mutamid, the future king of Seville.

1042 (24 January): Death of Abul Qasim, first king of the Taifa of Seville.

1042 (26 January): Al Mutadid ascends the throne of Seville, succeeding his father.

1042: Al Mutadid's offensive against the Carmonan taifa.

1043: Death by Sevillian troops of the king of Carmona, al-Birzali.

1044: Attack by Seville on the Arab Taifa of Mértola.

1044: Attack by the Sevillian taifa on the Arab Taifa of Niebla.

1044: Alliance against the Taifa of Seville of the Taifas of Badajoz, Granada, Málaga, Algeciras, Silves and Niebla.

1050: Attack by Sevillian troops commanded by Ismail, the first-born son of Al Mutadid, on the region of Évora, which belonged to the kingdom of Badajoz.

1050: Great victory of Ismail against the coalition of the kingdoms of Carmona and Badajoz. Death of Isaac of Carmona.

1051: Al Muzaffar, king of Badajoz, requests peace with the kingdom of Seville. The occupation of some southern territories of the Taifa of Badajoz by the kingdom of Seville is agreed.

1051–1053: Sevillian troops take the city and kingdom of Niebla.

1052: The Taifa of Saltés and Huelva falls under Seville's control.

1053–1054: The kingdom of Silves falls to the Taifa of Seville. Fall of the Taifa of the Algarve to Seville; the Sevillian troops are led by a 13-year-old son of the king of Seville, named Al Mutamid.

CHRONOLOGY

1057–1058: Meeting held in Seville in which Al Mutadid summons the lords of the Taifas of Arcos, Morón and Ronda, ending their lives through treachery. The seizure of these taifas by the Sevillian taifa begins.

1058: Surrender of the Taifa of Algeciras, after brief resistance, to the kingdom of Seville.

1060: Al Mutadid puts an end to the farce created to make it appear that Hixam II was still alive.

1059–1063: Various disputes and clashes between Ismail, the first-born son of Al Mutadid, and his father. Finally, Al Mutadid kills his son with his own hands in a fit of rage.

1063 (Possibly): Attempt by Al Mutamid, son of Al Mutadid, to take the Taifa of Málaga.

1063: Seville becomes tributary to the Christian King Ferdinand I, following a campaign of raids by the latter on Sevillian lands.

1063: 'Return' of the body of Saint Isidore of Seville to Ferdinand I by Al Mutadid.

1065: Failed attempt to take the stronghold of Ceuta by Sevillian troops.

1065: A small Sevillian army is sent to help the king of Zaragoza take the city of Barbastro.

1067: Definitive incorporation at all levels of the Taifa of Carmona into the kingdom of Seville, after years of attempts.

1068: Definitive overthrow of the lord of Arcos by the troops of Seville, the taifa being definitively incorporated by that of Seville.

1069 (7 February or 20 February or 29 March): Death of Al Mutadid of Seville.

1070 (Autumn): Takeover of the city and territory of Córdoba by the Taifa of Seville, after having helped the Cordobans against attacks by the king of Toledo.

1074: The city of Jaén is taken by Sevillian troops.

1074: King Alfonso VI demands tribute from the king of Granada, Abdalá.

1075 (Possibly): Estepa is returned by the kingdom of Granada to the kingdom of Seville. Alcalá la Real is handed over to the Granadans in exchange.

1075 (Possibly): The king of Granada hands over Martos to the Sevillians; the latter hand over Qastro in exchange.

1075 (Possibly January): Seizure of Córdoba by Al-Mamun, king of Toledo, with the help of Christian troops. Death of Abbad, son of Al Mutamid; his head is carried on a pike and 'paraded' around the city of Córdoba.

1078 (4 September): Córdoba is reintegrated into the kingdom of Seville after expelling the Toledans.

1078: The cities of Baeza and Úbeda are taken by the kingdom of Seville.

1078: Sacking of the lands of Seville by King Alfonso VI of Castile and León.

1078: Celebration of the famous chess match between Ibn Ammar and Alfonso VI, by which Seville is saved from the Castilian assault on the city.

THE FALL OF MOORISH SEVILLE 1023-1091

1078: The Murcian adventure begins between Ibn Ammar and the kingdom of Seville.

1078: The kingdom of Seville takes Mula and Cartagena with troops under the command of Ibn Ammar.

1078: The city of Murcia is taken by the kingdom of Seville. The kingdom of Murcia is annexed by the kingdom of Seville. Ibn Ammar becomes lord of Murcia, falling out of favour with Al Mutamid in the following years.

1078: Ben Rachic becomes the Sevillian king's new right-hand man in Murcia. Despite this, he begins to behave independently of the Sevillian kingdom, creating numerous conflicts with the Sevillian king.

1079: Rodrigo Díaz de Vivar, El Cid Campeador, goes to Seville to collect the tribute for that year for the king of Castile and León.

1079: Battle of Cabra. In it, the troops of El Cid and those of Seville defeat the troops of Granada and Count García, who were ravaging the lands of Seville. El Cid fulfils the aid pact that King Alfonso VI and Al Mutamid had sealed.

1082–1085: Constant attacks by Castilian-Leonese troops against the lands of Seville, to increase the pressure on King Al Mutamid. Sacking of the Seville Aljarafe.

1085 (25 May): The city and kingdom of Toledo fall to Alfonso VI.

1085 (May–June): Sevillian troops seize lands to the south and east of the now defunct Taifa of Toledo. Cuenca, Consuegra and Uclés are Sevillian.

1085: At the suggestion of Al Mutamid, he and the kings of Badajoz (Al Mutawakkil) and Granada (Abdalá) agree to ask for help from the Almoravid empire to defend them from the advance of King Alfonso VI.

1085: An Andalusian embassy made up of important officials from the kingdoms of Seville, Granada and possibly Badajoz goes to the stronghold of Ceuta to meet with Yusuf, the Almoravid emir.

1085 (Spring): Capture of the fortress of Aledo by the Christians.

1085–1088: There is a rapprochement between the kings of Granada and Seville, which culminates in the signing of a peace between the two kingdoms. This peace was never really complete. Al Mutamid helps Abdalá of Granada against Granadan rebels in Antequera, Estepona and Yarisa.

1086: First landing of Yusuf and his army on the peninsula, specifically in Algeciras. This place will be 'taken' as a base of operations for the Almoravids; it is therefore the first town on the peninsula under their control.

1086 or 1087: Al Mutamid executes his ex-friend and ex-vizier Ibn Ammar, having captured him in the fortress of Segura. Seizure of the fortress of Segura by Sevillian troops.

1086 (23 October): The Battle of Zalaca takes place near the city of Badajoz. The Castilian-Leonese army of Alfonso VI is defeated by the alliance between troops from the Almoravid empire under the command of Yusuf and Andalusian troops under the command of Al Mutamid of Seville.

1086: The sovereigns of the southern taifas stop paying taxes to King Alfonso VI.

1089 (Spring): Second arrival of Yusuf on the peninsula. After landing at Algeciras, he is joined by an Andalusian army with troops from Seville, Granada, Almería, Málaga and Murcia for the siege of the fortress of Aledo.

1089: Ben Rachic is deposed from his 'independent' kingdom of Murcia. Murcia nominally reverts to Seville, but Ben Rachic's second remains independent of the Sevillian kingdom. Final loss of Murcia to Seville.

1089–1090: King Abdalá of Granada returns to paying parias to the king of Castile and León.

1090: Abdalá of Granada meddles in the Murcian 'affairs' of the king of Seville, provoking the latter's anger.

1090 (10 June): Yusuf sets out for the third time in Al-Andalus after disembarking in Algeciras and heading for Córdoba.

1090: The Almoravid troops take the city and kingdom of Granada. Abdalá must go into exile in North Africa.

1091 (Possibly): Al Mutamid sends Zaida to the Toledo court of Alfonso VI, handing over several towns in the east of the peninsula that belonged to Seville to the Castilian monarch.

1091: The Sevillian towns of Úbeda and Segura fall under Almoravid control.

1091 (26 March): The city of Córdoba falls to the North Africans. The governor of the city, Al Mamun, son of Al Mutamid, is killed in the battle.

1091 (Early September): After the conquest of Carmona, the Almoravid army reaches the city of Seville, which it besieges.

1091: Pro-Almoravid uprising of part of the Sevillian population, which is put down by the Sevillian troops.

1091 (4 September): The walls of Seville are breached. Al Mutamid himself goes to the breach, and the invaders are repelled.

1091 (Friday, 7 September): The Castilian army under the command of Alvar Fáñez, which came to the aid of the king of Seville against the North Africans, is defeated by the latter near Almodóvar in Córdoba.

1091 (Sunday, 9 September): The Almoravid General Syr orders a new assault on the walls of Seville, which in this case will be definitive. The North Africans storm the streets of the city, sacking it and sowing chaos and destruction.

1091 (Sunday, 9 September): North African troops arrive at the palace where Al Mutamid and his family are staying. There is strong resistance from the Sevillians, who engage in several battles. Al Mutamid's son Malic is killed in one of them. Al Mutamid is finally forced to surrender to Syr.

THE FALL OF MOORISH SEVILLE 1023-1091

1091 (Mid-September): Under pressure from Syr, Al Mutamid writes letters to his sons Al Radi and Al Motadd, who had made themselves strong in the cities of Ronda and Mértola, respectively, with the aim of getting them to surrender in exchange for respecting the lives of the royal family. Both agree to surrender, but, while Al Motadd escapes with his life, Al Radi is killed by the Almoravid General Guerur, who broke his word to respect his life.

1091 (Possibly October or November): The Sevillian royal family, headed by Al Mutamid and Itimad, embark at the Seville salt dock for their exile in North Africa. They will first pass through Tangiers, then Meknes and finally Aghmat.

1093: Revolts take place in the Ronda highlands against the Almoravid invader. Their leader is Al Djabbar, son of Al Mutamid.

1093–1094: Death of the deposed queen of Seville, Itimad, in her exile in Aghmat.

1095: Al Djabbar's raids reach the vicinity of the city of Seville.

1095: The last king of Seville, Al Mutamid, dies in Aghmat at the age of 55.

Appendix II

Glossary

Meanings of certain words of Arabic origin used in this text.

Abbadids: A family of Arab origin (Yemenis) who gave three kings to the Taifa of Seville during the eleventh century.
Aceifa: Military incursions into enemy lands. In the time of the caliphate, they tended to be Muslim, whereas, during the century of the taifas, this tendency was reversed, being mostly carried out by Christians against Muslims. They were also carried out between Muslim taifas.
Adalid (al-Dalil): A person who led armies.
Adarve (al Darb): Dead-end alleyways formed by several dwellings. On ramparts, it corresponds to the walkway used for patrolling the ramparts.
Aftasid: A Hispano-Muslim dynasty that dominated the west of Al-Andalus during the taifa period as the Taifa of Badajoz.
Ajimez (al samís): Window or small balcony with wooden latticework that protected women's rooms from the outside world.
Al-Andalus: The name given by the Muslims to the portion of the Iberian Peninsula dominated by them.
Alcaicería (al qaysar): Place with shops dedicated to the sale of silk, textiles, earthenware and so on.
Alcazaba (al-qasaba): A citadel independent of the medina where the military authority resided.
Alcázar (al-qasar): Palace-fortress and residence of the caliphs and the various taifa kings. The governors of the various provinces could also reside there.
Alfaqid (al faqih): Doctor of Koranic law. His mission was to ensure that neither justice nor government deviated from Mohammedan precepts.
Algarve (al-garb): The west. Also refers to the southwestern region of Al-Andalus.
Alhondiga: Warehouse or market. It consists of a corral on the ground floor with rooms for merchants on the upper floor.
Aljama (al-yama'a): The main mosque of a city. This is where Friday prayers are held.

Almajeneque: Military device used for the siege of fortresses or walled cities. It launched projectiles from a distance by means of counterweights. They were used in the siege of the fortress of Aledo.

Almuédano or Almuecín (muazzin): In charge of calling to prayer from the minaret of the mosque.

Almunia (al munya): The name given to orchards and farms during the Muslim period.

Almuzara (al musara): An open field on the outskirts of the city, where various activities such as parades or public executions took place. It was also known as Sa'ria.

Alquería (al qarya): A place with its own boundaries and jurisdiction.

Alquibla (al qibla): Place in the mosque to which the faithful direct their gaze when praying.

Arab: Semitic people from the Arabian Peninsula.

Arrabal (al rabad): Group of houses or neighbourhood outside the city walls.

Atarazana (al sana): Arsenal for boats.

Berber: Name given to the people from the territory between Libya and the Atlantic, from the southern coast of the Sahara.

Cadi (qadi): Civil judge who was in charge of many legal situations such as lawsuits, divorces, marriages or inheritance matters among others.

Caliph (jalifa): Means 'successor' and refers to the successor of the prophet Muhammad. Caliphs were both political and religious leaders. The caliphate would be the territory under the jurisdiction of a caliph.

Dar: Arabic for 'house'.

Diwan: The various ministries of a government.

Emir (amir): Means 'prince'. The emir was a political leader but not a religious leader. The emirate corresponds to the territory ruled by an emir.

Faqih: Identical in origin and meaning to alfaqid.

Fetua: Legal ruling.

Fitna: Civil war, riots and disorder that endanger the purity of the faith of the Muslims.

Háchib or Hayib: He fulfilled the functions of a prime minister to the caliph. Under him were the viziers.

Hammam: Bath. It consisted of three parts: a cold area, a warm area and a hot area. It was often used as a public relations centre and by both men and women, although at different times so that they did not coincide.

Hisn: Fortified castle.

Imam: Guide or leader who leads the Muslims in prayer.

Isbiliya or Ishbiliya: The name given to the city of Seville during Muslim rule.

Khatib: Muslim preacher who delivers the Friday sermon.

Khutba: A speech delivered at Friday prayers or on some exceptional occasions. It was delivered by the khatib.

Mahdi: Arabic for 'one who is guided by God'.

GLOSSARY

Medina (madina): A city that was characterised by being surrounded by walls.
Minaret: Of the same meaning and origin as the minaret.
Minaret (al minar): Mosque tower from which the muezzin calls to prayer.
Mosque (masjid): Enclosure for Muslim worship. It consists of an ablutions courtyard and a covered enclosure, where the faithful pray in the direction of the qibla. As an altar, there is an empty niche known as the mihrab.
Mozarab (mustarab): Hispanic Christian who preserved his religion and lived in Al-Andalus, subject to the Muslims.
Mudejar (mudayyan): Muslims who remained in territory conquered by the Christians from the Muslims.
Muecín: Of the same origin and identical meaning as almuédano.
Qibla: In the mosque, the wall that points in the direction of Mecca.
Quba: A building that is covered by a dome.
Razia (ghazah): Has the same meaning as aceifa.
Sahn: Courtyard of the mosque.
Sheikh (shaykh): A superior among Muslims who rules and commands a territory or province.
Souk (suq): Square or group of streets used as a marketplace. Craftsmen and traders were usually grouped in guilds, which led to the existence of several souks within the same city.
Taifa: Means 'band' or 'banderries'. It refers to each of the small Muslim states that were created after the dissolution of the Caliphate of Córdoba.
Vali (wali): Governor of a province, who acted as the king's representative in that province.
Visir (wazir): This title corresponds today to the powers of a prime minister of a country.
Zalmedina (sahib al medina): Head of the city.

Bibliography

Amador de los Ríos, Rodrigo, *Inscripciones árabes de Sevilla* (Madrid: Extramuros Edición, 2008) [Facsimile of the original of 1875.]
Anon., *Crónica de España* (Barcelona: Plaza & Janes, 1988), vol. 1
Anon., *Gran atlas de carreteras de Europa* (Barcelona: Editorial Planeta, 1993)
Area Sacristán, Enrique, and Hervás Maldonado, Francisco, *Militia and Health in Al-Andalus* (Aguadulce: Editorial Círculo Rojo, 2014)
Ayuntamiento de Sevilla: Patronato del Real Alcázar (ed.), *Apuntes del Alcázar de Sevilla*, 1 (2000)
Ayuntamiento de Sevilla: Patronato del Real Alcázar (ed.), *Apuntes del Alcázar de Sevilla*, 6 (2005)
Aznar, Fernando, *España medieval. Musulmanes, judíos y cristianos* (Madrid: Editorial Anaya, 2005)
Balbás, Yeyo, '"Campidoctor". Tácticas y armamento en tiempos del Cid', *Desperta Ferro. Antigua y Medieval*, 40 (2017), pp.46–52
Barrucand, Marianne, and Bednorz, Achim, *Islamic Architecture in Andalusia* (Cologne: Taschen, 2007)
Bosch Vilá, Jacinto, *La Sevilla Islámica, 712-1248* (Seville: Universidad de Sevilla, 1988)
Bueno, Francisco, *Los Reyes de la Alhambra. Entre la historia y la leyenda* (Granada: Ediciones Miguel Sánchez, 2007)
Carrasco Manchado, Ana I., Quesada, Juan Martos, and Souto Lasala, Juan A., *Al-Andalus* (Madrid: Ediciones Istmo, 2009)
Cebrián, Juan Antonio, *La Cruzada Del Sur. La Reconquistaz: de Covadonga a la toma de Granada* (Madrid: La esfera de los libros, 2005)
Cómez Ramos, Rafael, 'Fragmentos de una mezquita sevillana: la aljama de Ibn Adabbas', *Laboratorio de Arte*, 7 (1994), pp.11–23
Conde, José Antonio, *Historia de la Dominacion de los Arabes en España, Sacada de Varios Manuscritos y Memorias Arabigas* (Valladolid: Editorial Maxtor, 2001) [Facsimile of the original of 1874.]
'Cultural Itinerary of the Almoravids and Almohads', *El legado andalusi*, <https://www.legadoandalusi.es/cultural-itineraries/cultural-itinerary-of-the-almoravids-and-almohads/?lang=en>, accessed 14 Feb. 2023
De Mena, José María, *Historia de Sevilla* (Barcelona: Plaza & Janes, 1991)
De Mena, José María, *Tradiciones y leyendas Sevillanas* (Barcelona: Plaza & Janes, 1988)